CW01024933

THE DOCTRINE OF ELECTION

THE DOCTRINE
OF
ELECTION

John Calvin

Selected Texts Translated from the French

by

ROBERT WHITE

THE BANNER OF TRUTH TRUST

THE BANNER OF TRUTH TRUST

Head Office
3 Murrayfield Road
Edinburgh, EH12 6EL
UK

North America Office
PO Box 621
Carlisle, PA 17013
USA

banneroftruth.org

First Banner of Truth edition 2022
© Robert White 2022

ISBN
Print: 978 1 80040 265 2
Epub: 978 1 80040 266 9
Kindle: 978 1 80040 267 6

*

Typeset in 11/15 pt Adobe Caslon Pro at
The Banner of Truth Trust, Edinburgh

Printed in the USA by
Versa Press, Inc.,
East Peoria, IL

CONTENTS

Q. What do you believe concerning 'the holy catholic church'?

A. I believe that the Son of God, through his Spirit and word, out of the entire human race, from the beginning of the world to its end, gathers, protects and preserves for himself a community chosen for eternal life and united in true faith. And of this community I am and always will be a living member.

The Heidelberg Catechism (1563), Question 54.

If you would honour God aright, you should know that he does not want the word that he has spoken to disappoint you, provided you do not profane it by your unbelief. He desires to show you clearly how faithful he is to his promises.

Calvin, *Sermons on the Acts of the Apostles* (*SC* 8:28).

INTRODUCTION

I F the doctrine of election were no more than a speculative attempt to explain why some accept and believe the gospel and others do not, it would be an interesting and perhaps intriguing hypothesis, but one incapable of proof. As it happens, election is writ large on the pages of both the Old and New Testaments, and is a doctrine difficult to avoid for anyone who regards Scripture as being, in any way, God's truthful and authoritative word. The God of Abraham, Isaac and Jacob is a God who chooses not only individuals to be his servants, but a whole people, Abraham's descendants, Israel, whom he calls to enjoy his provision in the land of promise, to bear witness to his mighty works, to observe his law, and to bring blessing to the whole world. That call, constantly repeated but obeyed by the few, is finally seen to devolve upon the One foretold by the prophets, the Saviour-Servant of Isaiah 53, the elect Son who, dying for our sins and rising for our justification, chooses apostles to herald his salvation, and who, through his life-giving Spirit, gathers his people of every age into his church.

For the apostle Peter, the church is 'a chosen race, a royal priesthood, a holy nation, God's own people', as befits those who are built into a spiritual house of which Christ himself is the 'elect cornerstone' (1 Pet. 2:6, 9). For Paul, the Thessalonian Christians to whom he writes have been 'chosen by God from the beginning to be saved, through sanctification by the Spirit and belief in the truth' (2 Thess. 2:13). He makes the same point elsewhere in his letters, most notably in Romans (8:28–11:36), in Ephesians (1:2-14) and in 2 Timothy (1:9, 10). Among the Church Fathers, Augustine (354–430) was especially attentive to Paul's message, which he employed to good effect in his battle with the Pelagians, who argued for man's free choice in the matter of salvation. Augustine's concern was not lost on a number of medieval scholars. The master theologians of the twelfth and thirteenth centuries, Peter Lombard and Thomas Aquinas, strongly defended the doctrine of election.[1] Despite the semi-Pelagian position of the official church,[2] predestinarian currents persisted into the fourteenth century, influencing the thought of Wyclif and Hus, before decisively emerging in the work of the first generation of Reformers led by Luther and Zwingli.

That Calvin was a staunch advocate of the doctrine of election can be easily shown. His treatise of 1552, *Concerning the Eternal Predestination of God*, where predestination assumes the double form of predestination to life and predestination to judgment, amply demonstrates the importance he attributed to the doctrine and his readiness to argue for it against all detractors, whether present or past. To contend, however, as many have done, that election is the very foundation of what is called his 'system', that it is the fixed centre around which all other doctrines are made to pivot, is patently false. Election, and its corollary, reprobation, are no more central to Calvin's thinking than is his understanding of the Trinity, the person and work of Christ, the Holy Spirit, the church, word and sacraments, sin and final judgment. All belong to the same body of truth, all are part of a common, God-given fund, knowledge of which is necessary for our establishment and growth in faith.

[1] Lombard, *Sentences*, III.20.3; Aquinas, *Summa theologiae*, Ia 23.1-8, 24.1-3. On the extent of Calvin's agreement with Aquinas' doctrine of providence and predestination, see Paul Helm, *Calvin at the Centre* (Oxford: Oxford University Press, 2010), pp. 140-43, 150-52.

[2] Semi-Pelagian because, then as now, conversion was not viewed as an exclusive act of the unfettered will, but as a cooperative work between prevenient grace and human liberty.

The issue of election appears almost incidentally in Calvin's first major theological work, *The Institutes of the Christian Religion* (1536), where it is part of a much larger discussion of the church. The author defines the church as the sum total of the elect, 'whether angels or men; if men, whether dead or still living, in whatever lands they live or wherever among the nations they have been scattered'. Chosen in Christ before the foundation of the world in order to be gathered into God's kingdom, they have been, in God's eternal providence, 'adopted as members of the church, and are made holy by the Lord'. In accordance with the pattern outlined by Paul in Romans 8:30, God's choice is said to be manifested by his call and subsequent justification, and the perseverance of the elect is assured: 'Their salvation rests on such a sure and solid bed that, even if the whole fabric of the world were to fall, it itself could not tumble or fall.'[3]

As a compendium to the *Institutes* which had appeared only in Latin, Calvin, in 1537, issued, in French, his *Brief Instruction in Faith*. The new work marks an important advance in his thinking, since it treats election as a doctrine in its own right. 'The seed of God's word,' we read, 'takes root and bears fruit only in those whom the Lord by his eternal election has predestined to be his children and heirs of the heavenly kingdom. For all others who, by this same counsel of God before the foundation of the world, are rejected, the clear and unmistakable preaching of the truth can only be an odour of death to death.'[4] With remarkable concision, the *Brief Instruction* outlines some of Calvin's most characteristic themes: election is a mystery which the human mind cannot fathom; since it is God's work, it is holy and just;

[3] Calvin, *Institutes of the Christian Religion: 1536 Edition*, tr. Ford Lewis Battles (Grand Rapids, MI: William B. Eerdmans/H.H. Meeter Centre for Calvin Studies, 1975), pp. 58-59.

[4] *Calvini opera quae supersunt omnia*, ed. G. Baum, E. Cunitz and E. Reuss, 59 vols. (Brunswick and Berlin: C.A. Schwetschke & Son, 1863-1900), 22:46. Hereafter cited as *CO*.

both election and reprobation redound to God's glory, the first by exalting God's mercy, the second by exalting his justice; all election is in Christ who, when we embrace him by faith, is the guarantor of our election. 'Possessing therefore Christ by faith, we also possess life in him, ... for he is not only a mirror which represents to us God's will, but a pledge by which it is sealed and confirmed.'[5]

The doctrine underwent further elaboration in the second edition of the *Institutes* (1539), written, like the first, in Latin, but translated into French in 1541. The new work reflects the influence of the Reformer Martin Bucer, with whom Calvin worked closely during his three-year residence in Strasbourg (1538–41).[6] It reflects, too, the author's debt to Augustine, whose works became increasingly familiar to him and whom he frequently cites. At the same time, his preparation of a *Commentary on Romans* (published in 1540) ensured that the issue of election remained firmly in view, but with the added advantage of placing it in a new, more concrete setting—God's providential ordering of salvation history.

The Reformer is well aware that a variety of views exists among his readers. He begins his new work by addressing the concerns of the over-curious who seek to understand the reason for God's choice. To delve too deeply into the mystery of predestination, Calvin warns, 'is to stumble into a labyrinth from which there is no way out'.[7] At the other extreme are critics who question the need for such a doctrine at all, describing it as 'perilous' on the grounds that it is unnecessarily divisive, is contrary to reason, and is either unsettling to faith or inimical to moral effort. Diverse as these positions are, Calvin in each case argues that only God's word can provide sure guidance in

---

[5] *CO* 22:47.

[6] On Bucer's influence, see Alexandre Ganoczy, *The Young Calvin*, tr. David Foxgrover and Wade Provo (Philadelphia: Westminster Press, 1987), pp. 158-68.

[7] Calvin, *Institutes of the Christian Religion (1541)*, tr. Robert White (Edinburgh: Banner of Truth Trust, 2014), p. 464.

matters where complete clarity cannot be hoped for, let alone attained. Citing Augustine, he affirms that the only safe course is to follow Scripture, which condescends to our lowliness, as a mother might to her child's weakness when she wants to teach him to walk. Everything else is idle speculation.[8]

Having established Scripture as his sole and necessary authority, the Reformer lays out the essential premise on which the whole of his doctrine is based. Election is an act of God's free grace: it does not rest on God's foreknowledge of our merits, of which, as children of Adam, we are totally bereft. That election depends on nothing we might do is shown by the example of Jacob and Esau (Rom. 9:11-13): God chose one and rejected the other before ever they were born. Paul, citing Malachi 1:2, 3, invokes no other reason for God's choice than his good pleasure, his sovereign purpose. What was determined in eternity was thus fulfilled in time. Those, Calvin argues, whom God has graciously chosen are effectually called by his Holy Spirit, who confirms their adoption into God's family (Rom. 8:15, 16) and guarantees their future inheritance (Eph. 1:13, 14). The faith which unites them to God is properly not theirs; it is the gift of God, not an act of the unaided will. They are indeed willing, but only because, illumined by God's Spirit and emboldened by his word, they have been made so.[9]

For the believer, few questions can be of more immediate relevance than the question of assurance. Is it possible to be sure of God's election? Calvin considers the call of God to be sufficient evidence of election. God's call is said to consist outwardly in the preaching of the word and inwardly in the illumination of the Holy Spirit.[10] And since both word and Spirit lead us by faith to Jesus Christ, it is in Christ, not in ourselves or in any quality of

---

[8] *Institutes (1541)*, p.466. (Unless otherwise specified, the references which follow are to this edition.)

[9] *Institutes*, pp. 484-85.

[10] *Institutes*, p. 485.

faith, that assurance is to be found. 'Christ,' writes Calvin, 'is like a mirror in which we may properly view our election and where it can be seen without distortion … We have firm and manifest proof that we are written in the book of life if we are partners with Christ. He fully proved to be our partner when, through the preaching of the gospel, he testified that he has been given to us by the Father, so that he and all his benefits may be ours.'[11] Being made one, therefore, with God's Son, we draw our life from him, and look for grace to persevere to him from whom no power in heaven or earth can part us (Rom. 8:38, 39).[12]

By contrast, God's word which calls the elect to salvation serves only to harden the reprobate: by a decree no less final than the decree of election, they are consigned to unbelief and death.[13] They are nevertheless without excuse: 'Whatever obscurity there may be in the teaching, there is always more than enough light to convict the consciences of the wicked.'[14] Sinning knowingly against the light, they are fully accountable for their actions, and thus 'suffer nothing which does not accord with God's just judgment'.[15] Here again, as in the *Brief Instruction in Faith*, reprobation, by testifying to the integrity of God's justice, redounds to his glory.

* * *

[11] *Institutes*, pp. 487–88.

[12] *Institutes*, pp. 488–90. That experience may serve, in a lesser sense, to confirm election, is suggested by this brief addition of 1559/60 (*Inst.* III.24.4): 'Let this be our method of inquiry: to begin with God's call, and to end with it. This should not, however, prevent the faithful from recognizing that the benefits which they daily receive from God's hand derive from his secret adoption, … since God wills this to be a token or emblem confirming to us all that we may lawfully know about his counsel.'

[13] *Institutes*, p. 467: '[God] does not create all men in like condition, but appoints some to eternal life, and others to eternal damnation.'

[14] *Institutes*, p. 496.

[15] *Institutes*, p. 497. Calvin's (qualified) determinism is thus compatible with the idea of uncoerced choice, which makes human beings wholly responsible for the acts which they perform, and which, in terms of their moral quality, deserve either praise or blame.

In essence, Calvin's understanding of election may be said to be fully formed and comprehensively stated in the *Institutes* of 1539/41. Whatever further refinements the doctrine was to receive over the next two decades, up to and including the final editions of 1559 (Latin) and 1560 (French), little new was added. Generally speaking, the author was content either to buttress his argument by fresh appeals to Scripture and to recognized authorities, or to answer yet again objections raised by his opponents.

That the doctrine itself should be contested was, as we have seen, natural enough. Advocates of free will could scarcely be expected to concede that the only freedom the human race enjoyed was the freedom to run from God. This issue had, after all, pitted Luther against Erasmus over a decade earlier, and no solution had been found. To the argument that free will alone made human beings responsible moral agents, capable not only of sin but of repentance, belief and the reception of grace, Calvin opposes the fact of man's loss of righteousness since Adam's fall, and the irremediable corruption of his natural endowments.

Other critics were more concerned to defend God against what they saw were the defamatory implications of the doctrine. Election, they contended, made God 'a respecter of persons': it denied the indiscriminate and impartial character of his mercy, representing him as capricious in his choice of a favoured few, and as unfair in the leniency extended to some but not all. By way of answer, Calvin points out that since there is nothing that prompts God to prefer one person to another—all being equally undeserving—there is no question of favouritism: nothing accounts for his choice except his sole mercy, 'which should be free to reveal itself where and when he pleases'.[16] As to the accusation of unfairness, he appeals to the biblical revelation of

[16] *Institutes*, p. 482.

God as holy, wise, gracious and just. Either God is as Scripture affirms him to be, or he is not. If he is not, he ceases to be God and we are left with only idols of our own making. If he is holy, he owes nothing but justice to guilty sinners; if he is gracious, he will exercise his mercy in a way which accords with his wisdom. Either way he cannot be made to conform to our sense of what is acceptable, limited as it is by our flawed reason and by our self-serving arrogance. 'God's rule,' says Calvin, 'is the supreme and sovereign rule of justice, so that whatever he wills must be considered just, inasmuch as he wills it.'[17]

Another objection voiced by the critics concerned divine foreknowledge. If, as Calvin claimed, God foresaw Adam's fall, why did he not intervene to stop it and to save the world from ruin? The complaint, Calvin replies, might have some merit if God's foreknowledge was simply the contemplation of a wholly contingent future. His foreknowledge, however, is not passive; it is not mere precognition or prevision: he foresees that what he has purposed will come to pass. God foreknows because he has pre-determined. He not only foresaw Adam's fall, he willed it—actively, not permissively. 'Just as it is part of his wisdom that he foresees all future events, so it is part of his power that he rules and governs all things by his hand.'[18] Was it then not merely remiss of God, but cruel, to allow Adam and his progeny to suffer loss? And does not election make God in effect the author of evil, since men must necessarily sin? 'How,' writes Calvin, 'could he who is the Judge of the world commit evil? ... Man stumbled according as God had ordained, but he stumbled through his own fault ... From where did man's evil

[17] *Institutes*, p. 474. In his text of 1559/60, Calvin adds (*Inst.* III.23.2): 'God is not accountable to us so that he must give us reasons for acting as he does; and we, on the other hand, are not able or competent to decide this issue according to our own understanding.'

[18] *Institutes*, pp. 478-79. On the denial of a permissive will in God, a concept favoured by Erasmus among others, see *Inst.* III.23.8.

come, if not from the fact that he had turned away from his God?'[19]

If, finally, election was allowed to stand, what, it was asked, were its practical consequences? Who among the elect could resist the temptation to pride, complacency and moral indifference, since regardless of performance salvation is assured? And who among the reprobate had any incentive to mend their ways, since they were inevitably lost? While conceding that the reprobate might well misuse the doctrine to that end—'certain swine defile God's predestination with such blasphemies'—the Reformer affirms that election has as its goal a holy, blameless life (Eph. 1:4). Far from encouraging spiritual sloth and moral laxity, it is the best possible incentive to good works, since it arises from a sense of infinite debt to divine grace. And is not the Spirit given to believers for sanctification?[20]

* * *

No one knew better than Calvin that this was not an easy doctrine to proclaim. It met with much opposition from both sides of the confessional divide. It could be, and was, caricatured as a message of doom for the damned. It was not this, however, which led the Reformer in his *Institutes* of 1559/60 to describe it as a 'dread decree' (*decretum horribile*).[21] The dread is not that felt by the offender about to suffer punishment for his crimes; it is the dread of mortal man brought face to face with God's power and holiness, and forced to confess his worthlessness and insignificance. It is here, perhaps, that we come closest to the heart of Calvin's Calvinism, which consists, in the words of one commentator who knew Calvin better than most, 'in a

---

[19] *Institutes*, pp. 476, 479-80.
[20] *Institutes*, p. 483.
[21] *Inst.* III.23.7.

profound apprehension of God and his majesty', accompanied by a poignant sense of our creaturely dependence upon him, and of our need as sinners 'to rest in self-emptying trust purely on the God of grace.'[22]

In proclaiming, however, God's sovereign will, prudence is required. The *Institutes* repeat Augustine's admonition that care must be taken to avoid all censoriousness, harshness and recrimination. No prior judgment as to a hearer's spiritual standing must be made. With no sure and certain knowledge of who belongs to the company of the predestined, 'we should be so minded as to desire the salvation of everyone, so that we try to make all whom we meet a sharer in our peace'.[23] Hence the necessity of a preaching ministry which addresses itself indiscriminately to all, and which in God's name offers the promise of pardon and life to all who repent and believe.

Never in his *Institutes*, his commentaries or sermons does Calvin pursue doctrine for its own sake. He lays consistent stress on the practical outworking of doctrine, on its power to inform, edify and correct—on what he calls its 'fruit'. In prefacing his discussion of election in the *Institutes* of 1559/60, the author identifies three uses of the doctrine. First, it reveals in the starkest terms the gratuity of grace: by excluding human merit it demolishes the notion of righteousness through works. Second, it serves to magnify God's glory, since redemption from first to last is seen to be the mighty work of Father, Son and Spirit. Third, it strikes down pride and makes humility man's only possible response to God's great goodness. To these, a fourth use may be added: election serves to reinforce faith. 'Christ bears witness to us,' says Calvin, 'that nowhere else do we have true

---

[22] B. B. Warfield, *Works*, 10 vols. (Grand Rapids, MI: Baker Books, 2003), 5:354-55.

[23] *Inst.* III.23.14. From the first edition of the *Institutes* onward, Calvin contends that the elect 'cannot be recognized with assurance of faith', but that 'those who profess with us the same God and Christ by confession of faith, example of life and participation in the sacraments, ought by some sort of judgment of love to be deemed elect and members of the church' (*Institutes: 1536 Edition*, p. 61). Cf. *Inst.* IV.1.8.

firmness or confidence to deliver us from so many perils; ... and to make us invincible, he promises that nothing which has been entrusted to him by the Father will perish' (John 10:27-30).[24]

Because doctrine is, in the most basic sense of the word, useful, it must be preached. 'It must be preached,' says Calvin, 'so that those with ears to hear might hear.' Just as we preach good works in order to serve God as he deserves, so we ought to preach predestination, 'so that he who hears should boast in God and not in himself.'[25]

To proclaim God's choice made before the foundation of the world is to proclaim a mystery, or as Calvin prefers to say, a 'secret'. Unlike the mystery of Christ preached by the apostles, election is not a wholly open secret. Half of it is hidden in God's eternal counsel, and will remain so until the last day. Ours is an age which dislikes mysteries; we resent anything which cannot be exposed to the cold light of reason. So when we speak of God's designs—if we speak of them at all—we do so in a matter-of-fact way, or, to use another's phrase, 'like cobblers who speak about their leather'.[26] We have no time for paradoxes. The notion that God's sovereignty and man's responsibility, that God's love and his justice are equally real and operative, baffles and vexes us. We are inclined to accuse God of inconsistency, of indecisiveness or worse, of bad faith. It requires more than a little modesty on our part to appreciate and approve the force of Calvin's question: 'Would it not be utterly unreasonable to judge God's works by the rule that we were free to revile them when they made no sense to us?'[27]

---

[24] *Inst.* III.21.1. In the *Institutes* of 1539/41 (p. 487), Calvin had written that while predestination is thought of as a 'dangerous sea' for those who choose to put their lives at risk, 'those who seek it rightly in the order which Scripture lays down draw particular comfort from it.'

[25] *Inst.* III.23.13.

[26] Lucien Febvre, *Un destin: Martin Luther* (Paris: Presses Universitaires de France, 1952), p. 43.

[27] *Institutes*, p. 476.

Half of the secret is revealed: Scripture assures us of the fact, but not of the reason for it. As Augustine saw long ago, to the question 'Why?', only one answer is possible: 'God willed it so.'[28] In the last analysis, we must let God be God. We, however, are not absolved of all responsibility. We are to see that the gospel is faithfully preached, to live by it ourselves, and to pray that all who have ears to hear, may hear.

* * *

In sketching the main details of Calvin's doctrine of election and of its counterpart, reprobation, we have followed the usual route of drawing on a single source, the *Institutes*. Supplemented by his treatise of 1552, *Concerning the Eternal Predestination of God*, and by certain of his commentaries—notably those on John and on Romans—our analysis would have certainly been longer but not necessarily more complete, since the Reformer rarely alters his course once it is set. The convenience of a single source cannot be denied. Other sources, however, exist, which are less often explored because less accessible, and which offer fresh perspectives on Calvin's teaching. All are records of the spoken word and are addressed to a mixed audience; they are not documents written with a view to immediate publication and with the needs of a select readership in mind. They have a directness and a pungency which are found elsewhere only in Calvin's personal correspondence and in some of his polemical works. There is not a hint of bookishness here: this is theology for Everyman.

The texts which are here translated are grouped under four headings: (1) a summary statement of the doctrine of election; (2) election and reprobation; (3) election in Christ; (4) election in the context of God's overarching providence.

[28] Augustine, *Letters* 186, 7.23.

The first text, *On the Eternal Election of God*, is an address given by Calvin in Geneva to a weekly assembly of ministers and laypeople known as a *congrégation*. The *congrégation* was modelled on the *Prophezei* practised by the church in Zurich; it met on Fridays for purposes of mutual instruction and to settle disputed points of doctrine. It was just such a dispute which prompted Calvin to choose election as his theme. The Reformer's teaching had been roundly attacked by Jerome Bolsec, a former Carmelite friar who was then working as a physician in the vicinity of Geneva. In the course of a *congrégation* held on 16 October 1551, Bolsec had accused Calvin of twisting Scripture to suit his own purposes. The resulting scandal had led to Bolsec's arrest, imprisonment and trial on a charge of sedition. The trial was nearing completion when, on 18 December, Calvin rose to defend his doctrine. In short order he reviewed the biblical evidence for the doctrine, examined the implications of what it meant to be chosen in Christ, answered common objections and concluded by affirming God's justice and equity toward the reprobate—all to the praise of his glory. Five days later Bolsec was found guilty. Condemned to banishment, he promptly moved to Bernese territory where he found a warmer welcome; from there he continued to snipe at his opponent.[29]

The second grouping consists of four sermons on Jacob and Esau, and on God's choice of the younger over the older (Gen. 25:12-28). The Reformer had begun his Genesis series in September 1559, and had reached the twenty-fifth chapter by July 1560. The sermons in question belong to a group of thirteen which were first published in 1560, together with the treatise of 1552 on predestination. No one who read the title page could mistake the book's intention: *A Treatise on the Eternal Predestination of*

---

[29] Bolsec's criticisms are detailed below in Appendix II. Calvin's address, *Congrégation sur l'élection éternelle de Dieu*, was published in 1562 by Genevan printer Vincent Brès. A full account of the dispute and trial is given by Philip C. Holtrop, *The Bolsec Controversy on Predestination from 1551 to 1555*, 2 vols. (Lewiston, NY: The Edwin Mellen Press, 1993).

God ..., to which likewise are added thirteen sermons treating of God's free election in Jacob, and of reprobation in Esau. A treatise in which each Christian may see God's excellent benefits toward his own, and his marvellous judgments toward the reprobate.[30] The narrative of God's dealings with Jacob and Esau is exemplary, in the sense that no clearer illustration exists of the absence of any compelling motive which would explain God's choice. As Paul demonstrates in Romans 9:10-16, the election of Jacob is an exercise in mercy which is grounded solely in God's good pleasure. 'The person of Jacob,' says the preacher, 'prefigures all of the elect: in him God shows that his unmerited gift of grace owes nothing to ourselves.'[31] He also prefigures the elect in another sense: contemptible in the world's eyes, God's people will inevitably appear weak and vulnerable. The church has small beginnings; only when sustained by the Spirit's power can it, the lesser, triumph over the greater. Election assures us that in every circumstance, God is faithful and will complete the work of salvation. His promises in the gospel are such that 'we are not deceived if we rely upon them'.[32]

The remaining texts come from the one source, Calvin's sermons on Ephesians, which were begun in May 1558, interrupted by illness in October, and not completed until the summer of the following year. They first appeared in print in 1562.[33] Of the forty-eight sermons which comprise the collection, four, on Ephesians 1:3-14, bear directly on the theme of election

---

[30] *Traité de la prédestination éternelle de Dieu ...* (Geneva: Antoine Cercia, 1560). A separate edition of the thirteen sermons (*Treze sermons de M. I. Calvin traitans de l'élection gratuite de Dieu*) appeared in 1562. An English translation by John Field was published in London in 1579; it has been republished in slightly modernized form under the title *Sermons on Election and Reprobation* (Audubon, NJ: Old Paths Publications, 1996). See further T. H. L. Parker, *Calvin's Preaching* (Edinburgh: T&T Clark, 1992), pp. 184, 191.

[31] Sermon 2 on Gen. 25:21-23.

[32] Sermon 3 on Gen. 25:21-23.

[33] *Sermons de Iean Calvin sur l'epistre S.Paul apostre aux Ephesiens* (Geneva: Jean-Baptiste Pinereul, 1562). Cf. T. H. L. Parker, *Calvin's Preaching*, pp. 186, 191. An English translation, done by Arthur Golding, appeared in 1577; a reworked version of Golding's translation was published by The Banner of Truth Trust in 1973.

in Christ, while another, on Ephesians 3:9-12, situates election within the broad sweep of God's all-embracing providence.

The first chapter of Ephesians played a key part in Calvin's understanding of election. He returns to it constantly in his *Institutes*, in his treatise of 1552 and in his sermons. It spells out what, in the story of Jacob and Esau, is barely hinted at: God's choice precedes not only birth but time itself—'before the foundation of the world'. It is a choice made apart from us, indeed, from God's point of view, despite us, since by nature we are part of the mass of perdition.

In his sermons on Ephesians 1, Calvin shows not a little warmth in his condemnation of those who are reluctant to admit the particularity of divine grace.[34] No doctrine, the preacher assures his hearers, is better suited to displaying the boundless riches of God's mercy. Furthermore, the arguments which are habitually advanced in favour of foreseen merit founder on the fact that the saved are chosen in Christ and not in themselves. They have no merit but his; they are not loved except in him. Their names are inscribed in him as in a register: 'He is the model and mirror in which God beholds his own.'[35] Although called to holiness, they are not instantly sanctified. 'God,' says Calvin, 'will not have us enter his kingdom in one bound.' By continual striving, prayer, repentance and correction, the elect are drawn toward perfection; they do not attain it this side of death.[36] They do not strive, however, unaided. They are doubly indebted to the Holy Spirit, who not only illumines them but gives them strength to persevere. The Spirit, to use Paul's imagery, is both the seal

---

[34] Bolsec was by no means alone in questioning Calvin's doctrine of election, which on occasion was critically received by Reformed and Lutheran commentators. Melanchthon, for example, Luther's associate and eventual successor, had said nothing about predestination either in his *Commonplaces* of 1521 or in the *Augsburg Confession* of 1530. In the second edition of his *Commonplaces* (1535), much to Calvin's disappointment, he expressed strong reservations as to the usefulness of the doctrine. See below, Appendix II.

[35] Sermon 1 on Eph. 1:3, 4.
[36] Sermon 2 on Eph. 1:4-6.

who authenticates the truth of God's word, and the pledge of a redemption embraced by faith, enclosed in hope and consummated in heaven.[37]

In his sermon on Ephesians 3:9-12 the preacher enlarges his perspective still more. The note he sounds is not entirely new, since in his comments on Ephesians 1:7-10 he had already spoken of sin's pervasive effect on creation, and had endorsed Paul's description of God's purpose as the summation of all things in Christ. In expounding Ephesians 3 he returns to that theme with renewed vigour, setting God's redemptive plan within the context of his providential governance of the world. Election is part of that context, a major part, admittedly, but it is not the whole. The redeemed are the first-fruits of an immeasurably great harvest. The Scriptures speak not only of God's continuous saving purposes in time, but of the goal to which he has always been working: to make an end of sin and death, to rescue creation from futility, to re-establish a new humanity under a new Head, to unite all things in Christ. When the Redeemer returns, it will be not only to a fully saved church, but, as Warfield reminds us, to a fully saved world.[38] 'It was as if,' comments Calvin, 'by Christ's coming, God had restored the world to the state it had before it was effaced by sin.' Those called by God into the fellowship of the church 'already share in the promised restoration… The world is given to us as our inheritance.'[39]

Election places believers (proleptically in the case of the Old Testament saints) between Christ's first and second coming; it places all of them between God's first and second creation. It situates them in a world which, though marred by sin, has never ceased to be the theatre of God's glory, and which in its height and depth and in all its parts has always been the object of God's

---

[37] Sermon 3 on Eph. 1:13, 14.

[38] B. B. Warfield, *The Plan of Salvation*, rev. ed. (Grand Rapids, MI: Wm. B. Eerdmans, 1955), p. 102.

[39] Sermon on Eph. 3:9-12.

decree. The world is to be radically transformed; it is destined to enjoy what since Adam's sin it has never known—peace, such that the wolf will dwell with the lamb and the leopard with the kid (Isa. 11:6), fullness of life, and an ordered excellence which God himself will delight to call 'very good' (Gen. 1:31). From every corner of heaven and earth God's works will praise him, joining with the redeemed in proclaiming 'blessing and honour and glory and power to him who sits on the throne and to the Lamb, forever' (Rev. 5:13). Election is both crowned by, and ends in, doxology.

* * *

The texts which follow have been newly translated from the nineteenth-century edition of Calvin's collected works, established by Baum, Cunitz and Reuss.[40] Modern conventions regarding sentence length, paragraph division and punctuation have been observed. Scripture references have been corrected where necessary, and further references added. When Calvin cites Scripture, often from memory, or when he paraphrases it, we translate in the form given. Sermon titles are our own, as are the sub-headings which accompany Calvin's address of December 1551 to the Church of Geneva. The short extempore prayer with which the preacher ended his sermons has been included, and a small number of explanatory notes are supplied.

We have added three appendices which seek to place the Reformer in a somewhat wider setting. The first outlines a number of representative statements on election culled from contemporary or near-contemporary sources; the second discusses critical reactions to Calvin's teaching in both Reformed

---

[40] See above, footnote 4. Texts are sourced as follows: Part I, *CO* 8:85-118; Part II, *CO* 58:17-72; Part III, *CO* 51:259-310; Part IV, *CO* 51:459-74. The four sermons on Gen. 25 retain their original numbering. Those on Eph. 1, originally numbered 2-5, have been renumbered 1-4; the single sermon on Eph. 3 is the eighteenth in the series.

and Lutheran circles; the third examines the place which the Reformer accords the doctrine specifically in his preaching, and the manner in which, as pastor of God's flock, he presents it to his hearers.

I wish to thank the trustees of The Banner of Truth for their willingness to publish, and am particularly grateful to the Editor, Jonathan Watson, for his encouragement, wise counsel and unfailing support.

ROBERT WHITE
Sydney
6 April, 2022

I.

ELECTION:
A SUMMARY STATEMENT

AN ADDRESS GIVEN IN
THE CHURCH OF GENEVA

ON ETERNAL ELECTION

AN ADDRESS GIVEN IN THE CHURCH OF GENEVA BY JOHN CALVIN

SINCE we are shortly to receive the Lord's Supper, and since we cannot receive it as we ought unless we are joined together in unity of faith; and since, as you know, Satan in these past days has attempted to sow discord and division in our midst, we have by common consent thought it good and profitable to discuss God's election, according to which he has chosen and elected us. Our aim is to give an understanding of these things to both great and small, so that we may have peace, and our consciences, rest.

Now this is a subject which would take much time to explain. I must therefore try to be as brief as possible, omitting many things which might be said, since time does not permit us to deal with everything at length. By God's grace, however, I will endeavour to give a summary statement to which we might adhere, so that no one, however uneducated or ignorant, should have any excuse for knowing nothing about the matter. If, finally, doubts or scruples remain, they can be brought out into the open so that a better and more reasoned explanation may be given, by means, that is, of holy Scripture.

Election in Christ, the source of saving faith (Eph. 1:3-5)

This, then, should be our starting point: belief in Jesus Christ does not come from our own efforts, or because our minds are lofty and keen enough to grasp the heavenly wisdom contained in the gospel. It comes instead from God's grace—grace which surpasses our nature.

We need, then, to see whether or not this grace is common to all people. Scripture tells us that the opposite is the case. God, that is to say, grants his Holy Spirit to whomever he wills; he illumines them in his Son. Experience shows this to be true; of this we are persuaded. We must therefore conclude that faith proceeds from a higher and more hidden source and wellspring—from God's free election, by which he chooses for salvation those whom he wills.

Paul deals with this question in the first chapter of Ephesians, where he blesses God not only for the fact that we believe or for his gift of Jesus Christ in whom our salvation is fulfilled and complete. In addition Paul says, 'Blessed be God who has called and illumined us, having chosen us before the world was made' (Eph. 1:3, 4). Accordingly we see how we may fully comprehend the grace of God if we know with certainty that he has not only granted us faith, but has given it to us because, of his free will, he chose us before the creation of the world. The apostle, however, is not content merely with this: he goes on to say that God has chosen us according to the purpose of his will which he determined in himself (Eph. 1:5). We should carefully weigh each of these words, for when he speaks of God's purpose he is contrasting it with whatever might be found in men, which would imply that God was induced to do as he did by something else. As for the word 'purpose', what does it signify if not God's own determination? It is as Paul says to Titus, 'God chose us with a holy calling, not according to our works but according to his own purpose and grace'—that is, according to his free counsel.[1]

Here we find Paul contrasting two incompatible things: on the one hand men's works, on the other, God's purpose. So when

---

[1] The reference is not to Titus, but to 2 Timothy 1:9.

4

we hear this word from the lips of Paul, we should understand it to be a decision which God made when he chose us for himself, without, however, taking account of anything in us, as if that was what persuaded or moved him to be gracious to us. The truth is that, in choosing us, God does indeed take account of what is in us. But what does he find? Nothing but wretchedness and utter want! It is this that moves him to pity us. Yet although he finds this wretchedness in everyone in general, he shows mercy only to whomever he pleases. And why is that? The reason is unknown to us. So let us be satisfied with what our minds can grasp—with what Paul says and reveals to us, namely that God has chosen us according to the purpose which he himself determined. In this way Paul seeks to overturn all the objections which might be made about God's lack of justice in the matter. All such objections must be dismissed. When Paul declares that God determined his purpose all by himself, he means that God did not go beyond himself, that he did not look to one side or another as if to say, 'I am moved to act this way.'

The elect called according to God's purpose

The apostle makes the further point that God chose us 'in Jesus Christ' (Eph. 1:4), meaning that we are unworthy in ourselves. This in truth is how things are, and those who refuse to acknowledge it are badly deceived by pride and arrogance if they think that God called them to himself because of something that lay within them. That is why Paul adds that God 'adopted us in his beloved Son' (Eph. 1:5). It is for very good reason that our Lord Jesus Christ is described as 'the beloved Son', for in ourselves we are objects of hate, deserving of God's abhorrence. Nevertheless he looks upon us in his Son, and it is then that he loves us.

For the rest, in order to show that faith is a step lower and that it depends upon God's election, Paul expressly says that God's purpose is that we should be holy and spotless (Eph. 1:4). We ought to remember Peter's words in the fifteenth chapter of Acts: 'God cleanses men's hearts by faith' (Acts 15:9). Thus, when Paul states in this verse that God has chosen us so that we should be holy and spotless, he includes faith as well. In effect he is saying that we are full of corruption, and that this corruption consists in part in our unbelief. As he says, the thoughts of unbelievers are corrupt and defiled in God's sight (cf. Eph. 2:2, 3). What then must we do? We must come to God's unmerited election if we wish to have one ounce or drop of purity. We therefore see that faith comes solely from God's election. God, that is, illumines those whom of his free goodness he chose before the creation of the world.

That too is what Paul affirms in the eighth chapter of Romans, declaring first that God makes all things work for good to those he loves (Rom. 8:28). Lest, however, we think that we can prepare ourselves for salvation and attain this blessing by our own powers, he adds this rider: 'to those who are called according to God's purpose'. What he is suggesting is that everything works to blight and destroy us if we fail to love God. God's love must be in us if we want all things to aid and assist us. We should not think, however, that it is for us to take the initiative; God must forestall us. Who, then, are those who love God? Those whom God calls, says Paul, according to his purpose. Once more the apostle brings us back to the word to which we drew attention, that is, to the immutable counsel which is in God who does not go beyond himself, but whose motive for doing this or that lies in his sheer goodness. That, then, is what we must understand by the term 'election', used by Paul of those who are called according to God's purpose.

Why this particular insistence on God's purpose? It is so that we may know that God's calling is sure and certain: it is done with power and efficacy. God will assuredly call the unbelieving, but his call does not suffice to convert them. He does not touch their hearts to the quick; he does not give such power to his word that it abides in them. But when he calls us according to his purpose, when he converts us to him, it is because he has chosen us. It is as Paul goes on to say: 'Those he foreknew, he chose and called; those he called, he justified' (Rom. 8:29, 30). Here Paul identifies different steps, but the first and basic step is this: God knew those who are his.

Election not based on foreseen merit, but wholly on grace

How, then, did he know them? There are slanderers, it is true, who maintain that he knew those he wished to choose because he foresaw that they would be faithful to him and would profitably use his gifts to them.[2] Now that is an utter absurdity, for here the knowledge in question is of the kind that Paul describes later.[3] No other expositor is needed than Paul himself, who makes his meaning plain; we should seek no gloss from any other source. The apostle says that God did not reject his people whom he had known (Rom. 11:1). What did he know of them? Did he find his people worthy of his grace? On the contrary, Paul says that, among so great a multitude, only a remnant will be saved 'according to the election of grace' (Rom. 11:5). This is the grace of which Peter spoke in Acts, where Jesus Christ is said to have been proclaimed according to God's foreknowledge (Acts 2:23). And foreknowledge implies deliberation.

In sum, in declaring that God chose those he knew, Paul says the same as is said in the fourth chapter of Galatians: '... after you

---

[2] Calvin's target here is Bolsec, for whom God's election was dependent on his fore-knowledge of future faith. The Reformer argues that Scripture nowhere supports this view, since it establishes no qualitative distinction between elect and non-elect. Calvin's fundamental position has been well put by François Wendel: 'To establish a causal link between foreknowledge and predestination, whether it be foreknowledge of man's merits or foreknowledge of the graces which God will grant him, is tantamount to making God's will dependent on a cause external to the act of will itself. It would therefore mean limiting his will, whereas by definition his will permits of no diminution.' (*Calvin, sources et évolution de sa pensée religieuse*, Paris: Presses Universitaires de France, 1950, p. 207.)

[3] That is, God's knowledge of Israel's declension, as outlined by Paul in Rom. 9–10, which prompts him to pose the question, 'Has God rejected his people?' (Rom. 11:1).

knew God, or rather after you were known by him' (Gal. 4:9). Paul allows that men indeed knew God by faith. However, to help us understand that this does not come from us, he qualifies his remarks by adding, 'inasmuch as you have been known by him'. In effect, he is saying that we have come to God only because he has drawn near to us. So too it is written in the prophet Isaiah: 'I was found by those who did not seek me; I showed myself to those who did not inquire of me; and to those who were far off, I said, "Here am I. Here am I."' (Isa. 65:1). Thus we see how the elect are known to God, and how he elects those whom he has known. That is, he marks them as his very own possession, as if to say, 'You are mine.' Now these, being known, are called by him, and his call is when he grants us faith.

It is clear, then, that there is very full confirmation of the point already made. God, that is, on seeing that the whole human race is lost and ruined, out of pure grace rescues those he wills, and in rescuing them he calls them to himself. That is the means he uses. Election, at any rate, is paramount: it must precede faith, and faith must follow in its turn.

Election is not universal, but is secure

Now the person who has set out to trouble this church displays appalling insolence by shamelessly insisting that the first chapter of Ephesians applies only to Paul and the apostles. Thus, when Paul declares that God chose us before the creation of the world and accepted us in his beloved Son, choosing us for adoption and making us his children—'Oh,' he says, 'all that means is that God chose the apostles so that they might preach the gospel.' So it is only the apostles who are children of God, who have been adopted by him and who alone are the objects of his love! A fine theology that is, which drags the whole world down to hell! Such people, we know, hold God in derision. They are barking dogs bent on demolishing and destroying all reason.

What then must we do? Let us carefully weigh what has been said, in order to discern Paul's meaning which is neither uncertain nor obscure.

By way of further proof, let us turn to what we have already seen in John, especially in the sixth chapter, where it is said that none can come to Jesus Christ unless the Father draws him (John 6:44). Consider whether all are drawn this way. It is true that God offers his word to all and that by his word he invites all without distinction to hear him. Nevertheless he does not speak to the hearts of everyone—a point again made by John: 'He who has heard and learned from my Father will come to me' (John 6:45).

I ask you then, do all come to Jesus Christ? It is the opposite that we see. If all do not come to Jesus Christ, it follows that not all have been taught by the Father, for it is said that all who have been taught will come to Jesus Christ. Here we have a passage which is sufficiently clear and easy to understand. Our Lord Jesus Christ provides proof of this by citing the words of the fifty-fourth chapter of Isaiah, where it is said that all the children of the church will be taught by God (Isa. 54:13; John 6:45). Without question, the prophet is speaking of the special gift which God grants to those who are called into his flock. It is grossly impudent to argue, as this hothead does, that all that is said here applies to everyone in general. So when God says in Ezekiel, 'I will cause you to walk in my commandments' (Ezek. 11:20), he claims that this is a universal promise which applies to Turks as well as to Christians. And again, when it is said, 'I will establish a new covenant with you; I will give you a heart of flesh' (Ezek. 11:19, 36:26, 37:26), this is a promise made to everyone! When Scripture says, 'I will engrave my law on your hearts' (Jer. 31:33), it is a promise to all without exception!

Now is that not to laugh at God and at his word, since we see God through Jeremiah outlining a new covenant different from the one made with his ancient people? God declares, 'This covenant will not be like the one I made with your fathers, and which they transgressed' (Jer. 31:32). Men cannot avoid at once betraying God and parting from him. So if God wishes to make a firm and lasting covenant with us, he must impress his law upon our hearts. Does he do that to all men generally? As I said at the beginning, the opposite is what we see, as experience shows. We must thus conclude that this does not come from any power, worth or merit in us, but from God's sheer grace. We find that all do not have God's law imprinted on their hearts; that a heart of stone remains in most, in whom we see an utterly desperate obstinacy. Let us recognize, then, that God's promise is particular, and that he works only in those who are of his house.

Further, the Lord Jesus relieves us of every difficulty, for when he cites that very verse (John 6:45), does he mean that God will teach all men? Not at all! He says that what the prophet announced is being fulfilled. What then is his purpose here? Observing just how mindless were those who fancied they were great teachers, but who rejected everything he proclaimed, observing also that the leading clergy of the church would not receive him, he declares, 'Do not be surprised if there are so many rebellious and stubborn men, for it is not given to all to believe. My Father must draw those who come to me' (cf. John 6:44). So this is what he says: all whom the Father has given him will come to him; he will keep all who come, and will allow nothing to be lost (John 6:37, 39).

There are three points here which we should note. First, when we come to Jesus Christ we are given to him as his inheritance by God his Father. It is not for us to give ourselves to him: we must be the gift which his Father makes to him. We must thus conclude that election precedes faith, for the Father gives to the Son what is already his. That is, although all creatures are his, all are not of the flock. He has his own whom he has chosen according to his good pleasure. God has already chosen all those whom he gives to Jesus Christ.

From this there follows a second point, namely that Jesus Christ takes into his care and protection those who have been given to him by the Father. He will permit nothing that he has been given to perish. When once we are in his care, he will give us such power that we will persevere to the end. This we saw also in the tenth chapter of John, where he says that no one will snatch the sheep which have been entrusted to his keeping (John 10:28). Now why will no one snatch them? 'Because,' he says, 'the Father who has given them to me is greater than all' (John 10:29). We must be careful to bear this in mind, so that we may fight against the many trials which Satan brings upon us in order to distract us. Otherwise, when we are attacked on all sides and when a hundred thousand dead lie round us, where will our strength and resilience be? God, however, is invincible. Understand, therefore, that our salvation is certain. Why is that so? Because it is in God's hand. And how can we be sure of this? Because he has placed it in the hands of our Lord Jesus, who clearly teaches that the Father who has chosen us seeks to give full effect to his determination and to bring it to completion.

For the rest, our Lord Jesus makes clear in this verse something we have said many times, and which it is vital to remember: God has made us his sheep; having indeed chosen us, he also calls us into his flock. Faith is the means by which he calls us: it is then that we are shown and revealed to be his sheep. For the only call which we find in Scripture is the witness which God bears to his determination, which was previously concealed and about which more will be said directly. At any rate, we were Jesus Christ's sheep before ever we knew him; later he calls us to himself, and then we begin to hear his voice (John 10:3, 4).

Paul's understanding of election (Rom. 9)

An even clearer treatment of the subject is found in Paul, in the ninth chapter of Romans (Rom. 9:6-18). There he completely resolves the issue, so much so that no one can argue against him. Everything he tells us there is perfectly plain. True, Satan has always tried to quibble and to invent much subtle nonsense to obscure what is said. Be that as it may, truth always prevails. Here, then, Paul argues that although God chose Abraham's children as his inheritance, all who descended from Abraham's line according to the flesh are not children of the promise (Rom. 9:6, 7). They are not, that is, included and comprehended in God's election, which would make them true heirs of God and of his kingdom. Likewise today we might say that Jesus Christ has been ordained king of everyone, so that all might come and pay him homage. This is the way so many passages in the prophets speak, and especially in Psalm 2, which is the most notable text and the one most commonly cited: 'Ask of me and I will give you the ends of the earth as your inheritance. From the rising to the setting of the sun, kings and rulers will worship you' (cf. Psa. 2:8, 10, 11). This is how all people are called to salvation in the name of our Lord Jesus Christ. Yet that is not to say that all are actually heirs of the promise. Why? Paul might well have argued that all do not believe. It is not that he forgot: he leaves the fact unsaid, the reason being that God elects those whom he wills (Rom. 9:18).

Now attend, brethren, particularly to this point. Notice in the first place who it is that speaks. It is Paul, who declares in another place—the twelfth chapter of Second Corinthians—that he was caught up to the third heaven, and beheld mysteries of God which it is not lawful for anyone to utter (2 Cor. 12:2-4). Does not Paul know the balance that must be kept when God's mysteries are made known? He affirms that it is not lawful to reveal certain mysteries which he saw on high. It follows, then, that this is one mystery which can be revealed to men, otherwise he would have strictly refrained from publishing it and would not have disclosed it as boldly as he does. For here, very deliberately and with nothing to compel him, he opens up the subject of election, and desires us to be so well taught that we are familiar with the argument he puts.

He speaks of two children who are in the same mother's womb, and who have been begotten by the same father, the patriarch Isaac (Rom. 9:10). Both possess the promise which had been outwardly proclaimed; they were born in the same house, which is the people and sanctuary of God, who is the Head of his church. Nevertheless, at the time when the mother still bore them in her womb, it was said: 'The older will serve the younger' (Gen. 25:23; Rom. 9:12). Now some, who seek only to slander, claim that it is an earthly blessing that is meant.[4] Really? This is merely to deride the Holy Spirit who spoke by the mouth of Paul. Is the apostle discussing which of the two would live more comfortably in this world, or would enjoy white bread? Is he discussing sensual pleasures and other such things? What an absurdity! His theme is rather the eternal salvation of every soul. They make such a claim only in order to pervert holy Scripture. It is clear, then, that the interpretation offered by these mockers of God is pure folly – in fact, brazen wickedness! For here it is a question of those who are heirs of the covenant, which is uniquely spiritual – the covenant which God made with Abraham when he said to him, 'I will be your God and the God of your seed after you' (Gen. 17:7). What does that signify? 'You will live forever in my kingdom', as Jesus Christ himself explains.[5]

---

[4] It is Erasmus who appears to be meant. In his treatise *On Free Will*, he argues that, strictly speaking, the story of Jacob and Esau does not convey a spiritual lesson. It teaches us instead that God is able to direct men's temporal affairs for good or ill, without excluding them from salvation. (Erasmus and Luther, *Discourse on Free Will*, tr. Ernst F. Winter, New York: Frederick Ungar Publishing Co., 1961, pp. 53-55.)

[5] Calvin perhaps has in mind Christ's words to the Jews: 'Your father Abraham rejoiced to see my day; he saw it and was glad' (John 8:56).

The apostle was also right to say that while Isaac had two children from the womb of Rebecca his wife, one was preferred to the other (Rom. 9:12, 13). He points to the testimony of the prophet Malachi.[6] Admittedly Malachi is speaking of the land of Canaan and of Mount Seir. But was not Canaan a symbol and image of the heavenly inheritance? Paul therefore shows us as in a mirror that God chose Jacob, preferring him to his brother Esau. Jacob, I say, who was the junior, was preferred to the one who was his senior. He was ranked above Esau, so that we might attribute nothing to the natural order, but rather to that eternal counsel which is our subject here. Nor is Paul content to say only this: he argues that before they had done either good or bad, God announced that he had chosen Jacob and had conferred the inheritance on him, having stripped Esau of it. 'Before they had done either good or evil,' says Paul, 'in order that we should know that it came from God who calls, and not from men' (Rom. 9:11).

There is a distinction commonly made by popish theologians, namely that God does not elect men according to the works they do; he elects those who he foresees will be faithful. Now that contradicts what we have already said about Paul, who asserts that we are chosen and elected by God to be holy and spotless before his face (Eph. 1:4). He would have had to say something very different if it were the case that God elected us because he had foreseen that we would be holy. Paul does not speak this way. Instead he says that God chose us in order that we should be holy. He thus concludes that faith depends on God's election. Those who think differently are ignorant of man and of our human nature.

Accordingly, let us consider for a moment what our nature is like, and what it might yield if God left it to itself. We are

---

[6] Mal. 1:2, 3: 'Is not Esau Jacob's brother?' says the Lord. 'Yet I have loved Jacob but I have hated Esau.'

assuredly so corrupt and perverse that we are capable of doing only evil. True, the point is well made that all things will work for good to those who love God (Rom. 8:28). Nevertheless, at the same time and in the same chapter, Paul says that every single power of our nature is at enmity with God (Rom. 8:7). So what does God foresee in us if he leaves us as we are? What will he find in us, except utter rottenness and loathing? Must he not be our mortal enemy, and must he not cast us into the very depths of hell? That is what he must inevitably foresee. When, therefore, God foresees good, it is because he has determined to put it in us: it is his gifts and graces that he foresees, nothing more. Who, then, can proudly boast? Who can stand up and say: 'I am something'?

That established, let us turn to another passage penned by Paul: 'Who are you to single yourself out? And what makes you superior?' (1 Cor. 4:7). Here Paul reveals two things. First, although we all share a common lot and nature, we are nevertheless distinct from each other, and this difference comes from God. That is what Paul's statement implies. To be singled out is to be superior. Then too, Paul teaches that none of this is our own doing. We do not take the initiative with God; we do not draw close to him; on the contrary, it is he who does everything; everything must be ascribed to him.

Such, we see, is Paul's meaning in the ninth chapter of Romans. When he states that Esau was rejected and Jacob chosen, he insists that this did not come from works, but from God who calls (Rom. 9:11). We are bound, then, to conclude that it is not of him who wills or who runs, but of God who shows mercy (Rom. 9:16). That is, men should not rise up and rob God of his glory, nor attribute anything of their salvation to themselves. Everything, says the apostle, is in the mercy of God.

Now there are those who quibble about this verse. 'It is not of him who wills or runs,' they say, meaning that running is not enough for our salvation, but that God helps with his mercy.[7] A pertinent remark, perhaps, but if that is the case, the opposite might well be said. For if there were collaboration between God and men—if, that is, God did half and we the rest—we would have to conclude that it is not wholly of us, but partly of God; and also that it is not wholly of God, but partly of us. Consequently we would be seeking to make God subject to us, which is a truly cursed blasphemy. It would horrify everyone, however wicked they might be.

Augustine himself expounds this verse, saying that in speaking of him who wills and who runs, Paul does not credit us with such will or power that we can do anything by ourselves.[8] He affirms instead that man is captive, so to speak, and can do nothing at all. What he does have comes from the grace of God, who has been holding out his hand to draw us to himself—yes, even when we were completely alienated, exiled and cast off.

Recapitulation: glory to the God of grace

We can now see that the remarks which I have made are fully confirmed by holy Scripture. God, that is, has chosen us, not only before we came to know him but before we were born, before the world was made. He chose us in his unmerited goodness, nor did he look elsewhere for a reason. He determined his purpose all by himself. It is important that we know this, so that we may glorify him as we should, otherwise we cannot give him the glory that is his due. This we see in the second chapter of Second Thessalonians, where the apostle says: 'We ought always to give thanks to God who chose us from before the foundation of the world, in sanctification and in spirit' (2 Thess. 2:13). How in this verse does Paul give thanks to God? Not simply, he says, for

---

[7] A probable reference to Origen (*Commentary on Romans*, VII.16) and Jerome (*Dialogue against the Pelagians*, I.5). Cf. Calvin's discussion in *Inst.* II.5.17.

[8] Augustine, *Enchiridion*, IX.32. The preceding paragraph directly echoes Augustine's argument.

the fact that they believe, but for the fact that God has chosen them. Furthermore he adds that God has chosen them in order to sanctify them by his Holy Spirit, and has brought them to the knowledge of faith. We have already noticed the same thing in Ephesians, which fully agrees with this verse (Eph. 1:4).

Objections answered: we cannot be wiser than God

There are of course objections which tend the other way. We know just how bold people are, and everyone with any experience knows how hard it is to tame our spirits, so that we receive calmly and humbly all that is explained to us. A man must be firmly disciplined by God before he finally comes round. That is why James urges us to receive the word of God as it is preached to us with meekness and a gentle disposition (James 1:21). We should not be surprised if people rise up against this doctrine and if it is so often denied. Whatever the case, all those who are God's children receive what they hear from God's lips without dissent, affirming: 'We must keep to it, for God has spoken.'

The fact is that this is how God desires to test our humility. It is true that every doctrine taught by Scripture has this as its aim, but there is no doctrine more calculated to humble us than this: the knowledge that God has chosen us in his unmerited kindness, since such was his good pleasure. We must therefore refute the objections that are made with this one word: God's authority—that is, his supremacy and pre-eminence over us. Supposing we had no more than that, it is enough to overthrow all the arrogance of those who clamour against this doctrine which we have determined from holy Scripture. It is enough also to rebuff all the wicked thoughts which, as we say, the devil might whisper in our ear.

I will begin with those objections which seem the mildest. We will indeed find some God-fearing people who may have certain doubts or mental reservations.[9] Even so, they have not really yielded such obedience to God as to exclude all hidden pride. God, then, must uncover the hypocrisy which has been in them up until now. Thus those who cry: 'Look, I am afraid to make God appear unjust by saying that he has elected those he wills. They had no notion of the evil hidden in them.' Or when they claim: 'I am afraid that I'm accusing God of cruelty by saying that he does not elect everyone in general', we might reply: 'Friend, you make it clear that there is secret pride in your heart; you do not yet know the hypocrisy that lies within.' Now why is this? Consider what Paul says in the fourteenth chapter of Romans. There he writes that we must not pass judgment on others unless we have been taught by God (Rom. 14:4). In that verse he is speaking not about sins which have already been condemned, and on which God's verdict is known; he is speaking about indifferent things.[10] In such matters we must not judge each other, for, as he says, we must all appear before the judgment seat of God (Rom. 14:10). We are brethren, so we must not presume to save or damn, asserting that this one will fall, for he has done evil, while that one will be raised up, because I say that he has done good. No, no. It is for our Lord Jesus to judge us, and just as he casts us down, so he raises us up, for this power has been given to him by God his Father.

If Paul asks us not to be so bold as to judge each other in this way, think, I say, of what it means to rise up against God, not wanting him to be known as just unless we know him to be

[9] The reference is to Reformed theologians in Bern, Basel and Zurich, who were in one way or another critical of Calvin's forthright defence of the doctrine of 'double predestination'. (See further, Appendix II.) The Reformed confessions of this and later centuries generally prefer to speak of sinners being 'left' in a state of corruption, or of God's 'passing them over' (preterition).

[10] By indifferent things (*adiaphora*), the preacher understands those practices which the Christian may freely accept or refuse without offence to God. Paul's chief concern in Rom. 14 is with foods. Here Calvin is arguing from the lesser to the greater: if it is wrong to pass judgment on our fellows in things that matter least, how much worse is it to pass judgment on God in things that matter most!

such—unless, that is, the reason is apparent to us. What kind of argument is that? This, however, is what those are like who say: 'I am afraid that God is unjust by acting as he does.'

So you fear that God is unjust unless he is beholden to you? Unless he is subject to your supervision, unless you understand his reason for doing this or that—unless, indeed, he is inferior to you? What arrogance is this! True, many do not see this fault in themselves, but we must look there for the real root. And we must not trot out our trivial questions, saying: 'I do not know if God is just, but let him show me how and why.' Since, however, we know nothing of his counsel, since we are not so lofty of thought that we can attain such heights, and since we cannot fathom why he does all things, we must walk humbly until the day when the books are opened, as we read in Daniel (Dan. 7:10, 12:1). Then, says Scripture, we shall see what we now understand by faith (1 Cor. 13:12)—why God chose Jacob, why he rejected Esau, and why he directs men the way he does. We will see, I say, the reason why. For now, however, let us be content to know that God is just, and let us be certain that he is the fount of all wisdom, right and equity. But let us also consider why this is so.

Some think that Paul was bereft of an answer when he declared: 'Man, who are you to rise up against God'? (Rom. 9:20). Nevertheless, that is the best possible solution. To prove the point, do not think that God cannot fully satisfy us, that he does not have what it takes when an answer is required, so that he can say to us, 'This is why I did this or that.'

In the first place, suppose that God chose to submit to us, like someone before his judge who enters a plea. 'You think me remiss in this matter? This is why I acted as I did.' If God should choose to submit to us, as if to account for all that he does, think for a moment of whether we could even bear his glory, his inherent majesty, since we would have behaved with such reckless abandon. Let us know, therefore, our own capabilities—the fact that we are so gross and ignorant that we cannot grasp the things that God has meant to hide from us. In any event, let us take it as settled that God has just cause to do as he does, however hidden it is from us, and that the things which we do not know nevertheless exist. We do not yet see face to face the things which God has done. We do not see them visibly, as Paul states elsewhere (1 Cor. 13:12). In short, we will never understand this present, secret mystery—so lofty and supreme!—unless we are meek enough to say: 'Well, although we do not see the reason why God works this way, it should be enough for us that he is just, and that we can keep on growing in the knowledge of his will.'

Now there are those who say that we could well do without this doctrine, and that faith and repentance can be preached without insisting that only some are God's elect. These people fancy that they are wiser than God himself. True, we must be sober, as I have just said, and we cannot be too careful in observing moderation as God has commanded, so that we do not exceed our limits. But by what measure is sobriety to be judged? From where are we to get it? From our own wisdom, or from God himself? It is certain that God knows what is needful for us to understand. Since this is so, let him show us the things we have already seen: we must know them, but we must not go beyond the bounds. As soon as God has blocked the path, we must call a halt. We should understand, then, that it is for God to show us what he wants to be clear and obvious to us; it is for us to accept it in all humility, and to inquire no further.

We turn now to the objections of those who loudly blaspheme against God. Some will claim that if God has elected those whom he wills, there is no need to believe that we should strive to lead holy lives, for God's election takes care of the lot. Swine like these thrust their snouts into everything, but where does it get them? Holy Scripture quickly and easily settles the question, pointing out that we have been chosen with a holy calling, so that we should no longer follow our unclean ways, but should be holy and spotless (Eph. 1:4). To make such a claim is to try to separate the sun from its light, and to assert that it is enough if we have sun but not light. What, then, do we gain by getting rid of the sun's light?

It is the same with God's election. Let us not separate what he has joined together, for when he chose us it was in order to make us holy. Those he chose, he separated from the faithless, so that they should not be caught up in their defilement, evil and corruption. For this reason it is erroneous to object that if God has chosen us, we are bound to throw over the traces and let ourselves go. The opposite is the case, for those who say: 'Oh, if we are the elect, we can do wrong, for we cannot perish', can give no greater proof that they are reprobates! The fact is that God rules by his Holy Spirit those whom he has chosen. And what does his election mean? It means that he has adopted us as his children, and that in choosing us he has given us the Spirit of adoption to rule and direct us, as is written in the first chapter of John (John 1:12, 13).

Now let us come to the chief blasphemy which is voiced by some: 'If it is true that God elects whomever he pleases while rejecting others, he would be unjust.' These people are not like the others of whom I spoke, and who fear that God might appear unjust. In doing so they mean indeed to honour him. They do not, however, know how to honour him: Satan is already preying on their minds. Of the others, however, he has taken full control. Yet both these and they have risen up against God, and what will finally happen to them? It is as if I were to toss a stone up over my head. Where will it come down? If we hurled ourselves one against the other, we might possibly avoid getting hurt; the blows might not touch us. But when we undertake to speak against God, who is it we are taking on? And when we shoot our firearms or launch our darts, arrows and other such above our heads, must not the lot descend upon us and cut us down? So let us fear lest we be overwhelmed, and let us learn to worship God's majesty alone. Let it be agreed that everything he does is well ordered, even though we may not know the reason why. That is what Paul is teaching us: we must not be wiser than the Spirit of God.

There are those who find it odd when they are not given easy solutions. 'I would like things to be explained more clearly,' they say, 'so that I might see why certain things are so.' 'Friend, you must look for another school, since, arrogant as you are, you will not give glory to God unless you have solid grounds for doing so. Go, look for a school which is different from that of the Holy Spirit!' We know how Paul puts it: 'O man, who are you?' (Rom. 9:20). If someone contends with us on a question which is not his concern, let him tackle God, for if we try to go beyond what he has told us in his word, we will be poor scholars in his school. Paul thus tells us how we should behave in this respect, and the balance we must observe. It is important that we be kept in check, and that we understand what our condition is.

Surely we want to be ranked above wild animals? Now if an ass or a dog happened to speak, saying, 'Why am I not a man?', every one of us would reply, 'Since God chose to make you an animal, should you not be content with that?' And who are we, compared with God? Without doubt we are as inferior to him as the animals are to us. So why should he not have as much authority over us as we would like to have over his creation?

What, therefore, remains to be said? Let those who would blaspheme consider the example which Augustine gives in a second passage, the example of our Lord Jesus Christ.[11] He is the

---

[11] Cf. Augustine, *The Predestination of the Saints*, X.19: 'The Saviour and Son of God is the most excellent mirror of grace and predestination ... How did he merit being taken up into unity of person with the co-eternal Father ...? What good work preceded in such a case as this? What prior good did he do? ... By grace he is such and so very great.'

very mirror and model in whom God has revealed the infinite treasures of his kindness, for he is the Head of the church (Col. 1:18). We must therefore begin with him, if we would know how God works in his lesser members.[12]

Here then is Jesus Christ, true God and true Man. His human nature was raised to extraordinary eminence: he is both God and Man, yet is also God's own Son—his only Son, I say, his natural Son. What did the human nature found in Jesus Christ deserve? For it came forth from Adam's race; it was necessary for him to be of David's seed, otherwise he could not have been our Saviour (Luke 1:32; Rom. 1:3). He was conceived by his mother in miraculous fashion, nevertheless he came from the line of David, Abraham and Adam. That he was sanctified and was not subject to the same corruption as we are, was due to the wonderful and extraordinary grace of God. Even so, if we consider only the human nature of Jesus Christ, it did not deserve to be exalted to the level of honour of which Scripture says: 'Behold him who rules over the angels, and before whom every knee will bow' (Phil. 2:10; Heb. 1:4, 6). Accordingly, when we consider God's grace shown to our Head, must not each of us look inwardly and say: 'God has elected me, who was banished and cast out from his kingdom. I had nothing in me that might please him, yet he chose me to be one of his.' Should we not acknowledge his grace and extol it? When, therefore, we ponder these things, we cry with Paul: 'What loftiness!' (Rom. 11:3). That should show us that we cannot truly be taught by the Holy Spirit until we have thrilled with wonderment. When we think of God's mysteries, let us confess that it is not yet possible for us to know them.

Calvin's point here, as he has said from the beginning, is that election is all of grace, and that this is most clearly seen from Christ's own example. He pursues his argument in the following paragraph.

[12] That is, in Christ's lesser members. Believers are united to Christ as members of his body, the church, of which he is Head.

Reprobation: God's hidden counsel

Lastly, we must come to the subject of the reprobate, for just as God has elected some, he has also rejected those whom he willed. One implies the other.[13] In the case of election, not all are included; a portion is chosen. Now as to the reprobate, we might find it strange indeed that God should reject them, since they are his creatures. We ought, however, to remember what we are like in Adam, and what we derive from him. In him, all of us are lost and condemned. If God were to reject everyone, from the first to the last, there is no way that we could argue against him. If he were to mete out justice to us, we would deserve to be cast into deepest hell.

Now if God has chosen some while rejecting others, must not our eye be evil when he exercises the authority which is properly his? Such is the metaphor which our Lord Jesus Christ employs when he says, 'Is your eye evil because I am generous and good?' (Matt. 20:15). There he is speaking of those who complain because the householder gave no more to those who bore all the toil than to those who had barely worked (Matt. 20:1-16). 'What?' he asks. 'Am I not free to use what is mine as I think fit?' So if men are free to dispose of their property as they like, is God subject to a stricter law than they are? Would that not be to tie him tightly down? Observe, then, that since we are all lost in Adam and all cast into hell, and since God nevertheless calls some whom he has chosen, it is a particular act of kindness which he shows them. He must certainly be free to do this, without anyone venturing to complain.

'Granted,' someone will say, 'but when God created Adam, did he not foresee what was to happen? And did he not direct events

---

[13] Calvin presents reprobation as the concomitant of election, since, as he writes in *Inst.* III.23.1, 'election would not exist if it were not set over against reprobation'. There is, however, this fundamental difference: reprobation is deserved, election is not. No exact symmetry exists, therefore, between election and reprobation.

as he pleased?' Yes, of course. That cannot be denied. The fact remains, however, that man was created naturally just, good and upright; but he stumbled and fell. That he disobeyed God and committed sin was his own work; it cannot be attributed to God. 'Yes, but if God had not decreed it, it would not have happened. He could surely have made provision. How did he allow things to turn out this way? Could he not have put them right?' He could! But let us be careful not to grumble at our Judge. And let us recognize that what, from eternity, he determined in his counsel is hidden from us. We can have no conception of it. Accordingly, let us remember the words of holy Scripture, that God's plans and mysteries are like the great deep (Psa. 36:6, 92:5; Rom. 11:33). What is the point of throwing ourselves in? If we saw a chasm before us, who would dream of jumping into it?

What else can we do but revere his justice in all of his works? That is what we must do. Paul brings us back to this, when he says that, in his time, there were some who grumbled at God, or who at least echoed what these blasphemers affirm: 'Why should God complain? Why does he find fault with men, since we cannot resist his will?' (Rom. 9:19). 'O man,' replies Paul, 'who are you to rise up against God?' (Rom. 9:20). He might well have set forth all the reasons advanced by the Sorbonists and blockheads who nowadays try to overthrow God's election.[14] He might well have said, 'Oh, God has chosen those who, he foresaw, would be faithful, those on whom he would bestow his favours and who, he saw, would accept them of their free will.' Yet he says nothing of the sort. On the contrary, he concludes that it is not for us to inquire. Nevertheless, he teaches that in granting grace, God gives it to those he wills. Is that not the plainest of statements? Let us be content, therefore, with the

---

[14] By 'Sorbonists', Calvin means the theologians of the University of Paris who, wedded to the Scholastic tradition, championed Roman Catholic orthodoxy. They were among the Reformer's most trenchant critics.

evidence of Scripture which we have already cited, and let us be sure that, even without that, all who rise up against God are already self-condemned, so that they need us to provide little by way of proof.

It is wonderful indeed to see how people are so presumptuous as to say: 'Look here, I will not be satisfied unless I am offered a very clear reason.' Then tell me, is there more ample proof than what we have already told you? Even if we had argued over and over and had pointed to specific details, is there surer proof than that which our consciences provide? Certainly not! So let each of us descend now into himself, and he will find his condemnation graven on his conscience. He will find that we are all guilty of death, and that each, having looked closely at himself, must condemn himself.[15]

How then can we go on to say, 'I cannot see why this should be'? These people clearly show that they have never searched their conscience. They flutter about in the air, never grasping with godly fear and reverence the things he shows us. They want to fly without knowing who God is and who they are. Now these two things should go hand in hand: if we would profit from what the gospel teaches, we need to know all about God and about ourselves. Yet these people want to know nothing about either.[16]

That is what we must remember concerning the reprobate. God rejects them because they have not been elected and chosen. Even so we must know that God is just, although we cannot comprehend the cause: he must not be held accountable to us. Let us be content, then, to know that all his judgments are

[15] Here as elsewhere, Calvin assigns a crucial role to conscience. A God-given faculty, it is diminished by sin but not extinguished. Cf. *Inst.* II.8.1: 'Our conscience does not allow us to feel nothing and to sleep a perpetual sleep, without bearing inward witness and warning us of our debt to God, without showing us the difference between good and evil and thus accusing us when we fail in our duty.'

[16] Compare the very first words of Calvin's *Institutes*: 'The whole sum of our wisdom— wisdom, that is, which deserves to be called true and assured—broadly consists of two parts, knowledge of God and knowledge of ourselves.'

right and equitable (Psa. 9:8), and that his justice will be clear to us once we see him face to face. That is why Paul, referring to Pharaoh's example, goes on to say that God has at least as much authority over men as a potter has over earth or clay (Rom. 9:20, 21). Thus if God should make us vessels of honour, reflect that it is out of sheer goodness. Remember, then, that he might also make us vessels of dishonour, and that when he does so, it comes from our own nature; it is not for us to do more.

It now remains for us to sum up all that we have said concerning God's election.

Notice that we cannot extol God as we should, or acknowledge the grace which he bestows upon us, unless we know that he has elected us, rescuing us indeed from the universal condemnation in which all of Adam's race lies, in order to lead us to our Lord Jesus Christ. He alone has redeemed us. However, when we consider the reprobate, let us learn to recognize ourselves in them, and to say: 'We would be the same, if God had not shown us his fatherly kindness and separated us from them.' By nature we cannot tell the difference: God alone has conferred this excellence upon us. Until the faithful reach that point, they will never, as I said before, exalt God as they should.

Contested scriptural passages (1 Tim. 2:4; Ezek. 18:23; Matt. 28:19, 20)

I will now briefly discuss all that might be cited against us, though I will not deal with every single point. It will be enough if I reply to one or two.

First, there are Paul's words in the second chapter of First Timothy: 'God desires all men to be saved' (1 Tim. 2:4). This same question has already been put by the person responsible for troubling the church. He received a full enough answer at an earlier meeting.[17] I raise the matter here because it is the basic

---

[17] The *congrégation* held on 16 October 1551. See our Introduction, p. xxi.

argument advanced by this muddler who has tried to confuse God's teaching in this church. 'There!' he says. 'According to Paul, God wants everyone to be saved and to come to the knowledge of the truth.' But if God wants all to come to the knowledge of the truth, why does he not send men to preach the gospel to the Turks? Why has he allowed the world to be blinded for such a long period of time? As Peter says in the tenth chapter of Acts, 'How was it that people were left to wander for so long?'[18] It follows, then, that Paul is not speaking of each and every person, but of people of all conditions. He demonstrates this by urging prayer for all rulers and for those who have been given authority (1 Tim. 2:2). Now someone might ask, 'How is it that we should pray for God's enemies?' Paul declares that it is not for us to restrict God's grace according to our fancies: God desires people of all conditions to come to know him. How fitting a verse is that, and how well cited, to overturn God's election! It is no surprise if muddlers like that can scarcely see. They think that they are most clever and sharp-witted: the devil is dazzling their eyes.

Then again, they argue this way: 'Yes, but has not God said that he does not desire the death of a sinner, but that he should be converted and live?' (Ezek. 18:23). Now let us see whether conversion is given to everyone. In the second chapter of Second Timothy Paul affirms that it is not a gift common to all: 'Perhaps God may allow them to repent and to be saved' (2 Tim. 2:25). He thus signifies that God bestows grace on whomever he wills. As for repentance, when God says, 'Let the sinner be converted and live', that, as all can see, is understood to mean that God invites everyone to repent. Nevertheless the promise is not universal. Similarly the threats that God makes to the Ninevites are conditional: 'They may not repent, but if they come to repentance, the evil which I resolved to bring upon them will not befall

---

[18] The reference is rather to Paul's address in Lystra (Acts 14:16): 'In past generations God allowed all the nations to walk in their own ways.'

them' (Jon. 3:8-10). The threat was thus conditional. So when the prophet Ezekiel declares that God does not desire the death of a sinner, but that he should be converted and live, it is as if he said, 'God is sending me to proclaim to all the promise of salvation, but you must be converted.' Yet the gift of conversion is not common to all. It is not in our power to turn from our evil lives unless God changes us and cleanses us by his Holy Spirit. Scripture is full of this teaching. It therefore follows that this promise is not made equally to everyone. Nevertheless this poor wretch ventures to ask 'Why?', as if in jest, as if he had never read one word of Scripture! Such impudence is worthy of curs like him when they thus set out to clash with God.

Despite this, they make a further claim: 'Yes, but is not the gospel preached throughout the world?'[19] It is! Think, however, whether all have been illumined by God so that they accept this message. Holy Scripture says the opposite, and Paul settles the question for us when he writes that the gospel is God's power to salvation for all who believe (Rom. 1:16). So let us consider who it is who believes. Paul tells us in the tenth chapter of Romans, when he says that faith comes by hearing, and hearing by the word of God (Rom. 10:17). 'However,' he adds, 'not all believe and not all are obedient, for Isaiah declares, "Who has believed our preaching, and to whom is the arm of the Lord revealed?"' (Rom. 10:16; Isa. 53:1). Seeking to explain why all do not believe, Paul expressly says that God's arm is not revealed to everyone; that is, God does not display his power toward all. Is that not a statement which is all too clear? How could we contradict it? All do not believe. Why? Because God does not display his power to all. That is what we so often read in holy Scripture. Luke, for example, writes in the sixteenth chapter of Acts that God opened the heart of a woman called Lydia, a seller of purple; he opened her heart so that she heeded what Paul was saying (Acts 16:14).

---

[19] As commanded by Christ, Matt. 28:19, 20; Mark 16:15, 20.

God's speaking to the heart of this woman was a particular gift given to her. Agreed! But is this not a general truth taught in Luke, when he says, 'All who were appointed to salvation believed'? (Acts 13:48). By its very nature the gospel is the power of God by which all who believe are saved. We, however, in our wilfulness, can only reject the gospel, unless God illumines us when he calls us. As Scripture says, all believed who were appointed to salvation.

Let us learn, however, that we cannot be assured of our salvation except by faith. Anyone who says, 'How do I know whether I am saved or damned?', shows by these words that he has never known what faith is, or the confidence which we should have in God, through Jesus Christ. Would you really know whether you are elect? Look at yourself in Jesus Christ. For those who, by faith, truly share in Jesus Christ, can be sure that they belong to God's eternal election, and that they are his children. Whoever, then, is in Jesus Christ and is a member of his body by faith, can be certain of his salvation, and in seeking to know it we do not need to ascend on high in order to inquire about what for now must remain hidden.

Here, then, God stoops down to us, and in his Son shows us what it is all about. It is as if he said, 'Here am I. Look on me and know that I have adopted you as my children.' When, therefore, we accept the witness of the gospel to salvation, we know and are assured that God has chosen us. The faithful, therefore, need not doubt their salvation: let them take it as settled that since they have been called to faith by the preaching of the gospel, they have been made to share in the grace of our Lord Jesus Christ, and in the promise he has made to them in his name. For our Lord Jesus Christ is the basis of both—of the promises of salvation and of unmerited election, given from the foundation of the world.[20]

---

[20] Elected in and through Christ, and effectually called by the gospel to repentance and faith, believers thus look for assurance of salvation not to themselves but to Christ,

Accordingly, we now see that all those passages which might be cited have been cited inappropriately in order to pervert the election of God. What we are taught concerning it must remain firm and certain. We see also that we must remain in fear and humility, without presuming to try to inquire about what God ordained before the creation of the world. Let us follow only what we are told by the Scriptures, and let us keep to the path we have already taken concerning God's election.

God's will is sovereign, and his purposes just

In the meantime, we must also remember as a general truth that God governs all things by his providence, so that his will is the source of everything. That is why we say that it is the necessary rule of all things. Not that we must therefore involve God in our iniquities, or that we can really do so. We must nevertheless hold to this doctrine as revealed to us in holy Scripture—the doctrine, that is, that God so arranges all things that he does no evil on his part, for he is just; that, on men's part, they corrupt all that is good and turn it into evil; and that the condemnation for all the ill they do remains on their heads.

Why then is that? Admittedly this subject would require extensive treatment if examined in detail. We will say only one or two words about it.

God, we see, has his will as sole cause, and his will is so much united with right and equity that he can will nothing but good. Men, we also see, are bent on enjoying their pleasures and desires; they can easily bend their wills to their evil dispositions and cravings; hence everything in them is perverted and corrupt. Why? Because man in himself is subject to evil thoughts and

---

their Redeemer, Mediator and Head. Cf. *Inst.* III.24.5: 'If we seek God's fatherly mercy and kindness toward us, we must turn our eyes to Christ … Those whom God has chosen as his children are said to have been chosen not in themselves but in his Christ, because he could only love them in him, and could honour them with his inheritance only if they had first become partakers of him.'

dissipation; he knows no moderation, he is completely undisciplined. God is quite the opposite. Why? Because God's will is the rule of all rules, the law of all laws, perfect justice, perfect equity, perfect integrity. In a word, it is the source of all goodness.

For that reason we must certainly condemn the teaching of the papists, for the popish theologians claim that God has two wills, one ordered and the other absolute.[21] What a devilish blasphemy is that! When they picture a will of God different from the will he has ordained, it is as if they were saying that his will is uncontrolled, immoderate, without balance, integrity or equity in all that he does. Is it not downright blasphemy to attribute these things to God? We, on the other hand, maintain that the will of God is ordered, and so well ordered as to be the source of all equity and justice. Nevertheless, as I said before, we will not have such knowledge of God's justice that we will see the reason why he does this or that. Even so, everything he does has a good and proper purpose.

For example, wars are waged in the world and much lawlessness is involved. Now a single murder is an awful thing, but in a war a hundred thousand are committed. To rob one man of his goods is most cruel, but in time of war a hundred thousand homes are robbed and plundered. Hearing two or three blasphemies might lead us to say, 'How deplorable!' But in war there are blasphemies without number, so abominable indeed as to fill us with horror; there is debauchery too, girls and women are raped, with other atrocities besides. The fact is, however, that wars do not take place apart from God's will and disposition. That is certain, and Scripture is full of such teaching, for it says that God shatters the spear, causes wars to cease, assembles

---

[21] While recognizing the Scholastic distinction between God's ordered and absolute will, Calvin denies that the latter is such as might allow God to damn even the angels if he chose. God, he contends, is no tyrant possessed of naked will. His exercise of power is never arbitrary, but is directed to ends which, in keeping with his nature, are holy and just. Cf. *Inst.* I.17.2.

armies and prepares them for battle; he makes kings and rulers his soldiers and puts them to work, directing them and leading them as by the hand; they are his darts, arrows, swords and axes (Psa. 46:9; Isa. 13:4). That is how Scripture pictures it.[22]

How is it that God does these things? Is there iniquity in him? Assuredly no! Still, he sends forth his rods upon the world, and by his just judgment he punishes us as he wills. And although we do not yet see the reason, we must nevertheless recognize that all that he does is just. That is why Job does not inquire why God has taken all his wealth from him and stripped him of everything. True, he argues a great deal about it and claims that it is not on account of his sins. Nevertheless he concludes that none of this has happened apart from God's providence, and that all the misfortune which he has suffered, grievous though it was to bear, has been softened by the patience which he derived from it. Does he, in fact, grumble at God? No! Instead he says, 'The Lord gave and the Lord has taken away. Blessed be his name!' (Job 1:21). And he does not speak hypocritically; he speaks the truth.

Let us learn, then, that when God does things for reasons which are not obvious to us, we ought nevertheless to worship his counsel and his judgment, confessing that he is just and equitable. If, for all that, our eyes are dazzled and the brightness is beyond our comprehension, God will make clear to us what is now unknown—when, that is, he has united us fully with himself, for that is the goal to which he calls us.

---

[22] For Calvin, God's sovereignty allows of no exceptions: success and adversity are both alike his work. He explicitly denies the notion of a 'permissive will' which might absolve God of responsibility: 'We have cited the Psalm, "God does whatever he pleases" (Psa. 115:3). If, as is written there, God directs both peace and war, who will dare to say that, unbeknown to him and without his intervention, men clash randomly and in reckless disarray?' (*Inst.* I.18.1). That 'man falls according as God ordained' is, in Calvin's view, true; it is equally true, however, that 'he falls by his own fault' (*Inst.* III.23.8). On the question of God's providence and the existence of evil, see Paul Helm, *John Calvin's Ideas* (Oxford: Oxford University Press, 2004), pp. 104-16.

I am well aware that I have spoken for too long, although I have endeavoured to be as brief as possible and to cut my comments short, so as to move from one point to another as quickly as I could. I have not been able to deal with the topic as fully as it deserves: to be profitable, it ought to be engraved upon our hearts! If I have passed over many things which it would have been good and useful to have heard—things which might have enhanced my argument—I ask the brethren to whom God has given grace to speak to say their piece, so that we may be more firmly grounded in this word received from him.[23]

---

[23] Twelve of Geneva's pastors spoke in the ensuing discussion, expressing their approval of the doctrine which they had heard expounded. No dissent was voiced. Calvin closed proceedings with a prayer of thanksgiving for the grace of election, and with a call for steadfast adherence to the truth of God's word (CO 8:119-38).

II.

ELECTION AND REPROBATION

SERMONS ON GENESIS 25

1

GOD'S PROMISE FULFILLED

*These are the generations of Ishmael, Abraham's son, whom Hagar the Egyptian, Sarah's maid, bore to Abraham. *[13]* These are the names of the sons of Ishmael, named in order of their birth: Nebaioth, the first-born of Ishmael; and Kedar, Adbeel, Mibsam, *[14]* Mishma, Dumah, Massa, *[15]* Hadad, Tema, Jetur, Naphish and Kedemah. *[16]* These are the sons of Ishmael and these are their names according to their villages and encampments, that is, twelve rulers among the tribes. *[17]* These are the years of the life of Ishmael, a hundred and thirty-seven years; he grew weak and died, and was buried alongside his people. *[18]* They dwelt from Havilah to Shur, which looks toward Egypt from the direction of Assyria; he settled close to all his brethren. *[19]* These are the generations of Isaac, Abraham's son. Abraham begot Isaac, *[20]* and Isaac was forty years old when he took to wife Rebecca, the daughter of Bethuel the Syrian from Mesopotamia, and the sister of Laban the Syrian. *[21]* And Isaac prayed to the Lord for his wife, for she was barren; and the Lord granted his request, and Rebecca conceived. *(Genesis 25:12-21)

HERE we must reflect on the distinction which Moses draws between Abraham's children. We have already noted that all the offspring whom he had from Keturah lived in a distant land (Gen. 25:1, 2). As for Ishmael, he lived apart, but fairly close to the land of Canaan. Nevertheless he had been cast off (Gen. 21:14), for it was necessary for Isaac to retain the inheritance appointed for him.

In the first place, we learn that Ishmael had twelve male children, who so multiplied that from them came twelve tribes. This shows us how justly God spoke when he told his servant Abraham that, as a favour to him, Ishmael would be in some way blessed (Gen. 21:12, 13). The blessing would be temporary and short-lived; the chief blessing remained with Isaac. Even so, God proved to be faithful and true to his promise which concerned this earthly life. If God wills to reveal his truth and constancy in the things of this world, fleeting as they are, and whose form, as Paul says, is passing away (1 Cor. 7:31), what shall we say of those promises which are so much more important, as when God calls us to be heirs of the kingdom of heaven? Do we think we will be disappointed if we lean upon him?

Thus the present passage can be profitable to us. If God desires to be known as steadfast and reliable in his plans for those who are estranged from him, and whom he has excluded and cut off from his church, what will he do for us who are his children, whom he has adopted and to whom he seeks to show his closeness? If God, in lesser things such as descendants and suchlike, desires his truth to be known, what will he not do in the person of our Lord Jesus Christ? He offers us heaven as our inheritance, showing us that he wishes to be favourable to us, and so pardoning our faults that we are reconciled to him and thus made brethren and partners with the angels, under one Head, Jesus Christ our Lord. Can God fail, then, in his promises? Will they be worthless, unfulfilled and ineffective? That is impossible! This is the first thing we must bear in mind.

Note at the same time that God desires to reveal himself to us not only in his most excellent and substantial benefits, but even in the things of this life. There is nothing so small on which he does not wish to leave the imprint of his fatherly goodness. And because he assures us that he will take care to feed us, let us look to him for all that serves to sustain this present life. We should not think that it diminishes his majesty to have us call on him for food and drink. He wants us to turn to him for help in each and every way. We should not doubt, then, that although our bodies are dust and ashes, rottenness—worthless carrion, so to speak—God will nevertheless provide for our bodily needs. That is the second point we need to make.

Next we must observe the contrast which Moses draws between Ishmael and Isaac. Ishmael has been cut off, and is no longer considered to be one of God's children. Yet he prospers, as we see, and he has many descendants, for from the twelve sons whom he begets come twelve tribes. What of Isaac in the meantime? He marries at the age of forty, and his wife is barren. Not just for a year or two, but for as long as twenty years he remains without offspring. God had said to him, 'I will multiply your seed like the stars in the sky and the sands in the sea' (Gen. 15:5). That was what God had said to his father Abraham, but it was also for his benefit. By now he might have expected to increase, yet he sees his wife barren, as if God were mocking him, showing that his hopes had come to nothing.

So when he sees his brother Ishmael, who has no root in the church and who is alienated from all hope of salvation—when he sees that his line is flourishing and that God's grace is showered on him, while in his household he remains alone and without an heir, he is bound to be deeply troubled, as if it would have been better for him to be like his brother Ishmael. It is enough to make him throw everything up in despair and in defiance of God. He might have gone completely astray had not rare forbearance held him back.

Here we should contemplate, as in a mirror, the state of God's church—how it begins, how God sustains it and causes it to grow. He does so in so strange a fashion that it seems that, at any moment, the spectacle of what God does is meant to disappoint us. For whereas the children of this world look prosperous and seem to multiply even as we watch, the church is hidden underground. We see the earth full of unbelievers, despisers of God and godless folk. Where then are the faithful? They are thinly scattered, imperceptible even; they are scorned and trodden underfoot. God, we might think, has little esteem for his church, and is glad to see the faithless, flushed with victory, strutting about in fine style!

All of this we see in the figures of Isaac and Ishmael, so that nothing we think of as novel should worry us unduly. We are to struggle constantly against whatever doubts we entertain, when we see only a few who worship God, and an almost countless number who resist him and who do not know what it is to bear his yoke.

Now this is a message which we need to hear today. How is God working at the present time? When he chose to set his gospel up again, where did he begin? What kind of people did he call? Even today, if we cast our eyes over the world, what do we find in Asia, which is a very large part of the world, and in Africa, which is the same? What do we find in Europe, in so-called Christendom, in events in Italy, France and other places? We find that the devil holds sway. There we find the ministers of Antichrist who are the church's deadly enemies, whatever the faith they profess. It is they who are like the stars in the sky and the sands in the sea! They seem to have it all, and indeed they boast about it, for they use it as a shield to challenge God and to grow hard in their pride. They deride us for being so few, and for nevertheless claiming to be the church. We, for our part, are despised and rejected, and we are a long way from being anywhere close to these nations which are ranged against us. In short, it is as if we were like three grains of wheat under a pile of hay!

For all that, we have testimony from God that he counts and reckons us servants in his house, for no church exists unless it is united to our Lord Jesus Christ who is its Head. If that is missing, all the rest lies scattered and wasted, as Paul says (cf. Col. 1:18, 2:19). We, however, are united to God's Son by faith in his gospel, which is the sure, unfailing bond. How, then, are we to judge whether we are of the church, since we are nothing in comparison with the faithless, who are proud of their size and of all their attributes, which they are able to trumpet out loud?

We should not be frightened by all these things, for God has testified to us in the person of our father Isaac that the church was like a derelict house, devoid of heirs, peopled only by a few and yet regarded by God as a hidden treasure. Let us be content with that.

For the rest, we should also attend to the figure of Ishmael. He had come from Abraham's house, which at that time was the only church on earth. He bore the mark of circumcision, as if he were God's heir. He was in fact the first-born and had a free hand in the house, so much so that, as we saw, he mocked his brother. It is the same today with the papists. They are not strangers to the church, but they are, so to speak, illegitimate children. They claim often enough that they have antiquity on their side and that they have precedence over us. We know the confidence they have in the apostolic succession, as they call it—namely that from the beginning they have had bishops and prelates in their church, and that we must therefore conclude that the name 'church' belongs to them. Well and good, but like Ishmael they have fallen away, since they were not begotten by the gospel which is the seed of freedom. Instead, they became corrupt, and we can thus regard them as Ishmaelites (cf. Gal. 4:22-26). For if they represent great nations, while we remain as those untimely born, understand that our Lord has given us such an example that we have no reason to feel ashamed. That, in brief, is the lesson for us here.

That said, we must also practise what we read in the prophets. It was not once, and once only, that the church shrank this way in numbers, or that it suffered awful devastation. What was it like, for example, under the Babylonian captivity? 'Rejoice,' says Isaiah, 'you who are barren and have not yet conceived. You will have many more offspring than all the married women. Although you were as a woman widowed, God will multiply you. You will be populated as by a miracle, beyond men's belief and understanding. When you have stretched out your tents in this place and that, all will be fulfilled' (Isa. 54:1-3). So when we hear such things said about the church, let us be sure that if today God reduces the number of those who worship him, either to humble us or to punish our sins, we must not faint on that account, but must continue to pursue our calling, having no fear of anything at all. And where the state of the church is especially concerned, let us heed what is said in Psalm 113: 'God fills the homes of women who were barren with fine children and numerous offspring' (cf. Psa. 113:9).

Let us wait, therefore, for the Lord to do his work. We will have reason to glorify him, knowing that it was not in vain that he promised to multiply Abraham's seed. This must come about, however, in a way that we will not understand, at a time of such small beginnings as to be almost nothing. If, then, we continue to be patient, God will surely work and will give us cause to be strong in his promises. They will prove to be true—truer, indeed, than anything we might think or wish. That is something else to remember about this passage.

We meet, however, a further difficulty here, which is this. Although Ishmael is raised so high that he sees a miraculous number of heirs—for he lived one hundred and thirty-seven years and had twelve male children—and although he already

beholds a whole people descended from his race, directly after-
wards it is, in a sense, lost to him. Moses indeed records the
children he had, but when the sacred story speaks of them, they
are cut off, having no connection with Abraham's true line, the
line that was blessed.

We note, then, that it is not enough to have the upper hand,
to look impressive and to have lustre in men's eyes, arousing even
wonderment. All this is nothing compared with the permanent
state of the church. God raises his house as if it were no more
than a child's plaything; but its foundations last forever. And he
continues his grace in such a way that he is clearly seen to be
the founder of his church, and the builder who completes and
maintains it. That is what we see. The faithless, in the meantime,
continue to plan and make decisions. They are like the grass
growing, as the Psalm says, on the housetops (Psa. 129:6, 7):
while the wheat is trodden down, thrown upon the ground and
left in a hollow, the grass grows tall on the rooftops; but since
it is closer to the sun and has no roots, it is bound to wither
without producing fruit.

Hence when we see that our Lord keeps us in a mean and
lowly condition, so that we are not merely despised but rebuffed
by almost everyone, let it be enough to know that we have our
roots in our God, and that we live forever by his grace. May he
uphold us, and may we be like a tree planted by a stream, always
watered and fed by it (Psa. 1:3). Let us be satisfied with that.

Moses is right, therefore, to speak explicitly of Ishmael, the
twelve sons whom he fathered and the twelve tribes into which
they gathered. There, however, Moses stops, and passes on,
saying, *These are the generations of Isaac.*

What then? Isaac's wife was barren until he reached the age
of sixty. Was that not strange? Yes, though as we will see God
ratified his promise that Isaac would increase. What would it
have been like to see so great a multitude of people in Egypt,

growing like grass in a lighted oven, for, as Scripture says, the tyranny and slavery endured in Egypt were like a furnace (Deut. 4:20). Here then are the people: they are like straw and a fire burns all around them, as we see in the image of the bush which was like a consuming fire, yet which remained whole (Exod. 3:2). We see, then, how the people multiplied, though oppressed and in anguish, so that they numbered not one, three or four hundred thousand: there were six hundred thousand who emerged from captivity. How was that possible? It was a miracle which should thrill us all and fill us with awe. We thus find that God so tested Isaac's faith and endurance that he finally took steps to fulfil his promise beyond anything men might understand. The manner of it was unknown; it exceeded human thought.

Today we should apply this lesson to ourselves, practising what is said in Psalm 37. If we see the wicked and the despisers of God raised high like the cedars of Lebanon, we should wait; we have only to turn our heads and they are cut down and felled; we do not even see the place where they grew (Psa. 37:34-36). Why? Because it was not God who planted them. We read also the words of our Lord Jesus Christ: 'Every plant which the heavenly Father has not planted will be uprooted' (Matt. 15:13). So we should not envy the children of this world when we see them in places of eminence, nobility, dignity or the like. Let us wait patiently and calmly accept our station in life. And if the world mocks us, shows us no respect and scorns us, it should be enough that we are of worth before God and his angels. Meanwhile let us wait for God to do as is said elsewhere: 'The righteous will prosper like the palm-tree and grow tall like the cedar of Lebanon'; or to put it differently, 'he will flourish in the courts of the Lord's house' (Psa. 92:12, 13). When Scripture speaks of those who are planted in the Lord's house, it means that they will be blessed by him. That is where our enduring happiness lies, so that from age to age we can still stand firm.

As Psalm 102 tells us, God is everlasting; he does not change or grow old like the world which wears away; he is always the same. The prophet concludes this way: 'The children of the faithful will dwell secure' (Psa. 102:25-28). Even though at first glance we do not see God's grace revealed to them, it will be made known in the end.

This is what we need to bear in mind when we consider the distinction which Moses makes between Ishmael's line and Isaac's. These were the beginnings of the church: they amounted to almost nothing, but their fulfilment was wonderful to see. The children of this world have great and noble beginnings, inspiring everyone with awe. Yet it all comes to nothing, because there is permanence only in God's promises. He is the fount of life, which is why we can persevere to the end. By this means, too, we can rise above the world. When, therefore, we are called to rejoice in God and to be content with the fatherly goodness he shows us, let us not be stupid enough to occupy ourselves with what the eye now sees; what is now present will fade and vanish away. We should gaze on what we do not see, for that, as the apostle says, is the true nature of faith (Heb. 11:1).

Ishmael, we read, *dwelt opposite—or facing—his brothers*. The word 'dwelt' has been translated 'die', since it means 'to fall'. Here, however, it has the sense of 'rest', 'live', 'settle'. The natural meaning is that Ishmael lived not far off from the children of Keturah. He remained in close proximity to the land of Canaan, which had been promised to Isaac. Isaac, however, had not occupied the land, having been expelled from it. Who was it who drove him out? After Abraham's death he could well have settled in the land, had he wished; all he possessed was the grave purchased by his father (Gen. 23:17, 18). He was no lord owning vast and broad estates: all he had was on loan, by permission of the inhabitants. Ishmael could have easily chosen to settle and make his nest there. Yet he moved away. Was it in order to obey

God? No, for he is full of pride and rebelliousness. He might have thought he could have defied God by living in isolation, apart from his father's house, while remaining in the country of his birth. But without reflecting why, he is led away by God, through some secret inspiration.

Such is the way God works in unbelievers: he turns them around and shifts them about. This is not something visible to the eye, but by faith we must view it as a providence of God. If we were really attentive, each day would bring us proof of what we are told here. How is it that we are not destroyed by these mad beasts who surround us on all sides? We know how cruel they are and how insatiable is their greed. Why are we not completely crushed, if not for the fact that God turns their fury aside and directs them to wherever he pleases? Sometimes he hurls them against each other,[1] or keeps them like lions chained and confined by iron bars. This is how, even today and without exerting force, God hurries the faithless along and drives them in any direction he wills. At the very least they are unconscious of the fact.

That was how it was with Ishmael. As we have pointed out, he was only too keen to overturn and ruin the promise made by God to Isaac. Yet he made no attempt to do so. Why was that? Because it was not allowed him from on high. God settled him in a distant location, as if to say, 'You will live alongside your brothers. Whatever happens, you will not stop them occupying the region which I have given them to inherit.'

Now although Scripture speaks of 'brothers', the only brother so far was Isaac. This shows that, by thus confining Ishmael, God was thinking of not just one or two; it was as if already the whole Israelite nation was living in the land of Canaan—a

---

[1] A reference to the intense—often armed—rivalry between Europe's two major Roman Catholic powers, France and the Hapsburg dynasty of Spain and the Holy Roman Empire.

nation, I say, as yet unborn, and only born a long time later. This is a point worth bearing in mind, and one which should strengthen our faith. Whenever we see our deadly enemies, the wicked and despisers of God, frothing and foaming, we should know that our Lord is well able to obstruct and restrain them, and to turn them toward something else. And when they seem about to drive us from the earth, our Lord will somehow keep them captive, but how they do not know.

To sum up, we will experience what is said here about Ishmael, as long as we are patient and as long as we call upon God, not doubting that he has the means to save us, though we may not perceive it at the very first.

Turning now to what Moses says concerning Isaac, we learn that *he took Rebecca as his wife when he was forty, and she was barren*. We mentioned this before, but a fuller explanation is required. It is likely that, while Ishmael married earlier, Isaac, when married at the age of forty, was less fit. He was somewhat late. Now time cannot have passed without his wondering about the promise made to him, that his seed would be like the stars in the sky and the sands in the sea. He finds no wife, for he dare not take a local woman (Gen. 24:3, 4). God, it seems, means to keep him childless to the end. Once he was married, however, God might at least have been expected to bless and increase him by adding progeny; yet his wife remained barren for twenty years. If such a trial had befallen any of us, even the most sensible at some time or other would not have been able to withstand. Why do we pass so lightly over what Moses tells us here? It is because we have little experience in meeting conflict; indeed we flee from it. God therefore spares us because of our ignorance and weakness. In any event, our inability to learn from such examples leaves all of us bewildered. When our faith is open to attack or is tested, we are not as well armed at the proper time as we ought to be.

So for twenty years Isaac seemed cursed by God, like a withered tree, with no hope of offspring. It was not just a question of children. When men and women marry they are happy to have offspring, who are evidence of God's grace. There was a particular reason in Isaac's case, however: not only did he look for tribes that would spring from him; he looked for the salvation of the world. Jesus Christ was, so to speak, in his loins, as the apostle says.[2] Isaac was childless, yet he had no other hope of being saved. Unless he had offspring he was like a man on the edge of hell. Even so, God appeared to mock him; he left him to pine alone. Whenever he looked at his wife, he thought: 'She is a mirror in which I see that God has rejected us, has no regard for us, has turned his back on us. His promise is vain, it does nothing for us.'

That, I say, is the kind of conflict which Isaac had daily to endure. Now because we do not see what the Holy Spirit intends when he speaks about Isaac, and because we cannot profitably apply what we are told about him, a mere nothing is enough to discourage us; it only takes a puff of wind to bowl us over. Why? Because we should have asked ourselves, 'How did Isaac manage to remain so staunch and steadfast for those twenty years?' He did not faint, but was long-suffering. He knew that he must not summon God to keep his promise, but that he should yield to him and honour him by acknowledging that his works are beyond our understanding; he knows the proper times and seasons to do as he has said. Isaac knew, in a word, that it is not for us to lay down the law to God. We must be silent, and must not grumble if things do not turn out as we would like. We should wait for God to complete his work, even if we see that everything is against it. Our faith must be victorious over all the world, as John says in his letter (1 John 5:4).

---

[2] Calvin may be thinking of Hebrews 11, where Abraham's faith (and, by implication, Isaac's) is tested by the absence of an heir, from whose line the promised Redeemer was to come.

However, because all this means nothing to us and passes quickly from our sight, we read this story in so cold a way that we get no benefit from it. That is why God punishes us for our thanklessness. We are so sensitive that as soon as something happens—not some great storm or whirlwind, a mere breeze!— we are shaken, and in the end we fall. We should therefore attend all the more carefully to what is said here: that Isaac kept on trusting God, even though for twenty years he seemed destined to have no progeny. The fact that he persevered is clear from Moses' account: *He prayed to God, and his request was granted, so that his wife conceived.*

Now when we read that Isaac prayed, we must not think that he waited till the very end. Seeing that his wife was barren, he sought help from God who was his sole remedy. Do we think that he wasted his time, casting his requests into the air without any of them reaching God? We might suppose so, for if God had heard him, would he not have fulfilled his promise in a practical way? Yet Isaac sees nothing of the kind. So he prays for one year or two, but it makes no difference, as if he has been speaking to a rock or wall! God pretends to be deaf, seeming not to lend a friendly ear to Isaac's requests. And so it goes on. After ten or twelve years, then, what would we think, except that the best course would be to give up? What an impossibly harsh trial it was to see God doing nothing about his promises after fifteen years had passed! Nevertheless, even after twenty years Isaac does not cease to pray. He perseveres, and his prayers bear sure witness to his faith. He did not pray as the faithless do, who rail against God. Instead he followed the rule—as yet unwritten— laid down for us by Paul: we are to join thanksgiving to our prayers, committing ourselves to God and patiently awaiting the result, which cannot yet be seen (Phil. 4:6). Accordingly, when Isaac continued to cast into God's lap all his sorrows, all the cares that burdened him, all the worries, the vexations and distresses that held him fast—when he laid all of that before God, he gave firm proof of his faith.

His example, then, reminds us that God is not bound from the very first to do all that he has said. Having spoken, he may give no further sign of completing his work, and we may feel that all his promises have been, as we say, empty words. So to hold us back we need patience, just as the apostle urges in the tenth chapter of Hebrews (Heb. 10:36). Day by day, year by year, all through life, let us remain quiet, as if nothing mattered; let us be silent before God, not skirmishing with him, not shouting or contending with him, or summoning him according to our nervous moods. We should also apply the words the prophet cites from Habakkuk: 'If the promise is delayed, let us wait, it will not tarry' (Hab. 2:3; Heb. 10:37).

Here two things are stressed. First, God's promise will not tarry; that is, God will certainly fulfil it at the proper time. Second, so far as we and our understanding are concerned, God's promise will tarry; thus we need to wait. In this way our faith must be tested, for if we hope that God will be faithful to us, and if we remain steadfast and firm, we must also learn the discipline of prayer and supplication. Faith should not be idle.

In short, if here below we have to live like simple peasants, so that some suffer illness and others poverty, if we each have to endure much affliction and misery, let us nevertheless move beyond these things. We must realize that although God promises to be a Father to us, it will not always be visible to the eye. He will indeed give us a taste of his goodness according to our need; we will even have enough to satisfy us fully, provided prayer is accompanied by faith. We will come to see that what God has said will not deceive us: 'Open your mouth, and I will fill it' (Psa. 81:10). Even so, we must always wait by faith for things not seen, things in a sense distant from us and seemingly impossible.

Furthermore, when we are grounded in God's truth and reliant on it, and when we willingly bear much misery while taking care zealously to pray to God morning and night—for relief comes only from him—we will not lightly dismiss Moses' story of how Isaac prayed on account of his wife's barrenness, and of how God heard and answered him. On the one hand we see how persistent Isaac was in trusting God and in calling on him; on the other, we see that God was not deaf to his requests, although this did not happen from the very first. God suddenly intervened after twenty years, in order to show that we are too hasty and impulsive in the things we want. This is why God's name is often blasphemed, and why we blame him for not acting as we would like. That, I say, is because of our impatience.

At the same time we should recognize that Isaac knew that the gift of offspring was a blessing from God. All things considered, when God said, 'Grow and multiply' (Gen. 1:28), it was to show that both men and beasts have offspring only by his power: we should not think that it comes about by chance. If bulls, horses and asses cannot produce young unless God grants his blessing and secret power, how is it with men? We are much nobler creatures, for God has made us in his own image. When, therefore, we see that both men and beasts increase by procreation, we should remember that the words which came from God's own lips, 'Grow and multiply', are still true today.

We must nevertheless go further, and reflect that God holds back his blessing and generosity, apportioning them just as he pleases. As we see, not everyone has offspring equally. Some have none, others one or two, and still others dozens! So when we see such inequality, we must acknowledge that offspring are a particular gift of God, as is said in the Psalm: 'The fruit of the womb is a reward from God' (Psa. 127:3). Here, then, we must look to God for help. Those who desire children should follow Isaac's example. Of course they might say, 'I'd love to have children', but not a word is said about God. He does not get a mention! That is why we see many who have no offspring, or if they do, it brings them even more harm, for they did not turn to God to obtain it from his blessing.

So from the story of Isaac we learn that, since his wife was barren, he turned to God, knowing that it was from him that children were to be sought. What objection could anyone have to God's blessing? Recall what is said in Job, that any child coming into the world is, in a sense, a living image of God, a work of God's unfathomable power which we cannot prize highly enough.[3] For of what is a child begotten, and when conceived, how does he live in his mother's womb? How does he come forth from it? If we consider all these things, who would be so mindless as to say that men are able to procreate by their own efforts and powers?

This is the lesson we must learn. Let those who are married and who desire offspring ask God for them, and for these two reasons. First, this is a thing reserved by God for his own hand. Second, it is not enough for our homes to be peopled by children, unless God is always in control. It would be better to have no offspring at all than to have seed that is corrupt, accursed and full of wickedness. Let fathers, then, follow Isaac's example in this matter. Note also, however, that Isaac did not only pray in order to have children, as men might naturally wish. He looked higher up, remembering that the world's salvation was to come from him, in the person of our Lord Jesus Christ. This we will explain more fully in due course.

Now let us cast ourselves down before the holy majesty of our good God, acknowledging our faults and begging him to make us feel them more and more. May we thus be humbled and led to true repentance, and may we be so moved by fear that we wish only to be rid of

[3] A reminiscence perhaps of Job 12:10 or 33:4?

our earthly passions and desires, to the end that we may be clothed with his righteousness, until we are brought to full and complete perfection.

2

GOD'S UNFATHOMABLE SECRET

Now when Rebecca had conceived, ²² *the children struggled together in her womb. And she said, 'If this is so, why do I live?' So she went to inquire of the Lord.* ²³ *And the Lord said to her, 'There are two peoples in your womb, and two nations within you will be divided. One will be stronger than the other, and the greater will serve the lesser.'* (Genesis 25:21-23)

WE saw yesterday how, for twenty years, God had tested Isaac's faith before he gave him offspring, showing that his prayer to God had not been in vain. God answered his request, intending that, through the seed promised to Isaac, he would send the Saviour of the world. Isaac was therefore able to rejoice, and not in any mundane sense: he saw that his wife who had long been barren had conceived, and that God had not forgotten his promise. Isaac's request was granted, because he had turned to God for help.

Now, however, he meets a new trial—a trial more severe and harder to bear than if his wife had remained barren. *Rebecca conceives two children, who struggle together in the womb.* This was an appalling thing, quite contrary to nature. So she says that *it would be better if she were dead.* It is not exasperation that makes her speak this way, as if she were coerced by feelings of pain or physical distress. No, she is looking higher up, for in her womb she bears all human hope of the salvation of the world. Yet here she sees such conflict that God appears to be upending everything and displaying tokens of his wrath.

In short, it is a hateful thing to see this struggle in a woman's womb. Nor did it arise from natural causes. God, as we will see, intended to show both her and Isaac that not all who came from their seed would be reckoned among the faithful; instead, there would be deadly warfare. So when Rebecca discerns in these things marks of God's wrath and a hellish battle with the enemies of God's church, she does not understand the whole. She thinks that if she has conceived only to witness conflict, it is because God is against her, and that he comes bearing arms, as if to say, 'You are a vile creature. I reject you and cast you out.'

What, then, is she to do, feeling as she does? We should not be surprised if, in her distress, she preferred to die rather than behold so monstrous and unnatural a thing. Nevertheless we are told that in her sorrow, *she did not fail to turn to God*. God indeed answered her and brought her comfort. Not that it was unmixed with lingering regret, but God assuaged her suffering and told her, '*There are two peoples in your womb.*' In effect he tells her that more is involved than the two children whom she bears. There is something more in view: *the children will be divided one from another.*

Although, then, both are offspring of Abraham, and although Abraham had been told that in his seed all the nations of the earth would be blessed (Gen. 22:18), from Isaac would come those whom God would cut off from his church, the reprobate, who would thus be enemies of God's church. True, this could well have brought mortal pain to Isaac and Rebecca, but even so they recognize that God's goodness is not extinguished, and that he has been faithful to his word once given.

Thus we read that *the greater will serve the lesser*. Here Rebecca learns that, in any event, from her would come the blessed seed which had been promised. This is the essence of what we are told, but its complete meaning will only be clear if we examine it in detail.

We should first of all observe that those who have been called into the church do not always remain in it, as we saw in the notable case of Ishmael. Although a son of Abraham, he was banished from his house. As Scripture says, he would not be an heir. It was not a question of worldly wealth or of Abraham's possessions: Abraham was rich in cattle, and in gold and silver, but he did not own a foot of ground. To what, then, did his inheritance point? It pointed to the spiritual promise, to God's choice of Abraham's seed, meaning that his people would be consecrated to God's service. 'Those who come from you,' says God, 'I will welcome and accept as my children, that I may gather them to eternal life.' Thus Ishmael, although the first-born, was excluded from the hope of life. Isaac alone remained.

It was the same with Esau and Jacob. Both descended from Abraham; in fact they were twins, born of the same pregnancy. One, however, was excluded and the other accepted; one was chosen and the other rejected. Accordingly we see that those who for a time find room in the church, and who bear the name of believers and children of God, may be deemed to be such by men, but they are not written in the book of life. God does not acknowledge them or reckon them as his own. We are therefore warned that if God has graciously ushered us into his church, we must not be proud or become drunk with foolish presumption. Let us walk in purity and be sure that we confirm our election, having the Holy Spirit's testimony in our hearts. We must not trust merely in outward appearance and in the name which we claim in the sight of men. We should note this, then; it is important.

In addition, however, we learn something even greater. Although God established his covenant with Abraham, he sought to show that the offer of his grace was not the only thing: he was free to choose whomever he wished, and to leave the rest aside (Rom. 9:10-13). This is why Paul quotes this passage, applying it to God's secret election, by which, before the creation of the world, he chose those whom he willed. Now this is a deep and lofty subject, but once it is explained, we can each benefit, provided we pay attention.

To begin with, let us soberly accept what we are taught in Scripture. Let us not try to be wiser than is lawful, but let us agree with what God has to say. We should also be humble, not answering God back or advancing our own ideas, as if we wanted to argue our case against God. Let us admit that his judgments are a deep abyss, and let us not inquire further than he allows us. What we must do, then, is try to deal with things so that what at first glance seems obscure becomes easy for us.

Now if we ask what led God to act as he did, we discover that Abraham was no worthier than others. This is a point we have already made at length. Here, then, we see a privilege granted to one family, but not one based on merits of their own or on anything in them which might attract God's preference. They are neither better nor more outstanding: it is simply a matter of God's pleasure. It is certain that, if we were to venture an opinion, we would find this hard to stomach, which is why there are many mad people who cannot accept this teaching. They fancy this gives them a reason to protest to God. But what good does it do them in the end? We contend that humility is essential here: we must worship what is hidden from us. Paul, moreover, demonstrates this by his example, for instead of arguing he cries, 'How wonderful are God's judgments!' (Rom. 11:33). The apostle expresses complete surprise; he is overcome with awe, he who had been caught up above the heavens and who had beheld

God's mysteries which it was unlawful for anyone to utter (2 Cor. 12:2-4). So Paul, a partner of the angels, so to speak, is here struck with wonder and utterly confounded. What then shall we say of those rogues who have barely touched a word of the gospel or law with the tip of their tongue, but who seek to outdo Paul? Yet this is the very pride we see in many people!

Let us come back, however, to the words of Paul: 'O man, who are you?' (Rom. 9:20). When we compare God and ourselves, who is God? With what will we measure and enclose him? With our brain? We do not have an ounce of common sense, but God has only to clench his fist to hold the whole world like a speck of dust, as Isaiah says (Isa. 40:12). Neither heaven nor earth can contain him. His is the power, the righteousness, the unending wisdom, and his purposes are beyond all understanding. Nevertheless we try to get him to bend to our foolish fantasies! Where will it end?

Then too, who are we? 'Mere men,' says Paul, implying by these words that we are nothing at all. It is as if he said, 'Must you so presume that you inquire into God's deep mysteries, since you are simply mud and mire? And what of your intelligence? You are full of sin and iniquity, wretched and blind. Yet you expect God to explain himself to you, and you conclude that if God's works are not deemed good and reasonable, you have the right to blame him and to call him to account!'

We ought, then, first of all, to heed this warning. Our Lord teaches us that on no account should we fail to open our ears when we inquire into what he wants us to know. But let us beware that we go no further, for there is no greater or more grievous folly than to want to know more than God shows us. Moreover what do we gain by working as hard as we like and by striving as much as we will? All that does is thrust us deeper and deeper into the labyrinth, unless God is there to guide us and to give us light. Let us keep, then, to the happy mean: we are to listen to what God tells us, and as soon as he closes his lips we are to keep our minds bound and captive. We must not set out to know anything more than what he has said.

Abraham's line was thus chosen in preference to everyone else, because God willed it so. That, however, is not enough: we need greater confirmation still of God's free election. This is what we see in the figures of the two brothers. Rebecca is carrying Jacob and Esau. Is one better than the other? When Paul expounds this passage, he affirms that they were not yet born (Rom. 9:11). How then could they have obtained grace and favour for their merits in the sight of God? Jacob had done neither good nor evil, nor had Esau, so why does he make Jacob greater? We must not begin to argue further: we can only stand in awe and worship God's secret counsel, by which those whom he wishes are elected, and the others rejected. By choosing Jacob over Esau, he sought to give greater lustre to his mercy. He could of course have arranged for Jacob to be first when the children emerged from their mother's womb. We know, however, that this is not a matter of chance, for as we read in the Psalm, 'You drew me from the womb' (Psa. 22:9). God displays remarkable power when children come into the world. Why then did he not permit and command Jacob to have the rights of the first-born? That would have been appropriate, since he had resolved to expel Esau from the church, while allowing Jacob to remain and to take the place of his father Isaac and of Abraham. Why does God delay his birth, making him inferior to his brother in terms of natural law? Yet he places the one born later above the other.

What this shows is that God chose to exclude all human boasting and to overthrow all loftiness so that men might bring nothing of their own, as if to say, 'I obtained this blessing by myself. I earned it by my own efforts.' Thus it is clear, as I said before, that here we have a mirror which shows that all who belong to the church have not entered in their own strength, or obtained grace by their own merits. God chose them before they were born. That is what we are taught here.[1]

At this point a possible problem may arise. Moses refers specifically to two peoples. More than a personal conflict between Jacob and Esau is involved; it is a question of their successors, of the descendants of each of them. Now it happens that many who descended from Jacob were not approved by God. Moses is content with the statement that Jacob's line was chosen and Esau's rejected. Nevertheless we see that God disavowed the greater number who came from Jacob. He calls them illegitimate children, sons of harlots: they are not his, and they vainly glory in his name (Isa. 57:3-5; Jer. 2:20-22). How are we to reconcile these things?

Notice, first, that God sets this vision before Isaac and Rebecca in order to show them the church's future condition. He bears witness that the church would come from Jacob, but not all who were begotten according to the flesh would be members of the church. It was enough that Jacob should remain, that God had reserved him for himself, and that Esau should be excluded, as we will later see. The explanation which Paul gives will help us better understand. He considers the verse, 'All who are of Jacob according to the flesh are not true Israelites'—they are not, that is, God's people (Rom. 9:6).

Jacob has two names, the second being, as we will see, Israel. So before the children are born, God divides them from each other, to show that they are not one, unified, body. One has been set apart while the other is banished. Paul understood that not all who were to be born of Jacob were God's elect. Paul

[1] As Geerhardus Vos observes, a consideration of the subsequent lives of Jacob and Esau could not itself remove the suspicion that Jacob's superior appreciation of God's promise qualified him for election. To allay this suspicion, 'the principle was established at a point where no such considerations, pro or con, could possibly enter into the matter. Even at the risk of exposing the divine sovereignty to the charge of arbitrariness, the matter was decided prior to the birth of the two brothers.' (*Biblical Theology: Old and New Testaments*, Grand Rapids, MI: Wm. B. Eerdmans, 1948, p. 109.)

takes us back to the beginning, telling us that one is separated from the other by God's secret counsel. God's reason we cannot grasp or explain; he remains free to act. So it is enough to know that from Jacob's line the church was born, although not all belonged to it.

As we previously pointed out, Abraham's line was the object of twofold grace. First, God made it clear that he would be a Father to them. Thus circumcision was common to them all. Now circumcision was not an empty rite: it bore witness to the forgiveness of sins and to the righteousness which believers must obtain through our Lord Jesus Christ. Ishmael is therefore circumcised; from God's point of view he received a sacrament which should have assured him that God reckoned him among his children, was a member of Jesus Christ and that the curse which came to him from Adam was wiped away.[2] Yes, but this was of no avail to him. The same is said of Esau and of all who are like him. Nevertheless we ought not to despise the benefit which God conferred on all of Abraham's line.

It is the same today, when we speak of God's priceless gift to us of the preaching of the gospel: it is preached indiscriminately to everyone. We might well say that God has been exceptionally merciful to us in enlightening us by his word, so that we may know the way of salvation, while we see others who wander bewildered and in darkness, as if forgotten and abandoned by God. This is how it is with the papists. Though full of pride and arrogance, they are driven about by Satan, knowing neither way nor path. We, however, daily hear God's call to come to him. He has remembered his covenant, so that we know that he is always favourable to us and that we can call upon him with true assurance, not doubting that he is a Father to us. That is

---

[2] Because God's covenant of grace is one, Calvin held that the faithful of every age are justified and saved on the sole basis of Christ's atoning work. The law and the rite of circumcision, no less than the gospel and the rite of baptism, point to him 'who takes away the sin of the world'. See further *Inst.* IV.14.20-23.

a blessing we should never revile. Yet there are many whom it serves to condemn. They are all the more ungrateful if they rebel against God and scorn to accept the fatherly favour which he offers. This, then, is a first grace already conferred on us, as it was on those of Abraham's line.

There is a second grace which is restricted to those whom God has been pleased to choose from Abraham's line. While he accepted Isaac, Ishmael had no place in his house. For a time, certainly, he was counted as a member of the church, but he was finally cut off. The same happened to the children of Keturah. We see this too in Esau: though the first-born, he was rebuffed by God. Accordingly this second grace was confined to Abraham's family. God reserved for himself those he willed, and Jacob was, as it were, the root of those descendants who came after him. Thus the person of Jacob prefigures all of the elect; in him God shows that his unmerited gift of grace owes nothing to ourselves, nor can we boast that we have attained salvation on our own initiative. The elect are drawn to it, having been chosen before the creation of the world, and thus before ever they were born. Hence, in the passage already quoted, Paul adds Moses' testimony by way of further explanation: 'I will have mercy on whom I have mercy, and pity on whom I have pity' (Exod. 33:19; Rom. 9:15).

That might appear to be a rather abrupt, indeed outlandish statement. It is nonetheless significant. It is as if God said, 'I know those whom I wish to set apart, and no one should argue a different case before me. In this I am entirely free.' There is nothing unclear about that if we think of everyday speech. Someone who says, 'I will do what I do', that is, 'I will do whatever I choose', means that he will not yield to anyone. He is not, that is, obliged to reveal what he plans or purposes to do. So when God declares, 'I will have mercy on whom I have mercy', he is effectively saying this: 'My mercy does not depend on this or that. Do not look for any other cause or bind me to observe a law. I know what I must do. Mercy is required: I will therefore have mercy on whom I have mercy. I take no account of anyone's worth, for none is worthy. I will nevertheless have mercy on some—on those, that is, whom I have chosen.'

That is exactly how God might speak. His aim is to refute whatever we might plead, to shut the door to idle curiosity and to put an end to all impetuosity. He means us quite simply to worship him and to allow him to keep what is his to himself. So when he saves, it is because of his free goodness; and when he condemns we are not to squawk or screech at him. Our mouths must remain shut, unless it be to glorify him.

Observe that this was said when the people had already multiplied in number and been rescued by God from Egypt. Here was a church descended from Jacob's race; from this barren and almost deserted house God brought forth so great a host that it is most obviously a miracle. God's promise, that Abraham's seed should be as the stars in the sky, had proved true. Is that not wonderfully clear to us? Thus God declares that from this great host he will reserve those whom he wills: 'I will have mercy on whom I have mercy, and let no one inquire as to the reason.' The reason is known of course to God, but this does not mean that we can comprehend it, or that we must delve beyond our limits into his secrets. We must understand that, so far as we are concerned, there is no reason. God's counsel must be for us the sole rule of justice, wisdom and equity.

Paul's exposition, therefore, corresponds exactly with what Scripture says, that there were two peoples in Rebecca's womb, and that from her would come two separate nations. It is as if God certified that there would be a divorce, but that Jacob would continue to be blessed. Not that all would be included without exception; only those whom God was pleased to reserve for himself, for he had chosen them before the creation of the world. That is the sum of what this verse contains.

Before we go further, however, notice carefully what we are told here. The main thing to note is that God desires that all the praise for our salvation should be ascribed to him. What, after all, is the source and origin of the church? It is God's election. This is the point to which Moses brings us back, according to Paul's interpretation, and this is the plain meaning of the text. This verse, as I have said, is not about some earthly, fleeting heritage; it is about the eternal salvation which Abraham hoped for, because of the promise he had received.

Jacob is thus the heir. Why? Had he entered so far into God's grace, or had he contributed something of his own which earned God's favour? Not at all! Here, then, is Moses' text, devoid of any gloss, proving that the church proceeds from God's sheer grace, and that the praise for our salvation must be kept for him alone.

Those, however, who try either to overturn or to veil this doctrine, argue that although God perceived no merit in Jacob, he fully foresaw the man he would become. So that was why Jacob was chosen and Esau rejected. In short, since many rascals do not dare to deny God's election outright, they wish for a higher cause, God's foreknowledge. What then is this fore-knowledge? It is when God foresees what each of us will be. God, they contend, elects those who, he foresees, will have a good nature and disposition: it is therefore not surprising that he accepts them in preference to the others. He acknowledges the good which is not yet in them, but which will later be.

People like this do not have one drop of godly fear in them! They plainly blaspheme against the Holy Spirit who spoke by the lips of Paul. They deride Paul's words as if they were mere fiction. If we accepted their solution, Paul would have been speaking thoughtlessly and in pure ignorance, for he reasons thus: although there was neither good nor bad in Isaac, Esau and Jacob, God nevertheless elected one and rejected the other. Now according to these madmen, there is an easy answer. What is it? It is true, they say, that there was neither good nor bad in them; but it was bound to come, and God simply foresaw it. Paul, on the other hand, assumes what is clearly true—that we are condemned, and that until God has chosen us we are left like snakes full of poison. We only give God cause to be angry with us and to exact retribution. We are put to shame, full of venom and iniquity.

That was what Jacob was like, and also Esau, for what do we find in Adam's race except corruption? We are filthy in God's sight, and because the root is cursed and defiled, because it is completely rotten, its fruit can only be the same. So when God leaves us as we are, we are bound to perish to the very last. Not one person remains: we are all lost and ruined. As Scripture commonly teaches, we are all children of wrath (Rom. 1:18, 2:5; Eph. 2:3). It follows, then, that there is no difference between Esau and Jacob, and that God did not distinguish one from the other, since he could find and foresee no good in either of them. What could he foresee except that corrupt mass in Adam, which bears only accursed fruit? That is what he foresaw equally in one as in the other.

Thus we find in Jacob only what God put in him; but he left Esau just as birth had made him. For this reason too, Scripture says elsewhere that God chose us so that we would be holy and blameless before him (Eph. 1:4). It does not say that we were chosen because God foresaw that we would be holy. On the contrary, it attributes all our holiness, righteousness and what-ever good there is in us to one sole source—God's election—to the end that we might walk in fear and live uprightly, being in some way keen and well-disposed to do good. If that is true, it follows that God cannot have foreseen anything in us.

Take away election, and what is left? As we have shown, we all remain lost and cursed, and rightly so, for God sees only corruption in us. He must disown us. As Scripture says, 'he repented that he had made man' (Gen. 6:6). That is all that we, for our part, can bring.

It is thus arrant nonsense to say that God elects his own according to what they will later be. It is because he has chosen them that he must put his good in them. This is the first step with which we must begin: we are no different from each other, except as God establishes a difference. Accordingly, Paul rules out all boasting which we might venture to employ. 'Who made you different?' he asks. That word alone must crush and demolish all pride. Why? 'Because,' he says, 'what do you have which you can call your own?' (1 Cor. 4:7). Thus Paul demonstrates that we cannot choose our rank, as if to say, 'I will get ready to do good, and God will have pity on me. If I mean well and am properly prepared, I will attain grace.'

Paul, by contrast, dismisses all such talk, affirming that we are all lost, that we are, all and sundry, ruined and bound for the deepest hell, unless God is pleased to make us different. Our sole worth and excellence comes from the fact that God has stretched out his hand to us. So let us hold fast to this principle, and let us make practical use of the teaching that has been given. God set Jacob and Esau before us as in a mirror. It should be enough to know that both these figures are like two living images, showing that the world is in a similar position. Some are called, others not, for such is God's good pleasure.

Notice in particular that, as I said before, because Jacob was the younger, he should clearly have been subordinate to his brother, according to the natural order. Yet we see him rise to the level of the first-born. And not only is Esau placed below him, he is completely cast out, for in the end he has no part or portion in the church. This shows that God means us to be absolutely sure that we have nothing to offer on our own account; we cannot meddle in things as if we had some value or worth of our own.

Now while God is not inconsistent in himself, here he seems to demonstrate a certain inconsistency or contrariness. He after all ordained that the first-born of the house should be the head; but having laid this law down he overturns it! All this, however, can be readily resolved, for God is above ordinary law, so that he chose to change what was customarily the common rule.[3] He did so to prove to us that, as Paul says, it is not of him who wills or runs, but of God who shows mercy (Rom. 9:16). Now when Paul says that it is not of him who wills or runs, he does not mean that we have some measure of good will. As he teaches in another place, it is God who does that (Phil. 2:13). Nor does he mean that we can put our best efforts into it. He means instead that we have nothing and so can offer nothing to God. God's mercy is all there is.

If, however, we did have something to offer, sharing would be necessary: God's share and ours. Thus we could claim that we did not get everything from God: there would be our willing, our running, our good zeal. Those are the sort of things that we might say. Paul, on the other hand, seeks to put an end to anything that we might bring. He insists that it is only God's pure mercy that prevails.

There are many people, it is true, who try to make the effort, and who even cite the example of the Jews who, infernally proud and puffed up like toads, thought they could put God in their debt and sought to be counted righteous by their works. There, however, they were mistaken, and instead of advancing they retreated. When we take too much on ourselves we undoubtedly rob God of his honour. They are thus guilty of sacrilege, and are worse, far worse, than thieves. There is no doubt that until God has made us new,

---

[3] God is above the law, not in the sense that he is lawless, since that would be to deny his righteousness and justice, but in the sense that, as sovereign lawgiver (*Inst.* IV.10.7-8), he is free to act apart from the rules which he has set down for the conduct of human affairs. When he does so, Calvin maintains, it is for purposes that are always wise, good and upright.

however good we look, we are rotten through and through. In God's eyes we are loathsome vermin. Let us not claim, then, that we are able to will or to run. God sees us as lost, so he must rescue us from that abyss. He must separate us from those who are lost, just as we were; we resembled them in every way.

The condition of all who belong to the human race is the same. True, some are children of wrath while others are blessed by God. But what accounts for this separation, this divorce? Mercy! We ought not to inquire further: we should be satisfied by way of explanation with this one word. That was why the first-born was expelled from his position, and why Jacob who was subordinate to him was put in his place, remaining indeed the sole heir.

When the prophet Malachi speaks of these things he upbraids the Jews for their thanklessness (Mal. 1:2, 3). It is true that he has the external sign in mind—God's choice of Jacob over Esau, and his gift to him of Canaan as his inheritance, whereas Esau was driven off into the mountains. The prophet does not, however, dwell on this idea: he has a much loftier thing in view. Paul, referring to the prophet's testimony and recalling how God gathered Jacob's descendants to himself, ascribes it all to God's sheer mercy (Rom. 9:18). The prophet for his part asks, 'Was not Esau Jacob's brother?', implying that the Jews were full of pride and arrogance, and were even bursting with it! Nothing was easier for them than to say, 'Oh, we are Abraham's holy, sacred line. We are the church, the people God has blessed and sanctified!' 'Yes,' replies the prophet, 'but where does it all come from? Was not Esau Jacob's brother? You see the Idumaeans who are your brothers. Are they a people of God? You claim they are strangers to the church, and that although they are circumcised, God has cast them off. What is the reason for that? Who made this separation? From generation to generation you see that you are Jacob's children. Of whom, then, was Esau the child? Did he not come just as much from Abraham and Isaac's line?'

Here Malachi is not speaking only of the land of Canaan. He goes further, saying that God loved Jacob and hated Esau. From where did this love for Jacob come? In himself, Jacob could not have been pleasing to God, for as we said he was a child of wrath, who from his mother's womb bore that awful curse thrust upon the whole of humankind. Nevertheless God loved him. Why did he love him? Because he rescued him from perdition. And why did he hate Esau? As we saw, God had just cause to hate the whole human race, for in us there is nothing but sin and iniquity. But let us go further, and ask why God, before the world was made and before Adam's fall, should both love and hate?[4]

Here is where we need to be both quiet and calm. This is not the place to lift up our horns! What would we gain by choosing to complain and to argue with God? We would surely be throwing stones above our heads; they would not fall randomly and certainly could not reach God's majesty. They would fall back upon *our* heads and break and shatter us! That is what we would gain by opening our mouths and casting our blasphemies at God. We would merely be throwing darts and stones into the air. They cannot reach God, but they could pierce and cut us to the quick! Since our rashness and arrogance will bring us down, let us be content with what God has said: he hated Esau but loved Jacob. So Jacob's children were clearly taught that they had nothing to boast about, and that all they could do was to be grateful to God for his generosity and kindness, for which they

---

[4] It is tempting to describe Calvin's position as 'supralapsarian', since he places election in order of thought prior to Adam's fall. Unlike his seventeenth-century successors, however, he is not concerned to determine a logical—still less temporal—sequence in God's cosmic and saving operations, or to establish his priorities in the framing of his eternal decree. He is invariably content to follow Paul's argument in Eph. 1:4 ('chosen ... before the foundation of the world'). In according priority, as here, to election, he simply wishes to safeguard God's absolute sovereignty in the work of redemption. Cf. his discussion of Eph. 1:4 in Part III below, and in *Inst.* III.22.1-3.

could see no reason apart from his good pleasure. They proved nevertheless impious where God was concerned, yet they wished to retain their privilege. God, however, declared that the privilege was not theirs: only if they held him to be their Father could they be his children.

We are thus warned that although our salvation comes from God's pure grace, and remains firm to the end, this is no pretext for breaking loose and for indulging in evil. Now there are two types of people who are hostile to this teaching: some are like dogs, others are like swine.

There are vile dogs who bark at God, and there are swine who subvert this doctrine by their dissolute living.

The first are those who bark and bare their teeth; they challenge God with their evil questions. We see rogues today who do not scruple to tear all of holy Scripture to shreds, corrupting, perverting, falsifying and cheapening everything, as long as they can obscure the truth of God's election and even wipe it out. That is their aim—to make this doctrine odious to us. They maintain that those who speak about election make no distinction between good and evil, and that God would therefore be unjust if he distinguished one person from another: he would be showing favouritism. These, then, are the dogs who bark and gnash their teeth in opposition to this doctrine.

Then there are the swine who do not object in quite the same way, but who say, 'Well, if I am elect, whether I am as bad as I can be is of no consequence: God is able to keep me safe and I can never perish. If, on the other hand, I have been rejected, why should I worry about doing good, since I can never be saved?' These people, as I said, do not spew their objections forth in order to overthrow God's truth. They are simply heavy with sleep and remain stupid and bemused in their sins.

We must beware of both these types, which is why Malachi reminds the people of all that has come from God's pure goodness, and urges them to be holy. Accordingly, whenever we are told that God is the author of our salvation, that we can contribute nothing, that he must keep us under his protection and complete the work he has begun, we are not meant to give free rein to our sins. Thus when Paul speaks of sealed letters, declaring that the identity of God's children is an unfathomable secret, he adds, 'Let him who calls on God's name depart from all iniquity' (2 Tim. 2:19). Know, then, that God did not intend to give us the opportunity for evil when he chose us with no regard for our merits, and when out of pure goodness he continues to uphold us. He does this so that we may honour him and may be even more careful about how we walk.

Returning, then, to the point already made, we note that God has chosen us so that we should be holy and blameless before him. He did not choose us because he found that we were already thus: he chose us so that this was what we should be. Let that be our aim, and may it be the goal we set before us as long as we live.

> Now let us cast ourselves down before the majesty of our good God, acknowledging our faults and asking that he may so make us feel them that we are humbled and brought to true repentance. May we forsake all our fleshly cravings and desires, and, becoming nothing in ourselves, may we be illumined by the power of his Holy Spirit, that we may serve and honour God all the days of our life, and may be led to give ourselves wholly to him. And recognizing that everything we have comes from his unmerited goodness, may we glorify his holy name not only with our lips but with our whole lives.

3

THE GREATER AND
THE LESSER

Now when Rebecca had conceived, ²² *the children struggled together in her womb. And she said, 'If it is thus, why do I live?' So she went to inquire of the Lord.* ²³ *And the Lord said to her, 'There are two peoples in your womb, and two nations born of you will be divided. One will be stronger than the other; the greater will serve the lesser.'* (Genesis 25:21-23)

WHEN we see the world in such a disturbed state, our minds are deeply troubled by the fact that there are many who openly despise God, and who seem to have plotted with the devil to indulge in every kind of evil. That God should have created men only to contrive their ruin seems contrary to reason. Why does he allow the majority to go astray like this? Even when we are told that this is not to be imputed to God but to those who, of their own accord, rush to their destruction, this still does not allay the worries we might feel. Can God not remedy affairs? Why does he not do so?

Those who argue for mere permission on God's part, so that the reins lie loose on our neck while we behave according to our free will—even they cannot solve the problem. Why did not God create a different sort of man? And why did he allow him to be so frail, so much inclined to evil and corruption? And since he knew men's infirmity, why did he not come to their aid and cure them? All this has the effect of deeply troubling and vexing us.

There is still more, however. As Scripture teaches, there is nothing that does not perish unless God in his unmerited goodness preserves it. How then does it happen that God should choose only a tenth or a hundredth part of humanity, and forsake all the rest, knowing that they are lost and ruined?[1] Why does he not hold out his hand to them, and why indeed has he ordained their loss, as Scripture says? For those are Solomon's very words (Prov. 16:4). Now that saying raises some very difficult questions. There are many who become entrapped in them, as if among thorns, and they delve so far into them that they become thoroughly confused.

We face an even greater test. What we find in the church is the same as what we see among men generally: when the gospel is preached to all we see many hypocrites, many who rebel and many who are completely bewildered. Very few make progress in God's school, although he summons everyone who hears, without exception. In particular we see many who out of contempt or thanklessness close the door to salvation and reject God's gifts. Not only that, we see them turn into deadly enemies of the truth, even though they may be servants in God's house. Isaiah, for example, first declares that God will gather a

---

[1] Calvin never ventures an explicit opinion as to the final number of the elect, which is a mystery known only to God. Here, as elsewhere, he speaks empirically, in terms of what he sees. Without doubt, however, he believes that what he sees is consistent with the Old Testament precedent of a faithful remnant which alone constitutes the true Israel. Cf. his comments in two sermons on Isaiah 53:1, dating from 1558, which directly address the problem of unbelief (*CO* 35:605-10). In this connection it is worth recalling Herman Bavinck's observation that Reformed confessions impose no limit on the wideness of God's mercy; no others so decisively locate God's saving grace solely in his good pleasure, which is both free and omnipotent. 'Aside from this,' Bavinck asks, 'where could we find a firmer and broader foundation for the salvation of a sinful and lost human race?' (*Reformed Dogmatics*, ed. John Bolt, tr. John Vriend, 4 vols., Grand Rapids, MI: Baker Academic, 2003–08, IV, p. 572.)

multitude of people of all nations into his church; but just when all seems flourishing and prosperous and when the banner is displayed to assemble all the people, he ceases to rejoice and discovers a hidden evil—an evil so entrenched in the church as to make it a medley of very different people. It nurtures its very enemies in its womb, as is evident in the figure of Rebecca (Isa. 60:3-5, 62:10-12, 64:5-7).

Now what are we to make of all that? If we were to turn these ideas over in our mind, we could not possibly resolve them. That we can all see. The devil would surely worm his way in and make us blaspheme against God; or else he would fill us with such bitterness that we would prefer to be blocks of wood rather than reasonable beings, made in God's image. As experience shows, many people become furious with God, raging at him because they cannot rid themselves of problems and scruples of this kind. We sorely need to seek a remedy.

It is true that we cannot free ourselves of every feeling. On first appearance and at the merest puff of wind we cannot help being anxious and upset. We cannot stop our thoughts from straying; we cannot avoid idly imagining many things and tossing arguments about. We are bound, in a word, to feel shaken, as if buffeted by storm or whirlwind. Our minds cannot be completely at rest or so composed as to feel no stress.

We see this in Rebecca, when she asks, '*If it is thus, why do I live?*' She wants to die, yet she is the mother of the faithful; she represents the church. Now if that was how she felt—she who bore in her womb the hope of the world's salvation—what shall we say about ourselves? Given, then, that our minds are so quick to imagine empty thoughts and follies, and given that we are so ready to fly off the handle and finally to snap at God, we have even more need of a remedy.

We find it in Rebecca herself. She does not nurse her sorrow or champ at the bit, as many do who sit and stew, who seek no way to satisfy themselves or to keep quiet and calm. They look aimlessly within, piling one idea on another and sinking so deep into their thoughts that the devil takes possession of them, and drives them in reckless fury against God himself. Rebecca, however, acts differently. On realizing that this is an intolerable source of distress to her, she withdraws to God and inquires of him. The answer is there; it is then given to her. She therefore has reason to be calm once she knows that this is God's good pleasure, and that she should continue to live. God requires that one of her children be cut off from the church and the other retained. Conscious of this, she can only agree to submit, which is what she does.

She does not resist God, nor do we read that she voiced any complaint at a later time. We learn that she heeded God and subsequently gave birth, always dwelling on what she had been told and giving Jacob her heartfelt love. Why did she do that? Because she knew that God had appointed him to be the blessed seed which she had hoped for—so much so that in this she behaved much more virtuously than her husband Isaac.

Here we are taught that, when we are worried, we should turn at once to God, for our minds are not competent to grasp hidden things. And even in those things which we regard as the simplest in the world, we will sometimes be struck by fear and wonder. What, then, of God's judgments, which surpass our comprehension and whose content is so lofty and profound that the Holy Spirit bids us worship them, and not inquire too carefully into them? Ought we to presume upon our reason and judge on the basis of what we think fit, prying into everything according to our own likes and tastes? Without question, such presumptuousness will not go unpunished, as we clearly see.

Why is it that nowadays so many riff-raff spew forth their blasphemies against the doctrine of predestination? It is because they do not deign to inquire from the mouth of God. They seek to voice their own opinions according to what their brains decree—as if we were fit and competent! Let us follow, then, Rebecca's example. That is, when all these questions come into view, and when we are troubled on every side, thinking, 'How is it possible that most of the world should perish and the rest be saved? How is it that one is chosen and the other rejected? How is it that the greater number is going to its ruin, and that God should reserve for himself only a handful of people?'—when all these things trouble and distress us, let us come to God. Let us listen to what holy Scripture tells us, and let us ask God to open our eyes and ears, so that we may learn what his will is. And once we know it, let us stop right there and be at peace. Further debate is out of the question once God announces his decree. Every day, therefore, we are reminded that we can never be ready to be taught by holy Scripture and to look to it for all our wisdom, unless we are sober and humble enough to want to know no more than what it contains.

Nowadays we do not need to have a revelation from heaven, as Rebecca did. Some, it is true, conjecture that she sought out some prophet or other, but at that time they were few and far between. We may readily infer that Melchizedek was dead, and Abraham and Isaac were no more. It is an illusion to think that schools of prophets existed. Rebecca received a revelation, as our text shows. We do not need one today, however, for our position is quite different. In those days there was neither law nor gospel, whereas we are fully taught. Earlier on, as Isaiah says, God did not speak to our fathers darkly or in secret (Isa. 45:19, 48:16). It was not in vain that he urged men to seek him, as Moses says: 'Here is the way: walk in it. I have set the way of salvation before you; heaven and earth bear witness that I have shown you what you must do to attain eternal life' (cf. Deut. 5:32, 33). In another place he says that while God has his secrets, 'The sum of the law is for you and your children, that you may be taught the way of salvation' (cf. Deut. 6:4-7).

Now since those times we have had the gospel, in which our Lord Jesus Christ fully illumines us, for he is the Sun of righteousness (Mal. 4:2). Seeing, then, that we have such convincing evidence, do we have to ask the angels to come down from heaven, and for God to reveal to us what still remains hidden? So let us be content with holy Scripture. And when it is a question of inquiring of God, if we truly want him to be our teacher, let us come to holy Scripture, remembering what Moses says: 'Do not say, "Who will ascend beyond the clouds? Who will descend into the abyss? Who will traverse the sea?" The word is in your heart and on your lips' (Deut. 30:12-14).

Given, then, that Moses uttered these words in his own time, we, today, have much less cause to wander here and there and to run unthinkingly about in order to seek God's will. As I said before, the gospel contains fullness of truth. It is the sole means by which we can be satisfied and have tranquillity and peace of mind. We must listen to God speaking, and we must be teachable, accepting what he says. It is certain that, just as our mother Rebecca received the answer which God judged necessary for her, so too Scripture will not fail us here, for it tells us loud and clear that God has chosen us in Jesus Christ before the creation of the world, according to his good pleasure which he determined in himself. We need no further gloss: God speaks in such a way that the most unschooled and ignorant may know the message that Scripture contains.

God, says Paul, has elected us and has distinguished us from those who are perishing. His mercy thus shines all the brighter for us, for what accounts for the fact that we were not left like the others to perdition? It was only because God was merciful to us, undeserving though we were. To explain the matter more completely, Paul states that we were chosen 'in Jesus Christ'

(Eph. 1:4)—chosen, therefore, quite outside of ourselves. If we had been chosen in ourselves, God would have found in us some reason for loving us, something disposing him to call us to salvation. What then? We have been chosen outside of ourselves. God, that is, took no account of what we were or might be: our election is grounded in Jesus Christ.

Paul goes on to elaborate the point by saying that this was all according to God's good purpose, which he determined in himself (Eph. 1:5). The words 'according to God's good purpose' show beyond all doubt that on man's side clearly everything is ruled out. And the words 'in himself' inform us that if we want to know the reason why, we are really trying to survey God's anatomy, looking into his very heart and probing all his secrets! Could we possibly do that? And how arrogant would that be!

It follows that if we allow God to teach us, he will most surely answer, according to our need, concerning all that has to do with our salvation. In particular we will grasp what now surpasses our understanding, namely the election of some and the rejection of others. Some, like the papists and unbelievers, have never been taught: God passes them over as poor blind souls. And among those to whom the gospel is preached, some obediently accept it; they are touched to the quick and persevere to the end. Others, however, remain bewildered, or are full of faithlessness and resist God; others still are fickle: having been put on the right path, they go astray and throw off every yoke. What causes this difference? We must come to the source revealed to us in Scripture: equal grace has not been given to all.

Here, then, is where our true wisdom lies. We are to be good scholars for God; and we will be good scholars if all we seek is to understand the things which he knows are good and necessary for our salvation, and when we remain quiet, learning to control our thoughts and to keep them on a tight rein. It is then that when mention is made of God's hidden election—his predestination to salvation of those he wills, and his reprobation of the others—it is then, I say, that we will leave off worrying. Why? Because, having inquired as to God's will, we will decide that we must stick to what he shows us and to what Scripture tells us, for there he has given ample testimony to what he knows is good for us.

For the rest, Scripture bears so much convincing witness to this doctrine that all who cannot be content with it seem only to have been inflamed by Satan, so that, stung by feelings of pride and rebelliousness, they will not yield to God's will. In short, they despise teaching and instruction of every kind, closing their eyes at high noon and blocking their ears, even though God's voice resounds so loud and clear that they have more than enough reason to be satisfied. To collect all the evidence is, at this point, unnecessary. It is enough to have seen it summarized, and with utmost clarity as I have shown. Moreover, when we rightly apply this doctrine to ourselves, we have reason enough to bless God and to rejoice in him. Instead of being like those madmen and rogues who, by warring against God, fancy they are being smart and sharp-witted, and instead of trying to deny his truth, we should consider how greatly God satisfies us, why he conveys this truth to us and how well it serves us. It is meant to assure us that we—though not all—are chosen.

To begin with, when we see that we cannot accept the gospel except through a particular gift from God, we are led to exalt his goodness to us all the more and to understand how just is his judgment upon the reprobate when he deprives them of this doctrine. For this is what we see in popery: people are like mindless beasts, roaming and ranging through the wilderness, keeping to neither track nor path. We, for our part, have sure testimony which should make us all the keener to prize God's exceptional grace to us; and also when we see some whose ears are deaf, even though they are daily told what is necessary for their salvation. Although everything is given to them in digestible form, as it were, they stay exactly as they were; or else they remain unmoved, and happily claim the freedom to indulge in evil, as if to spite God. When we see such things, the Lord most certainly binds us ever closer to himself, allowing us to feel his goodness and to taste the hope of salvation which he sets before us. We have renounced the world, and however infirm we are and however full of sin and corruption, we hate the evil within us and take pleasure in the good.

This is the goal which Scripture holds out to us. Nevertheless these rascals turn round and protest, 'Oh, God respects persons!' Really? As if in his election he had regard for the rich or poor! As if he distinguished between the eminent and the miserable, or between the wise and the ignorant! That is what it means to be a respecter of persons (Rom. 2:11; Gal. 2:6; Eph. 6:9). In Scripture the word 'person' has the sense of 'face' or 'look', and Scripture uses the word in that way. God, however, does not elect us for our good looks! 'Who sees anything different in you?' asks Paul, as we saw yesterday (1 Cor. 4:7). So when God elects those he wills, it is in his eternal counsel, in himself. He has, that is, his own secrets which we should worship, without inquiring why. Since that is the case, there is no doubt that God cannot be said to have favourites. Those who speak this way merely jest, not to mention the ill-will that is in them.

'Well then,' they say, 'if it all depends on God's election, why are some saved by faith and others not?' In saying this they show how gross and stupid they are. Where does faith come from, if not from God's election? They maintain that God's promises are general, and that God calls everyone to salvation; it therefore follows that everyone will be saved. God indeed desires everyone to be saved, but this is in order to deny the reprobate every excuse. The promises in the gospel certainly contain our salvation in themselves, and we are not deceived if we rely on them. What then? We must understand where the faith we have comes from. When the gospel is preached, why do some benefit from it, accepting it with due reverence and humble hearts, while others do not, but even grow worse as a result? It is because, as Luke says when speaking of Paul's preaching, those who were appointed to salvation believe (Acts 13:48).

Here, then, is Paul preaching. Without question, if there was ever a faithful teacher endowed with great skill, it was Paul. Even so, not everyone turned out to be a good scholar: only some accepted his teaching. What was the reason? Was it a matter of hard work? Were some better prepared? God, it is true, prepares people, but it is not their doing, as Luke shows when he puts an end to all human illusions. 'Those,' he says, 'who were appointed to salvation, believed.' This also is why our Lord Jesus Christ declares that all whom the heavenly Father has given him will not perish, but he will keep them to the end (John 6:39). Now when he speaks about those whom his Father has given him, he points us to eternal election. He says also in another place, 'Father, they were yours, and you gave them to me' (John 17:6). Why, then, do some belong to God and others not? It is not that some are mortal men: our nature is the same for all. We were all made by the one Father, but some belong to God and others have been rejected by him, for such was his good pleasure. God acknowledges and reckons some to be his own, and others, while they are his creatures, have no relationship with him. He does not count them as his servants because he has excluded them from his election.

Here, then, we observe that faith is a particular gift of God, which comes not from our free will, nor from our ability to make progress on our own or to be more skilled in understanding than are others; it comes rather from God's decision to reveal his secret to those he has elected. Hence it is said in Isaiah, 'Who will believe what we have heard?' (Isa. 53:1). Now Isaiah preached concerning the death and resurrection of our Lord Jesus Christ, raising the standard high, so to speak, declaring that all should be reconciled to God, that poor sinners would be mercifully received and that atonement and righteousness were made ready, since God's one wish was to be favourable to those who sought him. At the same time the prophet cries, 'Who will believe what we have heard?' Why does he say that? Because he had in mind the boldness and arrogance of unbelievers who cannot yield to God, but who are surly, always lifting up their heads to answer God back. They are addled in their thinking, so that they refuse to obey him.

Isaiah explains that there will be a large number of people who will not accept his message. He explains why: the arm of the Lord—that is, his power, his might—is not revealed to everyone (Isa. 53:1). He shows us that in ourselves we have neither motive nor entry nor preparation nor anything else, and that God himself must work. He does not work, however, on all in general. Faith thus comes from election which is its source. Once we acknowledge this, it is unthinkable that we should bury all that our Lord teaches us in holy Scripture. Having revealed his will to us, he exhorts us, reproaches us, threatens us.

Let us not be like those restless spirits who say, 'Why do we get so much preaching? If God has chosen us, we cannot perish, and if he has rejected us, what good will it do to hear all this teaching?' But everything makes perfect sense provided we keep a proper balance. Faith, we have said, comes from election. Just as God has chosen us, so too he calls us at a point in time. (We will deal with this more fully at a more appropriate time.) Whatever the case, God is not inconsistent. He testifies that of his free mercy he illumines us in the faith of the gospel and in the knowledge of our Lord Jesus Christ. By the same token he wants us to walk in fear and trembling, to be moved by his threats and to be gathered to himself. That is what he wants.[2]

---

[2] Calvin's point is that preaching serves a dual purpose: to convey God's offer of salvation to all who are willing to repent and believe; and, by exhortation, admonition and reproof, to urge believers to live lives worthy of God's call.

There are indeed two sayings which we, in our reckless-ness and boldness, find inconsistent. Jesus Christ says this in Matthew: 'Come to me, all you who labour and are heavy laden. I will relieve you, and you will find rest for your souls' (Matt. 11:28, 29). We have this invitation from the Son of God—not just for one or two, but for everyone in general. Yet in another place he says: 'No one can come to me unless he has been given to me by my Father' (John 6:44). When judged by the human mind, these things seem contradictory: everyone can come, yet no one can come unless the Father draws him! Yes, but as I said before, when God in general terms sets forth salvation in his only Son, it is to give the reprobate much less excuse for their ingratitude, since they despise so great a blessing. The elect, on the other hand, are deeply moved, for God speaks to men not only from the outside but inwardly as well. This also is why our Lord Jesus Christ says in another place: 'Whoever has heard from God my Father will come to me' (John 6:45).

As I said earlier, when the gospel is preached in God's name, it is as if God were speaking in person. Nevertheless all do not come to Jesus Christ. There are some who, on hearing the gospel, draw even further back, for the devil inflames them with such fury that they throw off all restraint. This is because there are two sorts of hearing. The first has to do with preaching. The voice of a man cannot enter into the hearts of his hearers. I speak, but I must listen to myself, being taught by God's Spirit. The word which comes from my lips will benefit me no more than it will benefit others, unless it is given to me from above. It must not come from my own head. The human voice is merely a sound which fades into the air, and yet, according to Paul, it is the power of God for salvation to all who believe (Rom. 1:16). When God speaks through the lips of men, he adds the inner grace of his Holy Spirit, so that what is taught is not useless, but bears fruit. This is how we hear the heavenly Father: it is when he speaks to us in secret by his Holy Spirit. It is then that we come to our Lord Jesus Christ.[3]

That is the essence of what we need to remember. When God reveals to us his eternal election and bears such witness to it that we cannot doubt it, and when he shows that this is for our blessing and salvation, we will gain much, providing we do not take the liberty of railing at him and of indulging in irrelevant or tortuous arguments. There is no doubt that to be taught the doctrine of God's election brings real joy to every believer.

We should not, therefore, think it strange when, to make this doctrine odious, we see the wicked hurling their insults and slanders at God. They are bound to show that they are reprobate. If they happen to war against God's truth, this is nothing new. To that they were appointed: they cannot avoid appearing as they are. We should recall the verse with which Hosea concludes his book: 'The ways of the Lord are just and good, and the upright will walk in them; but transgressors will stumble.' He also adds, however: 'Who is the wise man who understands these things, and who is the prudent man who knows them?' (Hos. 14:9).

Here the prophet teaches that, when we speak of God's judgments, we need a particular kind of wisdom in order to accept them. Is such wisdom found in the brains of everyone? Far from it! No, we need the wisdom which God gives us in his pure mercy. It follows, then, that it is quite exceptional to find people who are meek and teachable, who allow themselves to be led by God, to be ruled by his word and who fully welcome its instruction, which is sound food for their souls. When that is the case we should recognize that this is a particular act of God and a blessing conferred on us. That is why we should be equipped to face whatever might offend us. If we see evildoers

---

[3] On the distinction between the outward word and the Spirit's inner witness, cf. *Inst.* III.2.33: 'The bare word is of no avail without the illumination of the Holy Spirit.' On their necessary union, see *Inst.* I.7.4, II.5.5.

locking horns with God, or like mastiff dogs barking and baring their teeth when they are unable to bite, we should apply the prophet's words: 'God's ways are good and right; let the just walk in them.' It will always be thus, provided we do not have an evil and perverse spirit which turns us away from God. We should be calm, asking only that the Lord should show us the path to follow. If we are like that, we will always find ourselves on level ground where we can stroll and take our pleasure.

That, I say, is the enjoyment we will know when we walk in the Lord's ways. By contrast the wicked are said to stumble. But where? In the ways of the devil? No, we are told that it is in the ways of God—all God's judgments which are set before them, his eternal counsel, his providence, the fatherly love he bears his children. In all these things, says Scripture, the wicked will stumble. Let us, then, be so strong in faith that all the disasters and stumblings which we see before our eyes do not stop us from following the right path which our Lord traces for us.

You will recall these further words from Moses: *One will be stronger than the other, and the greater will serve the lesser.* The mention of the 'stronger' reminds us that when God's election is firm and beyond all doubt, and when we are upheld by his Holy Spirit, we have nothing more to fear. This is a most useful and most necessary point. What, after all, is our condition? It takes only a puff of wind to knock us over, and only a fly to dazzle our eyes! We are all the time exposed to an incredible array of conflicts. There are enemies in countless numbers. I do not speak only of those who are visible, but of spiritual foes. The air is full of devils who spy on us and who are even like roaring lions, not to mention their sly deceits (Eph. 6:12; 1 Pet. 5:8). Alas, what can we do? We would have to suffer endless, continual stress and worry; we would be like souls transfixed if we did not know that our Lord has our salvation in his hands and that he will preserve it. Peter declares that our hope is kept safe, and that faith is, so to speak, its protective cover (cf. 1 Pet. 1:3-5); nevertheless it is to God that he points. Our Lord Jesus Christ explains more fully still, when he says that all that the Father has given him will not perish, because, he says, 'The Father who has given you to me is stronger than all' (John 6:39, 10:29).

Accordingly, we can boast that God will be merciful to us to the very end, and that he will preserve us. And although he may allow us to trip and even to fall, with his hand he will bring us to our feet. How, then, could we trust that these things will be if it were not for election? It would be impossible! Once, however, we know that the Father has given us into the care of his Son, we can be sure that he will sustain us to the end, for we have his promise which binds him to keep us, as he says, 'to the last day'—until the resurrection (Matt. 28:20). We can rejoice in him because he is the beginning and the end of our salvation. Conscious, then, of our weaknesses and frailty, knowing that we are nothing, that we lack everything, we can only say, 'The Lord who has called us to himself will complete his work.' It is as Psalm 138 says, 'Lord, you will not forsake the work of your hand half way through' (cf. Psa. 138:7, 8).

Remember therefore what we are taught here: 'One will be greater.' Our faith will be victorious over all the world. And how is that? We must, I say, be wholly founded on God's election, and rely on it so firmly that we know God to be a Father to us: he will not allow us to perish, for we are his children.

Now Moses states that the greater will serve the lesser. This further confirms the point I have just made, which is that we should be so certain of our salvation that we banish all doubt, however weak we are, however much the world despises us and however little strength we display. Why so? It is because God desires us to be as the lesser for a time. He wants us, that is, to be small and contemptible, so that his glory should be better known and appreciated. For if we had greatness and eminence, if we had distinction, these would surely serve to cloak God's pure, unmerited goodness. When, on the other hand, we are feeble, then it is clear that it is he who does everything. His hand must be so upraised that we do nothing which will muddle things or make us spout our own ideas that we deny him all praise for our salvation.

Here, then, is a lesson worth remembering. On the one hand, despite our frailties, we must nevertheless walk freely on, knowing that our strength is found in God. And if he does not display his strength to us, it is so that our weakness should give us cause to humble ourselves. That is one point. The fact is that if we did not recognize our need, we would be reluctant to call upon him—indifferent even; but if we see that we are powerless, it is then that we turn for help to the one who can supply all our wants. It is then too that we give him the sacrifice of praise which is his due, once he has answered our request.

Notice, however, that God does not make our salvation immediately visible to the eye. It must be hidden, while we appear as men rejected, since the wicked tread us underfoot: they are incomparably higher than we are. Still, let it be enough that we are a precious treasure in God's sight, which is why our Lord Jesus Christ says, 'Rejoice, little flock; do not be like bewildered or baffled sheep.' Why not? 'Because the Father is well pleased with you' (Luke 12:32). That is the source of our rejoicing, and the means by which we arm ourselves to triumph over every trial. So when today we see the enemies of the gospel and Satan's ministers swaggering about as if the day were theirs, and heaping contempt on us; and when as well they regard us as hopeless creatures, worthy only, as the saying goes, of being fed to the dogs—when we see these things, when many are starving, short of bread to eat and devoid of comforts and necessities, let us recall what is said here: 'The greater will serve the lesser.'

Now Esau did not serve from the very first. As we will later see, Jacob came and knelt before his brother and called him 'lord'. He trembled like a poor lamb, and gave all his goods as prey into his hands (Gen. 33:3, 8-11). In what way, then, is Esau subordinate, and Jacob superior? For he humbles himself, and seems to surrender everything. Nevertheless he knows that God does not intend to fulfil his plan from the very first day. Thus he bears his misery patiently. God means him to crawl, so to speak, upon the earth. Yet nothing will prevent him attaining the salvation to which he has been called, because God does not depend on all these earthly things. Moreover, as I said, he wants us to start out this way and to humble ourselves before him. According to the words I quoted earlier from the lips of our Lord Jesus Christ, provided we know that the heavenly Father is well pleased with us, nothing else matters. Or else we should not be so upset that it makes us go astray, or so repels us that it stops us even doing good. In any case, we should not doubt that amid the problems and worries which we may meet, we will always have reason to rejoice, for who will separate us from the love God bears us in our Lord Jesus Christ? (Rom. 8:35)

Ever since God chose us in Jesus Christ, called us to faith in the gospel and engraved the proof of his fatherly love upon our hearts, we are able to defy our enemies, however small and feeble we are and however much we count for nothing in most men's eyes. For all that, we are firmly founded on the promise that 'the greater will serve the lesser'. Let us not seek, then, to be great in worldly terms, for while we know that we are contemptible and despised, we will not fail to inherit the earth (Matt. 5:5). Although we may have neither lands nor goods, all will be ours. The wicked, on the other hand, will have an awful account to render for having devoured God's good gifts and for having enjoyed the many blessings he has bestowed on them, without having ever given him the glory. That will cost them very dear.

So while we may be destitute of all goods and are abused and vilified, although we are small and lowly, since God's hand is outstretched to uphold us, we can boast in the face of all our enemies. In the meantime let us remember what Isaiah says: we are a precious crown in the hands of God; we are like a ring on his finger, or like a signet (Isa. 62:3); he prizes neither Egypt nor Assyria—all the world's great kingdoms—more than us. It is not because of any value to be found in us, but because he has been pleased to choose us, and to set us apart among those whom he wishes to make his. Of this we are sure, for by faith and hope we know that he has rescued us from the deep pit in which we lay, so that we might enter into the heavenly inheritance.

> *Now let us cast ourselves down before the face of our good God, acknowledging our faults and begging him so to make us feel them that we may be rid of all our evil desires and rebelliousness, and may be so renewed that we confirm our calling by leading holy lives which accord with his righteousness. May he uphold us in our weaknesses so that we do not fail, however many the enemies that surround us. May he remedy all our infirmities, and give such power to his election that we, seeing its fruit, may have cause to glorify him both in life and death.*

4

THE DAY OF SMALL THINGS

When the day came for Rebecca to be delivered, behold, there were twins in her womb. [25] *The first came forth red; he was hairy like a hairy mantle, and his name was Esau.* [26] *Then his brother came forth, and his hand had taken hold of Esau's heel; and his name was Jacob. Isaac was sixty years old when the boys were born.* [27] *When they grew up, Esau was a skilful hunter and a man of toil; Jacob was a simple man, dwelling in tents.* [28] *Isaac loved Esau because he brought him game from the hunt; but Rebecca loved Jacob.* (Genesis 25:24-28)

BECAUSE God's election is, in itself, secret, it must manifest itself in time, for God knows when to fulfil his works. It would not be enough for him to have chosen us and marked us out; he must continue to the end, demonstrating that his election is not in vain, and that it has energy and power which will bring us to salvation.

There are different ways, however, in which this happens, for God is not obliged to work always in the same fashion. He has his means which he ordains as he pleases. Sometimes he demonstrates his election very early, and sometimes he waits for a long period of time. Those, therefore, badly err who believe that there is some seed or other in those whom he elects, permitting him to distinguish them from others since they are inclined to goodness and are disposed to serve him.[1] Experience also condemns them. While John the Baptist was sanctified from his mother's womb, a different circumstance applies to many others.

God may sometimes allow his elect to be like wayward sheep; they seem entirely lost. He does this to give all the more lustre to his grace. Some such sign we see in Jacob, whom God had chosen, having rejected his brother Esau. *Jacob took hold of his brother's heel*, as if he were fighting him. This did not happen by chance, nor was it nature's doing. God was clearly pointing out that although Esau was the first-born, he would nevertheless be rejected, and that Jacob who was inferior to him by birth would be preferred in time to him. God thus sought to give proof of what he had said. That is what we gather from this passage. As we saw yesterday, the greater would serve the lesser, which was already seen in the birth of these two boys.

From this example we gather a general truth, namely that God foresees those whom he has chosen, and that he confirms his counsel and decree by implementing them. Although, then, we cannot enter far enough in as to know those who have been elected before the creation of the world, nevertheless, to the extent necessary, witness will be borne to our election. For if God keeps the original records, as we say, to himself, it is not that he fails to testify to them, assuring us that he is, and ever will be, a Father to us, and that we, fully trusting, may call upon him.

Despite the fact that Jacob was, to use Scripture's expression, called, it is not said that God informed him of his choice. That would come in time. Scripture simply says that God visibly confirmed that his answer to Rebecca had not been given lightly.

[1] An allusion to the belief of Strasbourg Reformer, Martin Bucer, who in his commentary on the Gospels (1530) held that the elect, before conversion, possessed 'seeds of piety' which marked them out from others. In *Inst.* III.24.10-11, Calvin dismisses the idea as contrary both to Scripture and experience.

How was that? Its effect was plain to see, in that Jacob held Esau by the heel. God uses this image to show that the elect will not reach their goal without many struggles. Jacob naturally did not know the significance of this, nor did his age allow it. Even so this is useful to us, for it is meant to teach us that God wills us to fight, although we are under his care and guidance and although we hope in his salvation, knowing that he will complete what he has begun. Although all this is true, God does not want us to be idle; he wants us to strive in order to be brought to the goal to which he is calling us. This is what Moses means when he records that Jacob took hold of Esau's heel.

Next it is said that *the name of the elder was Esau, and the name of the other was Jacob*. In the latter case it is as if his name was 'the Pursuer'.[2] Esau, we learn, came forth all hairy from his mother's womb. He is like a well-formed man, for that is what his name suggests. We notice a clear difference between the two. Esau could be said to be much more mature than his brother; he is sturdy and very vigorous. Although he is but a child, he appears almost a man. As for Jacob, all we are told is that his hand held Esau's heel; he is like one stillborn. And it is the same when the boys grow up. *Esau is a hunter, and a hard worker*—a man full of strength, we might say. In Jacob we see a simplicity which contrasts completely with Esau's more obvious qualities. According to Moses, *Jacob kept to the house*, like some layabout, crouching over the ashes! That is what we are meant to think about Esau and Jacob.

What we are taught here confirms what we discussed earlier: God does not choose people according to their looks. On the contrary, he passes over what we judge to be outstanding: he despises it; he gives preferment to the things that we reject. We see this all the time, but we cannot doubt that the Holy Spirit

---

[2] French: *le Talonnier*, a play on words impossible to render in English. The French for 'heel' is *talon*; the verb *talonner* means 'to follow on the heels of', 'to pursue closely' and thus 'to press hard' or 'to harass'.

sought to make this clear in the person of our father Jacob, so that we should learn to suppress all foolish pride, and not to seek reasons for God's election in ourselves and for his continuance of grace to us. We must recognize that he wishes to be glorified in our smallness. If this doctrine is etched upon our hearts we will have made real progress, for there is nothing which turns us away from God more than our claim to have qualities which are worthy of praise. We must completely abandon such claims, otherwise we are full of wind and God's grace has no way of entering in to us.

It is all the more necessary, then, that we remember this essential point. When God chooses us, he does not do so, as we say, for our good looks. And if the world despises us, we should not lose heart. As we stressed before, it should be enough for us that we are pleasing to God, however much the world may deride us. For we see how it was with Jacob. He lives at home—a lazy-bones, as it were. True, he is a decent man, but is his simplicity valued? Does he draw attention to himself? Is he esteemed? Not at all! Esau, on the other hand, has been streets ahead of him ever since birth. He is a grown man, full of energy; he is hard-working and seems set to perform miracles!

We are taught here that it is God who does everything. If our election were all our doing, we would all doubtless give Esau our vote. Yet God prefers Jacob. Why? It is the very opposite of what we would expect. What, then, we need to understand, is that God so dispensed his grace as to seek to show that his goodness alone moved him to love Jacob. This is a message we should certainly ponder all the days of our life. It is designed, as I said, to overthrow our arrogance and to allow God's pure mercy to shine forth. The lesson for us is that the church has always had small beginnings, and that God moves it forward in such a way that it appears weak in human terms. We should acknowledge that this is so and become used to our condition.

For the rest, be sure that God will not cease his work until he has brought it to full perfection, even though this may not be immediately apparent to us. It does not have to be, and it would be of no advantage to us. If God, then, gives some sign that he has chosen us and if this has been obvious since childhood, we have even greater cause to praise him, for the longer his grace has endured, the more praise it deserves. If, however, we seem for a time to have been rejected, if God appears to have no concern for us and to have forgotten us, but if he then calls us back and rescues us when we have long gone astray, then we have reason to give him twice the glory.

In a word, since God is at work in us, we must always open our mouths wide and acknowledge his goodness and mercy. There are some who from childhood give evidence that God has set them apart, as if his hand were outstretched to them and as if he were bringing them forward, declaring, 'These are mine.' From childhood indeed they have been taught so well and so profitably that people, seeing it, will say, 'They are God's seed.' Such people, I repeat, are very much obliged to confess that this is a great privilege from God. For what do they possess more than others? In Adam we are all corrupt! So when God has continually guided them from childhood to old age, they owe him an even greater debt.

Conversely, others are poor miserable creatures who seem to be completely cast off by God. Some may have been dissolute in their youth, and others wretched idolaters. And whatever devotion they may have had, its effect was to estrange them all the more from God and to provoke his wrath. They may even have been enemies of all truth, as we see from the example of Paul. Like a wild beast he shed innocent blood; his only aim was to scatter, like a ravening wolf, all the churches (1 Cor. 15:9; Gal. 1:13; 1 Tim. 1:13). Or there were the Corinthians who were immoral and given to every form of villainy, as Paul points out

(1 Cor. 6:9-11). It was the same with the Romans. 'In time past,' writes Paul, 'you were immoral, drunkards, given to theft and deceit; you gave your members to serve evil and sin' (Rom. 6:17-21). To the Ephesians, he says, 'You were formerly without God and without the hope of life. You were complete darkness and dwelt in eternal death' (Eph. 2:12, 5:8).

Now when our Lord, to humble us, allows us to be scattered for a time, but suddenly calls us to himself, we should extol him not only for his choice of us and for allowing us to see its fruit, but for having plucked us from the pit where we once were. We should strive all the harder, then, to make up for past time, as Paul says in the passage we have mentioned (Eph. 5:16). 'You were once darkness,' he says, 'but now you are light in the Lord. Walk, therefore, as children of the light' (Eph. 5:8). Recall also the words of our Lord Jesus Christ: 'There are many sheep which are not yet of this fold' (John 10:16). He was speaking of the Gentiles who were excluded from all hope of salvation. He calls them 'sheep'—not that they were that in themselves, for they were wild animals—but with respect to God's election. Although they had strayed, he says that he will gather them in. Accordingly, since God was pleased to rescue us when we were widely scattered, let us learn to heed the voice of our great Shepherd, not simply by signalling our approval with a nod of the head, but with the intention of following him and of obeying him in everything. That is what we should remember about this verse.

In addition, let us not be ashamed if our Lord does not give his church and faithful people an imposing presence or great esteem in men's eyes. As long as God is glorified, we must not be ashamed of our littleness. Today, for instance, the church seems set on being trampled underfoot. We also know that the ungodly and the children of this world take no account of those whom God has gathered to himself. Let us bear this patiently like our father Jacob, and let us not care if the world spits in our face, so to speak, as long as we have God's approval.[3]

This is the way we must put this doctrine into practice, both individually and in the whole body of the church. So what Paul wrote has been fulfilled. God has no time for the lofty and superior things of earth: they are an abomination to him (1 Cor. 1:26-28). Men will certainly deem them worthy of praise, as were Esau's qualities. Jacob's simplicity, however, is more highly prized by God and his angels. Let us walk, then, as our Lord commands, and let us not worry if the gifts that God has put in us are not apparent from the very first.

There are many who are worthless in God's sight, though they may be high in rank and station, expert managers who have it all their own way. They may be acclaimed and honoured—not too greedy, even! So upright are they that they seem like angels; on all sides they are praised. On the other hand there are poor tradesmen, workers who toil and the illiterate who have little chance to impress. The workshop or their small household takes up all their time. They have to labour to feed their children. Not much is heard from them: they have no eloquence to demonstrate their good sense. Yet God has chosen and elected them! He accepts what appears to have no value. Although a man who spends his time stitching, toiling or doing something else may appear abject and mean, it is a service dearer to God than we imagine.

Knowing, then, that in appearance we are nothing, we should not think that we are the worse off for that. We ought not to be ashamed of our weaknesses, but should raise our eyes above, so that, though crouching over the ashes, we remember that the

---

[3] Calvin's comments on the church's precarious position should not be dismissed as rhetorical exaggeration. The preacher frequently warns his hearers against taking for granted the gains made by the Reformation in sixteenth-century Europe. Such gains, he argued, could be easily reversed by external oppression and internal dissent, or worse, by indifference. In particular, the persecution unleashed against evangelicals in Calvin's native France, as elsewhere in Europe, showed how bitter the struggle for survival could be.

same was true of our father Jacob, who prefigured all of God's elect, all of his children.

We go on to read that *Jacob was loved by his mother, and Esau by his father*. Here we learn that Isaac was not as mature as he should have been. He was not ignorant of what God had said: 'The greater will serve the lesser.' He is aware that Esau, the elder, must yield his position and place of honour to his brother. Nevertheless Isaac loves Esau and seems bent on resisting God's counsel. But what difference will it make? Even if he devotes all his love to Esau, God will rule supreme. His election stands firm, even if the whole world is against it.

Isaac, then, is a man bemused. There is, however, more: his attitude seems brutish. Why does he love Esau? Because he brings him game! He loves him for his tasty food! Now Isaac is already old, and his age should have made him a man of calm and steady common sense. He should not have been driven by his foolish, fitful appetites. On account of his desire to eat and of his fondness for food, he forgets the irrevocable decree which God has pronounced: that Jacob must prevail and must be heir to the promise. Isaac nevertheless takes no notice and overturns God's election. He does not mean to do it. If anyone had said: 'What? Must you resist God? Will you stop him from doing as he has said? Will you alter the words his lips have uttered?', he would have replied: 'No!' He had no such intention. Nevertheless he is a man driven, a man beside himself. He cannot be said to have tried to aid and advance God's election; on the contrary, he tries to set it back.

What this shows is that, just as God's election is free in its origin, in its first foundation and in its effect, so too God must demonstrate to the very end that it is all of mercy. Anything that comes from men must cease and vanish. As Paul says in Romans, it is not of him who wills or who runs (Rom. 9:16). This is what we have to bear in mind.

We see also how firm is God's counsel by which he chooses those he wills. We must resolve, then, that however much the world tries to overthrow our salvation, it will never fail us, provided we rely on what we learned before, that our Lord Jesus Christ guards all that the Father has given him, for it is his; nothing will perish (John 6:39). This is the point to which he keeps bringing us back: 'The Father who gave you to me is stronger than all' (John 10:29).

Let us learn, then, to rely on God's invincible power whenever we need assurance. When we call upon him, he will hear and answer; and we should never doubt that having set us on the right path, he will enable us to persevere. Despite our weakness and our frailty, he will never allow us to fall, but will always guide us and more and more increase his power in us.

This should be true of us, for Jacob did not only have as enemies those without religion and godly fear; he had his own father, Isaac, the very man who at the time was, in a sense, head of the church! God had given him his covenant in trust, that he might administer it and keep it safe. Yet Isaac was hostile, so it seems, to Jacob's election. Consequently, if we face much antagonism and if there are many things that set our salvation back; if we can see no way out, we should know that God will be victorious in the end and that he will continue to work despite our weaknesses. Whatever resistance and opposition there may be on earth, he will overcome it all and achieve his ends.

Nevertheless Isaac's example serves to warn us that we must keep ourselves in check, for if it could happen that so superior a man, a man of angelic holiness, actually resisted God, how would we fare in comparison? No doubt some idle thought would so engross us that we would daily clash with God, even if that was not what we intended. We need, then, to distrust our own judgment and to pray that God may rule us by his Holy Spirit. Otherwise, as I said, we are like poor lost souls, aimlessly wandering here and there. We might think we were wise, but there would only be folly and rebelliousness in us, even if these were not wilfully or consciously meant. Enough said, however, on that point.

Consider now what Moses says regarding Isaac's motivation: 'Isaac loved Esau.' He loved him, as we saw, because he brought him game. So if we would submit to God, we should be careful not to be led by our earthly, fleshly appetites. Food and drink are not, it is true, condemned. God placed us in this world so that we might enjoy what he has made. We certainly do not offend him when we desire to have the necessities of life and when we seek to use the good things he has prepared for us. Scripture rightly tells us to eat and drink everything in his name (1 Cor. 10:31). However, because we are corrupt, our appetites are bound to be excessive, and our excess makes us forget our duty to God. We are thus in a state of continual excitement, and although we think we are doing our duty, we fall far short.

Isaac should have borne these things in mind; they should have been written on his heart. He should have heard the voice sounding in his ears: 'The greater will serve the lesser.' He should have constantly reflected, 'Well, since God wished his election to lie with Jacob, I must consent to it.' Yet his desire for food distracts him and drives him in the opposite direction. Let us beware, then, and avoid all excess and over-indulgence. Let us make sure, I say, that we rebuke and master them so that they never distract us or stop us yielding to God's will. That is the lesson for us here.

It is clear, on the other hand, that Rebecca's feelings were better ordered than her husband's. Admittedly, as a general rule, if a father loves one child in particular, the mother will go the other way and love another. These tensions are to be seen in almost all marriages. Rebecca might have felt some jealousy on seeing that Esau was preferred, and might have loved Jacob since he was less pleasing to his father. But she was also mindful of God's election, and still recalled what he had said. Some women skirmish with their husbands when their affection goes to a child who is not well thought of. Rebecca, however, is not to be seen in this light: she always looked to God and sought to obey what had been told to her. Doubtless she would have desired both her children to be reserved for the church, but because she knows that one has been excluded and that it is only the lesser that God accepts, she acquiesces.

Here we learn that our Lord sometimes allows those who have greater qualities and gifts of his Spirit to err, while those who are less advanced outstrip them in one way or another. If we compare Isaac and Rebecca, it is clear that he who had been taught from childhood in his father's house had, overall, more faith than Rebecca. Yet here is a particular instance where he fails and is seen to be at fault. Rebecca, however, who had but lately emerged from a den of idolatry—for superstition reigned in her father's house, and the country was thoroughly defiled—this poor woman, having known nothing of God in her youth, is so well instructed by the Holy Spirit that she surpasses her husband. That is why those to whom God has, early on, stretched out his hand, and who have been brought up by him to be mirrors, as it were, should always walk in fear and trembling. Why? Because it takes only one false step for them to stumble so badly as to fill everyone with shame.

We must learn that although our Lord so forms and fashions us that, generally speaking, others may marvel at us, individually we may stumble. We should always be on our guard, and when those who most stand out among us happen to fail in one way or another, let them not take as their shield the excuse that they have done a great many good and praiseworthy deeds. Let them not sing their own praises, as we say. They should see themselves as they really are, confessing that God means them to acknowledge their weaknesses and to realize that men cannot sustain themselves: it takes only one offence to cut us off from the church. And once God forsakes us, what will happen to us? All this we should learn from the person of our father Isaac, who was so dazzled that he could not see that, by cherishing the one whom God had rejected and by scorning his younger son, he was rebelling against God.

Now while Rebecca's feelings were well controlled and while she sought to obey God, there was inevitably some ill-will between her and Isaac, as always happens. Moses says as much when he records that Isaac loved Esau but that Rebecca loved Jacob. He implies that there was conflict and disagreement in the house. We are thus warned that although our feelings may be valid and well-intentioned, obstacles arise which do much harm.

For example, I may be trying to follow God and to act always according to his will. Opposition may arise, and in doing my duty I may fall out of favour with one and make an enemy of another. I will have begun well by seeking to do good and by looking to God; but if we are excessive in our zeal, human emotions are bound to be unleashed. Even those who are best disciplined and most mature may certainly go too far and react as men. We ought thus to be suspicious of our feelings, and even when we know our purposes are bad we may well stumble. This is a salutary warning: we should cease our quarrelling, for Scripture rightly urges us to be united, to be one in spirit and in word. Why? Because when we agree together, each of us encourages his neighbours and helps them to obey God's will. When, on the other hand, there is ill-will between us, when there are arguments and disputes, not only does one obstruct the other—as the proverb goes, it takes only one bad horse to throw the rest off course—but worse occurs: in fighting for God's cause we are sure to forget ourselves and to do things we would not do if released from combat.

We daily see examples of this sort in the church, for God's best servants, those endowed with outstanding gifts and busy contending for the truth, cannot always restrain themselves: when stung, they react like men. They begin well and their aims are good, but, as I said, there is always an element of weakness involved. The examples of Isaac and Rebecca should remind us of these things.

Yet for all their notable failings, Isaac and Rebecca continued to serve God, and Isaac never sought to overturn God's decree that Jacob should prevail. It was, after all, a matter of God's eternal election and of the church of our Lord Jesus Christ, who is its Head. Although husband and wife were at cross-purposes, Isaac did not intend to turn everything upside down. He simply did not understand and was inwardly confused. When, therefore, through ignorance or error, we sometimes find ourselves upset, and when the devil interferes to stop us speaking with one voice, we must always observe this guiding principle: we are of one mind in believing that God is our Father, and that in Jesus Christ alone we have our true and holy unity. Let us hold, I repeat, to these principles of our faith, and if we do not grasp everything as clearly as we would like, let the weak and ignorant humble themselves and not lose heart. May those who are more mature support them, until God brings them to a better mind and dispels the ideas in which they are ensnared.

This is what Paul says to the Philippians, when he points to the things that bind us together in harmony and brotherhood (Phil. 2:1-11). He concludes by saying that we should not have divergent views among ourselves, nor should our words be different. 'But,' he adds, 'if you cannot achieve perfection, if there is one among you who still limps along, do not try to be smart and to comprehend everything. Wait for God to reveal it' (cf. Phil. 3:15). That, then, is the first thing to be done: we must agree upon the pure and simple truth of God. However, because it is not given to all to have a firm and immediate grasp of every article of religion, we should lend a hand to those who may be confused through ignorance; and they, for their part, should not be stubborn. Sometimes—more often than not—those who know least are the boldest and most headstrong. They prove to be so obdurate that it is impossible to win any point with them. To solve the problem, Paul declares that we must wait for God to reveal it. We should remember this, then. But we should also remember that Paul says that when we are of one mind in Jesus Christ and when we seek only his glory, we may continue on our way. Thus if there is some small dispute it should not separate us from each other. Although, on some things, we may not be as resolved as we should be, it is enough if nothing separates us from our Lord Jesus Christ or turns us away from him.

For the rest, when we aim to glorify him, even those who are furthest forward will see that they are still far from the goal. Why is it, then, that those who are most skilled and knowledgeable in holy Scripture despise the brethren who they think are ignorant? It is because they believe them to be at fault. If, on the other hand, we know what it is to yearn for our Lord Jesus Christ and to seek to attain his glorious resurrection, we will confess with Paul that we have not yet attained it (Phil. 3:12). So when we realize that we are all at fault, we will not find it hard or strange to call to our brethren, even from afar, 'Come, let us press on!' Naturally there is quite a distance between those who have the gift of interpreting Scripture and those who are unschooled and ignorant. The latter know that there is a God who, in Jesus Christ, is their Father, but they cannot expound one verse of Scripture. Even so, they should keep to the same path, and those who are most advanced, though they might reach the goal sooner, should continue to wait for the others. That is what we must do, as we are taught here, and as we learn from the example set before us.

Section II. Election and Reprobation

Now let us cast ourselves down before the majesty of our good God, acknowledging our faults and asking him so to make us feel them that they may cease to please us; and may we, mindful of our condition, take refuge in his mercy. May he be pleased mercifully to receive us and to rule us by his Holy Spirit, so that we may be freed of all earthly desires. And since there are so many hidden faults in us, may we examine ourselves all the more closely, and turn to him who can cleanse us of them. May we strive against all that stops us engaging fully in his service, knowing that he accepts our striving only because he sustains us in our weaknesses. May we look only to his power, conscious of how much we need his help, and may we boast in him alone. May we not doubt that he, having once stretched out his hand to us, will continue to strengthen us so that, in all our battles with the devil, we will prevail.

III.

ELECTION IN CHRIST

SERMONS ON EPHESIANS 1

1

A CHOICE MADE IN HEAVEN

Blessed be the God and Father of our Lord Jesus Christ, who has blessed us in Christ with every spiritual blessing in the heavenly places, 4 *even as he chose us in him before the foundation of the world, that we should be holy and blameless before him in love.* (Ephesians 1:3, 4)

WE saw previously that Paul exhorts us to praise and bless God, because he has blessed us, not in any earthly fashion, but spiritually, making us glad that he has shown us his goodness and love. The gate to the kingdom of heaven is opened to us by hope, and although in this world we may be subject to much misery, we have cause to be content that God has chosen us and has called us to faith, and has testified to us in the gospel that he is our Father, for he has united us to our Lord Jesus Christ, as members to their Head.

Paul now takes us back to the origin and source, to the principal motive which moved God to accept us, for it is not enough that God should have poured out the riches of his goodness and mercy upon us, drawing us by the gospel to the hope of the heavenly life. That was fully sufficient in itself, but if Paul had not added what we now see, we might assume that God's grace was common to everyone, and that it was offered and presented to all without exception. In that case it would have been for us to accept it of our own free will, implying that we somehow deserved it. If the only difference between us was that some accepted God's grace while others refused it, what could we say, except that God's generosity had been shown to the whole human race?

Paul, however, in order to exclude all merit on our part, and to show that God's sheer, unmerited goodness is all there is, declares that *God has blessed us, even as he chose us beforehand.* What he means is that we must ponder the difference that exists between us, in order to exalt God's grace, as is our duty. For the gospel is preached to some, while others have no idea what it is. They are excluded from it, as if God had caused it to rain in one area but had left another completely dry. And if we ask why God should have compassion on one group and why he forsakes and passes over another, there is no answer except that such is his good pleasure. Or again, when the gospel is preached in a certain place, the hearts of some are touched with a living faith, while others return home just as they came, having gained nothing; or else they are hardened against God and display a rebelliousness which was previously hidden. What is the source of this difference? It is because God directs some by his Holy Spirit, but leaves others in their natural state of corruption.

That is why God's goodness to us shines all the more brightly. The fact that the gospel is preached to us is already a token that God has had compassion on us, that he loves us and calls and invites us to faith. In addition, when we accept with readiness of heart the message preached to us, we have a more specific token still by which we see that God desires to be a Father to us, and that he has adopted us as his children. Paul is thus right to say in this verse that we have been blessed by God, since he had already chosen us. It was he who chose us: we did not come to him or seek him out. What Isaiah the prophet said must be fulfilled in all of us: 'God has revealed himself to those who did not seek him, and those who were far from him saw him draw near. To them he said: "Here am I. Here am I. Although you have scorned me I condescend to come to you, for I care for your salvation"' (cf. Isa. 65:1).

It is clear what Paul was aiming at in this verse. In sum, observe that we will never know the source of our salvation until we raise our minds to God's eternal counsel by which he chooses whom he wills, leaving the rest to their shame and destruction. If some find this teaching strange and harsh, we should not be surprised, for it scarcely agrees with our natural understanding. Look at the philosophers; ask them their opinion. They will always say that God loves those who are worthy of him, and because virtue is pleasing to him, he takes note of those who practise it and selects them to be his people. So, in our judgment, God distinguishes between us, and therefore loves or hates us, only because one is worthy and another not.

Consider this, however: our understanding is entirely futile. We must not judge God by our own measure. We are impossibly arrogant when we try to lay down the law to God, thinking that he may do only those things we deem to be lawful and just. Here, then, it is a question of worshipping God's secrets which are beyond our comprehension. Otherwise we will never appreciate the first principles of faith, for we know that the first step to wisdom and humility is that we never come with our scales in hand to weigh up the judgments of God. We must not try to act as judge or referee. We must be sober, given the littleness of our minds, our coarseness and our stupidity. Let us exalt God, as holy Scripture teaches. Let us say, 'Lord, your counsel is too deep an abyss; none can tell of it' (Psa. 36:6).

That, then, is how it is with those who, being too fixed in their opinions, find this teaching harsh and grievous. They cannot humbly submit to God's wisdom and accept his words with sober moderation. So let us make good use of Paul's instruction: 'The unspiritual man does not understand God's secrets, for they are folly to him' (1 Cor. 2:14). This is because we are not privy to God's counsel: he must reveal to us by his Holy Spirit what would otherwise remain unknown. Let us judge according to the measure which he supplies.

In this verse Paul speaks of something which is familiar to us from experience. We learn that we are children of God; he rules us by his Holy Spirit, comforts us in our afflictions and gives us strength to suffer patiently. We would not understand these things if we were not illumined by his Holy Spirit. How then could we comprehend something which is much loftier—that God has elected us before the creation of the world? Since this is so, let us learn to dismiss everything our brains conceive. Let us cast it all aside, and let us be ready to accept what God tells us, emptying ourselves of all ideas and knowing that we can contribute nothing but our foolishness. That, then, is what we must remember.

We see just how firmly Paul urges us to come to this point. 'O man,' he says, 'who are you to answer back to God?' (Rom. 9:20). Having stated a number of objections which we are accustomed to make, 'Man,' he says. The word he uses is meant to make us feel our frailty. We are no more than earthworms and rottenness. What temerity it is to open our mouths and to answer God back! Is that not to corrupt the natural order? Are we able to pluck the sun from the sky, or to seize the moon with our teeth, as the saying goes? It is even less lawful to argue with God and to raise objections critical of his unfathomable decisions.

Now there are some who admit the truth of Paul's teaching concerning predestination. They do not dare to contradict the Holy Spirit, but would rather nothing was said about it and that it was buried.[1] Yes, but they should have been born much

---

[1] The preacher's principal target appears to be Melanchthon (see Introduction, p. xxii.

sooner if they wanted to criticize the Holy Spirit, who spoke by the prophets and apostles and indeed by the lips of God's only-begotten Son. For our Lord Jesus Christ takes us back to God's eternal election when he wants to assure us of our salvation, and when, in the sixth and tenth chapters of John, he wishes to celebrate the gift of faith (John 6:70, 10:14). These people, then, have come too late to shut God up or to erase this doctrine from holy Scripture. 'All Scripture is useful,' says Paul, speaking of the law and prophets (2 Tim. 3:16). We may likewise infer that the gospel contains nothing that is superfluous, is not of benefit or is incapable of building us up in faith and godly fear. Now the gospel contains this doctrine, and the Holy Spirit proclaims it loud and clear. We would have to be like the Manicheans who sought to cut into the gospel and to clear things out. They suppressed anything that was not to their taste and invented a gospel of different parts, only accepting the things they liked.[2]

If heretics like these rebelled against God by separating things which were indissolubly linked, those today who want us to be silent about election are similarly evil and perverse. They would like to gag God if that were possible, and to shut his mouth whenever they disapproved of what he says. Moreover their stupidity is clear to see, for Paul has no better grounds for extolling God's goodness than this. If this were the only reason we had, it would be better for the whole world to be destroyed than for this doctrine to be wrapped in silence. Is it right, after all, for God visibly to display the boundless riches of his mercy, and for nothing to be said about it and for it to be trodden underfoot?

---

note 34, and Appendix II). Calvin's criticism here is decidedly severe. Advocates of a policy of silence are termed 'evil and perverse' and reproached for their 'stupidity'.

[2] The Manicheans were a heterodox sect chiefly of the third and fourth centuries. Combining Christian, Gnostic and Mithraic beliefs, they held to the opposition between body and spirit, soul and matter, and sought release for the soul through ascetic practices and superior knowledge. They rejected the Evangelists' witness to the person and work of Jesus, and condemned the text of much of the New Testament as corrupt.

Besides, there are two reasons why it is necessary to preach this doctrine, and why it is so useful to us that it would be better never to have been born than to be ignorant of Paul's teaching here. There are two things which should be our chief aim, and which sum up all that God teaches us in holy Scripture. We should apply our minds and all our energy to this end, first, that all praise should be given to God as he deserves; and second, that we should be assured of our salvation, so that we can freely call upon God as our Father. Woe to us, for we are devoid of faith and religion if we do not do these things! We might well talk about God, but it would be no more than a lie.

Concerning the first point, I have already said that we do not acknowledge God's grace enough unless we behold our election, as it were, before our very eyes. Supposing God were to draw men on exactly the same terms, so that those who wished to obtain salvation came of their own free will and on their own initiative. If that were so we would earn the right for God to accept us and to deal with us as we each deserved. How could that serve to exalt his goodness? God loves us only because he generously forestalls us, and because he finds nothing in us or in our works to make him love us. In that case there has to be election, with God taking some since that is his choice, but leaving others out.

The issue is therefore settled. God's glory is visible and only shines as it should if we confess that he displays his goodness and love just as he chooses. As I said before, it is a particular gift God grants us when his word is preached to us. That is why we read so often in the law and the prophets that God did not treat all other nations as he treated Abraham's descendants, when he was pleased to choose and adopt them (Deut. 4:7). The law bore sure testimony to this, which was why the children of Israel were urged to praise God for deigning to give them the law, even though he left out the unhappy Gentiles who in no way belonged to him. It is an even greater and more special privilege, however, when he allows his word to benefit its hearers.

The fact is that although his word is daily drummed into our ears, it does us no good until God speaks inwardly to us by his Holy Spirit. Here, then, is a twofold grace of God. First, he raises people up to preach the gospel to us, for no one is competent in himself to do this (2 Cor. 2:16). Thus God must send those who call us to him and who hold forth the hope of salvation. Notice, however, that we cannot believe unless God reveals himself to us by his Holy Spirit. Accordingly the prophet Isaiah declares in his fifty-third chapter: 'Who will believe our report? And to whom will the arm of the Lord be revealed?' (Isa. 53:1). Here he teaches that faith does not exist on earth until God has worked in our minds and hearts by the power of his Holy Spirit. In the same way, our Lord Jesus says that no one comes to him unless he is drawn by the Father (John 6:44). 'Whoever,' he says, 'has learned from my Father, he will obey me' (John 6:45).

We see, then, that God shows his compassion for us when he is pleased to illumine us by his Holy Spirit, so that we are drawn to the faith of the gospel. If that were true for all of us without exception, we would already have cause to exalt God. When, moreover, we see that some are hardened and others fickle, so that they return home having gained nothing from what they have heard, while others are simply mindless, this surely gives greater lustre to God's grace, as we see when Paul, according to Luke's record, declares that those who were foreordained to salvation believed (Acts 13:48). Here we have a large number of people who heard Paul's preaching. Undoubtedly he, for his part, spoke with such grace as would almost move stones! Yet there were many who persisted in their stubborn unbelief. Some, however, did believe. Luke insists that it was not because they were clever people or were predisposed to virtue; it was because God had ordained them to salvation.

To sum up, therefore, it is clear that all our merits must cease and be swept away, otherwise God will not have the praise he deserves. At the same time we must understand that faith does not come from us, for that would mean that our works were somehow meritorious. True, by faith we confess that we are totally wretched, condemned and accursed, and that all we bring to God is the awareness of our sins. At any rate, faith would have some merit if we attained it of our own accord. We must thus conclude that we cannot believe unless faith is given us from on high. This is exactly what Paul says when he writes, '*Blessed be God.*' Why does he say that? Because in Jesus Christ God has made us rich, so that our lives are happy and blessed. And he adds, '*according as he has chosen us.*' Among the spiritual riches which Paul has in mind, is not faith included? Better still, it has the principal place, for it is by faith that we receive the Holy Spirit, by faith that we are patient in adversity, by faith that we are obedient to God, and by faith that we are sanctified for his service. In short, faith always remains the foremost of all the spiritual blessings which God pours upon us.

Consider carefully the sequence described by Paul. He tells us that since God has chosen us, he has given us faith with all the rest. Faith thus depends on God's election, otherwise we would be making Paul a liar. As regards our first point, then, all who cannot bear to hear, loud and clear, about predestination, are deadly enemies of God's grace: they are doing all they can to obscure it. As I have said, this is how all religion is destroyed.

We mentioned as our second point the assurance of salvation. The papists will tell us that we must remain in doubt, and that we can only come to God hoping that he will receive us. We cannot be sure, however, for that would be to presume too much.[3] Now when we pray to God we must call him 'Father'—if,

---

[3] In its decree on justification (January 1547), the Council of Trent asserted the impossibility of certainty regarding the forgiveness of sins and justification by faith.

that is, we are scholars in the school of Jesus Christ, for that is what he taught us. Do we call God 'Father' more or less haphazardly, having no certainty in ourselves? We would be nothing but hypocrites if we prayed like that, and the first word we uttered would be a lie! The papists have never understood what prayer is about, because they say that we cannot be sure of our salvation. Scripture, on the other hand, shows—as we will especially see in chapter 3—that real prayer means that we trust in Jesus Christ who grants us faith, and it is this faith which emboldens us.

Consequently we must never be unsteady or in doubt. We should be wholly resolved and convinced that God reckons us as his children. And how can that be if we do not by faith embrace his mercy, as it is offered to us in the gospel, and as we know we are reliant on his eternal election? If we relied for faith upon ourselves, it would soon slip away and take flight if it were not protected from on high. And although, as Peter says, we are guarded through faith (1 Pet. 1:5), it is God himself who guards us. If our faith were not based on God's eternal election, Satan would certainly snatch it away from one moment to the next. Today we might be steadfast, but tomorrow we could fail! Our Lord Jesus Christ, however, teaches us the remedy which fortifies us against every trial, when he says, 'You came to me only because the heavenly Father brought you. But since I have taken you into my care, have no more fear, for I know that you are the inheritance of God my Father, and he who entrusted you to me and put your souls into my hand, is stronger than all' (cf. Luke 12:32; John 6:44, 10:29). So as well as God's glory, there is the certainty of our salvation, which should encourage us to heed what Paul says here concerning God's election.

Chapter 9 ('Against the vain confidence of the heretics') concludes thus: 'Each one, when he considers himself and his own weakness and indisposition, may have fear and apprehension concerning his own grace, since no one can know with the certainty of faith … that he has obtained the grace of God.'

Now as I said before, there are many people who are up in arms as soon as they hear that God has chosen whomever he willed, and has rejected all the rest. We see that only the smallest portion comes to God.[4] Why has he forsaken all the rest? As if God's will were not a sufficient rule and guide for us!

Observe, in the first place, that God is under no obligation to anyone. If we worked on the principle that he was in the smallest way indebted to us, we might have some reason to quarrel with him. Since, however, he is not duty-bound toward us, since we owe him everything and since he owes us nothing, what is the point of our objections? If we wanted to force God to treat everyone equally, he would be less free than his own mortal creatures! If a man is rich, he can do whatever he likes with his wealth. If he gives to one person, can another pursue him at law for doing so, and can all and sundry demand a similar sum? Or supposing a man wanted to promote someone he liked, if every wretch demanded he do the same for them, as if it were his due, would that not be absurd? Again, someone might adopt as his child and heir the weirdest person in the world: that would be within his gift. Here, then, is God, who is generous to all and who causes his sun to rise on good and bad alike (Matt. 5:45). He sets aside one part of humanity, giving them the privilege of being his children by adoption. What would we gain by grumbling at him?

To those who say that God appears to be a respecter of persons (Col. 3:25), we would answer 'No', since he does not choose the rich in order to forsake the poor; he does not choose the noble in preference to those who are lowly and of little repute (1 Cor. 1:26-28). We cannot say that God has favourites. In choosing the unworthy God's only concern is his pure goodness. He does not consider whether one is better than another; he takes those

---

[4] A practical observation ('we see'), not a dogmatic statement ('we know'). See above, p. 74, note 1.

he pleases. What more, then, do we want? We are right to be satisfied with God's will, and to keep ourselves in check; it is right for God to choose those he wills, for his will is the supreme rule of all equity and righteousness. In this way the mouths of all will be stopped (Rom. 3:19). And although the wicked and the worldly may complain, fume or even blaspheme, God is mighty enough to defend his boundless justice and wisdom. When they have clamoured long enough, they will finally be put to shame.

We, for our part, can see what Paul is saying here. There is nothing obscure in what he teaches. 'God has blessed us,' he says—blessed us indeed by enlightening us by his Holy Spirit in the faith of the gospel, and by allowing us to share in the gifts of our Lord Jesus Christ. If we would extol God's grace, it is to this source that we must come—to the very first cause: election.

Proceeding further, we are told that God chose us *before the creation of the world*. Paul's aim here is to exclude more clearly still any consideration of worth which men might claim. We always tend to attribute something or other to ourselves; we cannot bear to be reduced to nothing! Since, then, we fancy we have what we do not have, it was necessary for Paul to overturn all such foolish opinions. He thus points out that we could do nothing to attract attention because we were not yet born. God chose us before the world was made. What could we possibly bring to him?

It is true that on this point the papists attempt a clever argument. They affirm that God chose for salvation the undeserving, but that he chose those who, he foresaw, would have merit! So while they concede that merits do not precede election in time or sequence, they say that God knew those who would be worthy, since everything is open and plain to him. Nevertheless the papists confess that God elected and predestined those he willed before the creation of the world—which shows just how much worse, how much more appalling is the godlessness of those today who will not hear a word about election. They are devils in the flesh!

In affirming the doctrine of election, the papists go even further—at least those among them do who walk a straighter path, even, I say, the monks and charlatans who are called Scholastic teachers![5] They hold that God's election is free, and that he chose no one whom he was not pleased to choose. Straight away, however, they muddle and confuse everything, asserting that when God chose those he willed, it was in order to make them worthy. It is on this that they base their merits, so much so that they conclude that men can attain the kingdom of heaven in their own strength. They indeed maintain that election is a free gift, but they always go back to their idea that God foresaw those who would do good.

Now how could he have foreseen that which cannot be? The whole of Adam's race, as we know, is corrupt; we cannot have one good notion of doing good; we are even less able to initiate it. If God were to wait a hundred thousand years for us, and supposing we were to live that long, there is no way that we could come to him. All we would do is add to our evil and condemnation. In short, the longer we live in the world, the deeper we sink into condemnation.

Thus God cannot foresee what is not in us until such time as he puts it there. How, then, do we come to God? How do we give him our obedience? How do we have a heart which is at peace, and which yields to him in faith? It all comes from him: he must do everything. Remember, therefore, that when Paul says that God chose us before the world was made, he assumes

---

[5] In general, Calvin has little good to say about the Scholastic theologians of the Middle Ages, whom he reproaches for their neglect or misuse of Scripture and their speculative excesses. He does, however, recognize among the earlier Scholastics 'more wholesome' expositors such as Peter Lombard and Thomas Aquinas (cf. *Inst.* II.2.6). On Aquinas' understanding of election and merits, see his *Summa theologiae*, Ia 23.5.

what is actually true, that God saw in us nothing but the evil that is there. As to goodness, not a drop could be found!

The fact that God chose us is another and very obvious evidence of his goodness toward us. Accordingly, in the ninth chapter of Romans, Paul speaks of Jacob and Esau (Rom. 9:11, 12). They were twins. While still in their mother's womb and before they had done either good or bad, Scripture says that the greater would serve the lesser (Gen. 25:23). This was to show that everything came from him who called; it was not of works. So Paul discusses in detail what I have only touched upon, namely that in choosing us before the world was made, God amply demonstrates that no one is superior or more deserving than another, and that questions of worth are of no concern to him. All praise, then, must be ascribed to God, and nothing set aside for man.

The apostle affirms the point even more strongly when he declares that *all this was in Jesus Christ.* If we had been chosen in ourselves, we might have said that God had found some secret virtue in us of which men knew nothing. Since, however, we are chosen outside of ourselves, since, that is, God loves us outside of ourselves, what can we say in reply? If I do good to someone, it is because I love him. If we seek the reason for this love, it is because I resemble him in conduct or because of some other consideration. But we cannot think the same of God, which is why it is expressly said that we have been chosen in Jesus Christ.

So when God chose to love us, did he look us up and down? Not at all! We would have been hateful to him. Of course, in seeing our wretchedness he had pity and compassion on us, and therefore helped us. That, however, was because he already loved us in Jesus Christ. Before God chooses and calls us, he has a model and mirror in which he beholds us—our Lord Jesus Christ.

Paul, having said that we have brought nothing to God, but that he, in his unmerited goodness, has forestalled us, now adds as a more certain reason that we have been chosen in Jesus Christ, who is in a sense an authentic register. For when God was pleased to elect us from all eternity, he wrote down our names, as it were. That is why Scripture calls God's election 'the book of life' (Phil. 4:3; Rev. 3:5, 13:8, 21:27). Thus Jesus Christ serves as a register: it is in him that we are inscribed, and in him that God acknowledges us to be his children. It follows, then, that because God beholds us in the person of Jesus Christ, he finds nothing in us which we can claim to be the cause of our election. That is a point we should ponder.

The verse concludes with these words: *to the end that we might be pure and blameless before him, in love.* The word 'love' may refer to God, meaning that God had no other reason to set us apart as his children than his unmerited love. It is more likely, however, that Paul is thinking here of what constitutes the righteousness and true perfection of the faithful—the fact that they walk uprightly before God.

We cannot expound the whole verse now, but it will be enough if we briefly outline Paul's purpose here. He argues that although God's election is free, and although it strikes down and destroys all human worth—all our works and virtues—it is not meant to leave us free to do evil, to lead a shameful life and to throw caution to the winds. It is meant instead to rescue us from the evil in which we were immersed. By nature we can do nothing else than provoke God's wrath: iniquity will always have dominion over us, and Satan holds us captive in his bonds and tyranny. God must therefore work to change us, for as Paul says, all goodness comes from his election. It is to this point that he seeks to bring believers back, so that, as God chose them of his free goodness, they should know that he does not give them leave to indulge in evil of any kind. He wants to keep and preserve them undefiled for himself, for his election is bound up with, and inseparable from, his call to holiness. As Paul says in another place, 'We are not called to uncleanness and corruption, but to godliness and holiness' (1 Thess. 4:7). More cannot be said for now, but let us resolve to make the most of what we have been taught.

At present we must prepare ourselves to receive the Supper of our Lord Jesus Christ, which is a token both of our election and our hope of salvation, and of all the spiritual blessings which flow from the source of God's free love.[6] Let us be clear that in it God displays his riches toward us. We must not misuse them. God desires that he be glorified by us, not only with our lips but with our whole lives. And since all that we have comes from him, let us learn to be his people and to give him our obedience, so that he may peaceably enjoy us. May that be our constant goal. If, then, we would have sure proof that he counts and reckons us as his children, let us display his signs. When we call upon him as Father, let us show in actual fact that we are truly ruled by his Holy Spirit. Until we consider the remainder of this passage, reflect on what has been said.

Now let us cast ourselves down before the majesty of our good God, acknowledging our faults, and praying that we may truly feel them, to the end that we may grow in godliness and be firmer in the faith. And may he continually uphold us in our weaknesses, so that we continue to enjoy his grace, until we are brought to full possession of it, when he will blot out our sins and sweep them all away, for the sake of Jesus Christ our Lord.

---

[6] The Lord's Supper was celebrated four times yearly in Geneva: at Easter, Pentecost, on the first Sunday of September and on the Sunday nearest Christmas day. This sermon, which can be dated 22 May 1558, was preached at Pentecost.

2

LOVED IN THE BELOVED

God chose us in Christ before the foundation of the world, that we should be holy and blameless before him, in love. [5] He predestined us to be adopted as his own through Jesus Christ, according to his good pleasure, [6] to the praise of his glory and grace by which we are acceptable to him in his Beloved. (Ephesians 1:4-6)

WE began this morning to explain that it would be wrong, on the pretext that God chose us before the world was made, to give free rein to dissolute behaviour as if evil did not matter, since we cannot perish, for God preserves us as his own. We ought not to separate what God has united and joined together. Since, therefore, he has chosen us to be holy and to walk in purity of life, election must serve as a kind of root which produces good fruit. As long as God leaves us as we are by nature, we can only commit evil, because there is so much wilfulness and corruption in us that whatever we think and whatever we do is contrary to God's righteousness. The only remedy is for God to change us.

What, then, is the source of this change, if not the grace of which we spoke—the grace, that is, by which God elected and chose us to be his children, before we were born into the world? We should be aware, however, that God may well let his elect go their own way for a time, so that they seem to be lost and far away; but when he wills, he brings them back into his flock. His purpose is to humble them still more, so that his goodness and mercy may be better known to everyone. If he caused all of his elect to lead upright lives from their earliest childhood, we would not be able to judge so readily that it was all the gracious work of his Holy Spirit. When, on the other hand, we see poor wretches who were dissolute and prone to evil completely changed, it is only because God has been active and at work.

This is why he holds off calling these he has elected—holds off, I say, from cutting them to the quick by his Holy Spirit, that they may walk in obedience to him. For when we see that suddenly, against all our expectation and belief, they are reformed, then we know God's powers have been displayed in them. Experience moreover convinces us that we owe God whatever goodness we possess, for when some natural failing in us is corrected, we are led to think that God has been merciful to us. We thus have cause to humble ourselves all the more, since, until God rescued us, we were on the path to perdition.

We should be careful to note this, because there are madmen who think that God so guides his elect by his Holy Spirit that they are sanctified as soon as they are born into the world or emerge from their mother's womb. The opposite is true, which is why Paul, speaking about believers in another place, says to them: 'Among you some were steeped in greed and others given to cruelty; some were deceivers and others profligate and disso-lute; some were gluttons and others drunkards' (cf. Rom. 1:29). 'You were full of defilement,' he says, 'but God changed you, and having cleansed you of filth and pollution he consecrated you to himself.' He declares that the Romans should be ashamed of the life they led before God drew them to him.

Accordingly, although we are told in this verse that God chose those who are his for a life of holiness, he was not obliged to rule them by his Holy Spirit from childhood on. As I said, experience tells us that he allows them to go astray until the time is right for him to call them. At any rate we must remember that, in choosing us, God meant to call us to holiness of life. If he had left us as he did the poor reprobate, we would have only been capable of evil, on account of the corruption within us. Goodness thus comes from God's free mercy, which he showed us even before we were born and before the world was made. That is the lesson for us here.

This, then, is an end to the blasphemies of those who seek to veil God's praise by proposing some kind of tension or divorce between God's free election and the impulse to lead a good life. 'Is that so?' they cry. 'If God has chosen us, we are all free to do as we like, for we cannot perish. And why does it matter whether we worry about good and evil, since our salvation is founded on God's pure grace and not on any virtue of our own?' There is an easy answer to that. If there were no such thing as God's election, every single thought of ours, and every single desire, would be a rebellion against all righteousness, for we are all inclined to evil—and not only inclined, we seethe with it, we rush to it with wild abandon, since the devil possesses all who have not been remade by God's Spirit. We thus conclude that if we are determined to do good, it is because God guides us to it by his Holy Spirit, all because of his election.

Let me repeat: we must not separate what God has joined together. We have been chosen, not to allow ourselves complete freedom, but to demonstrate that we are indeed God's children by adoption, and that he has taken us into his care in order to live in us by his Holy Spirit and to unite us to himself in perfect righteousness.

It is nevertheless important to note that, although God has remade us and put us on the right path, and although we feel him already at work in us, making us submissive to his word and obedient in his service, we are not fully remade from the very first, nor will we be as long as we live. Paul does not say that God brings his elect, his faithful people, to the goal of perfection; he says that he draws them toward it. We are, all the while and until death, on the way. While we live, then, in this world, let us learn to profit and to make continual progress, knowing that there is still much in us deserving criticism. Those who imagine perfection of some sort are bewitched by pride and hypocrisy, or else they have no sense or fear of God in them, being only scoffers.

Now anyone who examines himself will discover so many faults that he will be dismayed once he truly knows himself. Those who argue that we can attain a measure of perfection while still in this mortal body, amply demonstrate a hellish pride which completely blinds them, or else they are worldly people devoid of religion and piety. As I have said, God has chosen us so that we may be blameless. Not that we can be blameless before we are stripped of all our infirmities and have come out of this prison of sin in which we are now confined. So when we are conscious of our failings, let us fight boldly against them and not lose heart, as if we were not God's children, for we are not yet blameless before him; rather, we see all too well the sins which make us guilty. Let us nevertheless press on, knowing that as long as we live in this world below we have a path to tread. We must move forward, for we have not yet reached our goal.

This is how believers, though not at all perfect, should rouse themselves and take fresh strength. Yet at the same time we have cause to groan and sigh, being conscious of our burden. The only perfection open to God's children and to the faithful is to know how weak they still are, so that they are led to pray not only that God may correct their faults, but that he may sustain them in his boundless goodness, and may not hold them to account with utmost rigour. We must therefore seek refuge in God's mercy, by which he covers and buries all our sins, for we have not yet attained the goal to which he calls us—the goal of a holy and blameless life. Whatever the case, let us keep walking on, being careful not to depart from the proper path.

'Blameless before him,' writes Paul, '*in love.*' If the word 'love' refers to men, it is meant to describe what for the Christian constitutes a righteous life. It means that we walk faithfully and uprightly, for we know that hypocrites are always trying to placate God with their pomp and ceremony, as we say. Now some of them are given to theft, or are full of envy, ill-will, cruelty and treachery; others are drunkards, lechers and profligates who give free rein to all manner of villainy. Yet they fancy that when they have gone through a few devotions, their rituals give them an appearance of holiness. Paul, however, disposes of that idea by telling us that if we want God to commend the life we lead, we must walk in love, for love is the bond of perfection and the fulfilment of the law (Gal. 5:14; Col. 3:14). Such is the message of this verse.

Paul urges us moreover to pay homage to God for all the virtue and goodness which are in us. If, then, we have some worthy motivation, if we fight against our sins and if we walk in obedience to God—where does it all come from? From the source which the apostle sets before us: God's election. Let us not rob God of his due. We may lead an angelic life, but if we foolishly believe that it comes from our own free will and from our own resolve, we miss the principal thing. What is the point of all our good works, if not to glorify God? If we think that they are all our doing, they become faults instead because we are defiled. It is a question purely of self-interest. Such is Paul's meaning here. He brings us back to God's unmerited election, on which all goodness depends.

That said, Paul now adds: *We have been predestined to be adopted by him, through Jesus Christ, according to the good pleasure of his will.* The words 'predestined to be adopted' reveal that if we are

God's children, it is not by nature but by grace. As I mentioned this morning, grace does not mean that he foresaw anything in us; it means that he marked us out and reserved us for adoption beforehand. We must look for no other cause than that which is in him. Paul declares that God did it in himself, according to the good pleasure of his will. He also repeats the point we saw this morning, that it was all in Jesus Christ.

We must understand the verse this way. We are made children of God only because he chose us for himself. As we read in the first chapter of John, our worth comes not from birth or inheritance, not from flesh or blood (John 1:13). Anything we might look for in ourselves is ruled out and excluded. We have nothing in common with God as long as we are left in our earlier condition; we are wholly cut off from his kingdom. Admittedly, our father Adam was created in God's image and he was pre-eminent when first created, but ever since sin came in we are totally destroyed. And even Adam, as we know, had no stability in himself, and the free will which had been given to him served only to strip him of every excuse. He fell voluntarily and through his own wickedness. As a result, we are now all born children of wrath, cursed by God. If we remain in our first and native condition, only everlasting death is ours. Hence God must call us to himself. Can we attain such worth ourselves? Where is the silver or gold with which we might purchase it? Where are the virtues with which we might repay God for so great and magnificent a privilege?

In short, as John says, this comes not from flesh or blood; it comes, that is, from nothing that might be found in this world. There is nothing except God's adoption—Paul's word means instating as a child—as when a man, in adopting a child, makes him his heir, and it is in that capacity that he enjoys whatever wealth will later come to him. In the same way we are heirs of the heavenly life, for God has chosen and adopted us as his children.

The apostle is not content, however, to end God's praises there. He adds that he has predestined us, that this was an appointment made beforehand. Thus Paul piles one upon another all the things which overturn our vain hopes of bringing anything to God, of moving toward him or of winning his acceptance. All such things must be reduced to nothing, so that only God's grace is made known. That too is why Paul repeats the phrase, 'through Jesus Christ', for if we ask how and why God has predestined us to be his children, it is because he deigned to look on us in Christ. He, as we have said, is in a sense the register in which we are inscribed, that we might be made heirs of life and of salvation. While it is true that God takes pity on our wretchedness, we are accursed in his sight unless Jesus Christ anticipates our need, since all who have come from Adam are exactly equal and alike.

Now some are reprobate. Why? Because God sees them as they are and has no regard for them. He chooses us, however, in our Lord Jesus Christ, and sees us in him as in a mirror which is pleasing to him. That is why there is this difference. To better explain this idea, Paul says that 'this was in himself'. This is not how it is with God's ordinary works, for in choosing us he is motivated solely by his will. But by saying that God elected us in himself, Paul sets every other consideration aside. Thus when he shuts up in God's counsel all that concerns our salvation, Paul clearly shows that we are greatly deceived if we presume on our own worth or claim that we are ready to receive God's grace. We must be caught up to high heaven if we would know the basis of our salvation, its source, its beginning, its supreme and only cause.

Paul concludes by saying 'according to the good pleasure of his will'. Had he merely written the word 'will', that would have been enough, as we saw last Sunday when Paul states that he was chosen 'by the will of God' (Eph. 1:1).[1] There, in all humility, he does not claim that he acquired his apostleship by himself; he acknowledges that it was a free gift of God. That is the significance of the word 'will', as is found not in one verse only but throughout holy Scripture. When God's will, then, is set before us, it is to teach us that we can bring nothing of our own.

The phrase the apostle uses is rather overloaded: 'the good pleasure of God's will'. What he really means is that, since God's will is the cause of our salvation, we must not flit aimlessly about looking for means and reasons. But because we are so evil and ungrateful, always wanting to veil God's goodness, puffed up with foolish pride and claiming more for ourselves than we should—let us understand that it is by the good pleasure of his will, by his free will, independent of anything else and with never a glance this way or that, that he has freely chosen us, since such was his good pleasure.

It is now obvious that those who set out to find the reason for God's election do their very best to overturn his eternal counsel, for one cannot be separated from the other. If some think it strange that the reason for God's choice is his good pleasure, it is because they want to make God their little friend. This shows how devilishly bold they are. They will not allow God to be supremely free, so that, without a shadow of dissent, what pleases him should be considered good, right and just. These people may bark like dogs as long as they like. By the mouth of Paul the Holy Spirit has uttered an irrevocable decree, that we are not to look further for the cause of our election than God's good pleasure, his unmerited goodwill, by which he chose us, unworthy as we were. God's only consideration was to say, 'This is what pleases me.' This is what we need to remember about Paul's words.

[1] A reference to the first sermon in the series, delivered on the afternoon of Sunday, 15 May 1558.

Our text goes on to say, *to the praise of his glory and grace.* Here we learn the ultimate reason why God chose us: it was so that his grace might be praised, not in any ordinary or commonplace way, but gloriously. Since Paul combines glory and grace, we ought to thrill that God has plucked us from the depths of hell and has opened the door of his kingdom, calling us to the inheritance of salvation. Again we see the point we made this morning, which was that all who want to do away with God's predestination, or who get angry when it is mentioned, are deadly enemies of God's praise. They think that it should fade away and vanish. Yes, but who here is the responsible judge? Do they fancy they are wiser than God, who says the very opposite to what they maintain? They say that we are opening the mouths of many and making them blaspheme. Yet the wicked will undoubtedly always find ways to blaspheme, and no one can prevent them! God, for his part, has plenty of ways by which to justify himself, and all who seek to challenge him and his justice will be put to shame.

Be that as it may, God's praise is rightly said to be properly acknowledged when we know that he has freely elected those whom he willed, that this is the sole reason why some are distinguished from others, that the reprobate deservedly perish and that those who are called to salvation must seek the cause solely in his unmerited election.

With these two words, then, Paul urges us to be more ready and more ardent in our praise of God. It is not enough for us to confess, coldly, that our salvation comes from his sheer generosity. We must be inflamed as it were to give ourselves to his praise, as if it is to this that we are wholly devoted. Peter likewise exhorts us, since we have been rescued from the darkness of death, to tell forth the unutterable praises of God (1 Pet. 1:8). So when believers have tried their hardest to give God his due by praising his goodness, they will inevitably fall short, for it is beyond comprehension.

Now supposing all remembrance of God's election were lost, would he continue to be praised? No—at least, only in part. If all we said was that God causes his sun to shine upon us (Matt. 5:45), that would be cause to extol him. And when we open our eyes to behold, high and low, the marvellous works he displays, there we have ample cause to give ourselves to praise for as long as we live. When, in addition, his gospel is preached to us, we have further cause to praise him, even without a word being said about election. That would be enough from our point of view, but we would be denying him the chief part of his praise, and we would be giving him only part of what we owed him. Why? Because believers would think that they had faith of their own volition, whereas, as we said this morning, faith is a fruit of election. We are distinguished from the faithless only because God stretched out his hand to us and drew us secretly, even while we turned our backs on him and were estranged from him.

In essence, Paul is telling us that God will never be glorified as he deserves until we realize that his election is the reason for all the blessings he showers upon us. If he had not adopted us in his boundless mercy and according to his eternal counsel, we ourselves would have part of the praise which is owed to him. This would have demeaned and diminished him accordingly. We must disappear entirely if God is to have his rights: no one can share them with him. Let us confess that he is the beginning and completion of our salvation.

Consider now Paul's final words: *that by his grace we should be acceptable to him in his Beloved.* Here we have an even better explanation of why our salvation is grounded in God's free election and in his unmerited kindness. Men will never abandon their foolish arrogance unless they are so fully persuaded that they can no longer answer back. Paul tries to make us see this by showing that in ourselves we stand condemned before God. When a thunderbolt like that falls on our heads, we are in no position to protest! If men are therefore mad enough to run round in circles looking for something of their own, but which only God's grace can supply, this one word can make them change course: we are not acceptable to God until we are in Jesus Christ, for in ourselves we are totally condemned and cursed.

This truth would have been perfectly clear already except that we are so slow to grasp a thing that is so necessary to us and so self-evident. We ought, indeed, to have learned it from experience. If we were not so blinded by hypocrisy, we would know by intuition that we are evil through and through. The wrath of God would strike fear in us and we would feel ashamed. God, however, is obliged to make us submit by force, otherwise we cannot ascribe to him all praise. That, then, is what it means to be acceptable to God in Jesus Christ.

But why is Jesus Christ called God's Beloved, as we read in the seventeenth chapter of Matthew, in other places, and as he is described by the prophet Isaiah? (Isa. 42:1; Matt. 17:5; Mark 1:11; Luke 3:22; 2 Pet. 1:17). What this shows is that God rightly hates us and regards us with abhorrence as long as we remain in our natural condition. If the title 'beloved Son' truly applies to Jesus Christ, it cannot be shared with any created being. However much God loves his angels, he can only love them perfectly through Jesus Christ. He is the Mediator who makes peace between the angels and God, for they have no consistency or stability unless they are upheld by him.[2] Nor is their righteousness complete, unless they are blessed and elect in him. That is one thing to note.

We, for our part, are alienated from God by sin; we can only be his enemies, and he can only be the hostile party. Jesus Christ is thus the only one on man's side who is beloved. As for us,

---

[2] A marginal note refers to Col. 1:20: 'through him to reconcile to himself all things, whether on earth or in heaven'. On Christ and the angels, see Calvin's comments in the following sermon, and in *Inst.* I.14.10.

God rejects and disowns us, even to the point of repenting that he made man (Gen. 6:6). We ourselves are not worthy to be counted even as donkeys, dogs or other wild beasts, for while they remain God's creatures just as he made them, we are so foul and perverse that we should be wiped out; our memory should be accursed and hateful in God's sight. So are we now to give glory to ourselves? Will we be looking for coats of arms in order to achieve nobility? Well, we see how the Holy Spirit shames those who think that they amount to something! If we are God's enemies, we are worse off than if we had never been created.

As it is, God accepts us in his Beloved. And since our Lord Jesus is received in love by God his Father, not only for his own sake but because that love extends to every member of his body, we, who before were hostile and totally abhorrent to him, are gathered in and embraced by God as his children. We must in any case keep coming back to God's election of which we have spoken, for the gifts imparted to us by our Lord Jesus Christ come from that very source. Thus we are taught how great is our need to be loved in Jesus Christ. Here we repeat a point already made, for unless we were fully convinced, we could never admit—sincerely, I mean—that we owe everything to God. Our inclination is always to claim some sort of worth: all of us think of ways to keep something for ourselves, even if it is no more than a pin-head! Paul, on the contrary, shows that God must love us outside of ourselves, and that if he considers us acceptable, it has nothing to do with anything in us, for we are slaves to sin, under Satan's yoke and tyranny and trapped in bondage to death, until we are redeemed by our Lord Jesus Christ.

Here we have the sum total of Paul's teaching. We are told to come out of ourselves and to seek our salvation in God's pure goodness, through the means set before us here—by turning to our Lord Jesus Christ. For there are two equally bad extremes of which we must beware. First, we must not think that we come to Jesus Christ because we deserve to share in his blessings. How can this fault be corrected? By being brought to God's unmerited election. People presume too much on their free will, on which they base their belief in their personal merits and worth. They must recognize that they are nothing unless God, having chosen them in his eternal counsel, accepts them in his sheer goodness. We cannot attribute the origin of our salvation to God unless we confess that we were condemned and accursed when he adopted us, and that he began his adoption because he had already predestined us before the creation of the world. That is the first point.

The second extreme, equally bad, is to speculate, as many madmen do, who say, 'Oh, I will never discover for myself whether God has chosen me. I must therefore remain in a state of perdition.' Ah yes, but that is because you have failed to come to Jesus Christ. How do we know that God chose us before the world was made? By believing in Jesus Christ! As we said, faith comes from election; it is its fruit, which shows that the root is concealed within. Whoever believes thus has the assurance that God has been at work in him. Faith is, so to speak, the copy that God gives us of the original of our adoption. God has his eternal counsel; he always keeps the original for himself—the principal register, we might say, a copy of which he gives us through faith.

Here of course I speak in human fashion, for we know that God has neither paper nor parchment on which to write to us. And we have already said that the register in which we are inscribed is, strictly speaking, our Lord Jesus Christ. God, at any rate, reserves to himself the knowledge of our election, just as a ruler might retain the first and original register. However, he gives us certified copies when by his Holy Spirit he engraves on our hearts the fact that we are his children. So it is our faith in Jesus Christ which gives us assurance of our election. What more, then, do we ask? Jesus Christ is, as we said, the mirror in which God beholds us when he chooses to make us acceptable to him. For us, too, he is the mirror into which we should look if we would attain knowledge of our election. Whoever believes in Jesus Christ is a child of God and therefore an heir (John 1:12; 1 John 5:1). It follows, then, that if we have faith, we have also been adopted. The reason God gives us faith is because he chose us before the creation of the world.[3]

Here, then, is the infallible sequence. Believers, because they receive grace and accept God's mercy, and because they hold to Jesus Christ as to their Head in order to obtain salvation through him, know that God has adopted them. It is true that election in itself is a secret, part of God's deep and hidden counsel which we must worship. Nevertheless he reveals it to us as is necessary for us and is useful for our salvation. This he does when he illumines us by faith in the gospel. That is why Paul first speaks of God's eternal election, then sets Jesus Christ before us as the one to whom we must turn, in order to be sure that God loves us and has adopted us as his children. He adopted us indeed before we knew him, before the foundation of the world.

For the rest, this passage reminds us that the doctrine of predestination is not meant to send us off into wild speculations, but to crush all our pride and our enduring belief in our worth and merits. It is meant to demonstrate that God's freedom and privilege are such, and his dominion so supreme, that he can reject those he wills and elect those he pleases. In this way we are led to glorify him, conscious that it is in Jesus Christ that he has chosen us and preserves us in the faith of the gospel.

If we are members of him, and if we hold to him as to our Head, since he has joined himself to us in a sacred union

---

[3] Faith, when informed by the gospel and when sealed within us by the Holy Spirit, is both the fruit of election and an authentic witness to its reality. The call which God issues, in time, to each of his elect, is answered by the confession, 'I believe in Jesus Christ.' Cf. Calvin's commentary on John 6:40: 'For each of us our faith is sufficient witness to God's eternal predestination' (CO 47:147).

which cannot be broken, we must come to him for assurance of salvation. Through experience we both know and feel that God, having adopted and elected us, now calls us. He shows us that the witness he has given us, and which he daily gives us in the gospel, is not given in vain, especially when he engraves it upon us by his Holy Spirit. The gospel is preached to all, even to the reprobate, but they are not given the particular grace which touches them to the quick. When God's adoption, therefore, is engraved on our hearts, it is a sound and certain pledge that God will guide us to the end. And since he has set us on the path of salvation, he will bring us to the perfection to which he calls us, for without him we could not persist for a single day.

> *Now let us cast ourselves down before the majesty of our good God, acknowledging our faults and begging him to make us feel them more and more. May we be ashamed of them so that, hating both our sins and our evil and perverse life, we may turn to him who alone can cure us. And as we have communion with him through our Lord Jesus Christ, let us not stray to one side or another, but let us go direct to him. And since we have been chosen in Christ, may we know that it is for his sake that we are upheld and preserved. May God more and more display his powers in us, until we have finished our race and attained the eternal inheritance which is our goal. Since it is still far off, may God give us invincible strength always to persevere, until, fully renouncing the world and ourselves, we are so renewed in the image of God that it may perfectly shine forth in us, until we come to that glorious immortality which has been so dearly won for us.*

3

CHRIST OUR SURETY

Through his blood we have redemption, the forgiveness of sins according to the riches of his grace, ⁸ which he abundantly poured out on us in all wisdom and prudence, ⁹ having granted us to know the mystery of his will, according to his good pleasure which he purposed in himself, ¹⁰ that he might dispense it when the time was fulfilled, gathering together all things in Christ, both those that are in heaven and those that are on earth, even in him. (Ephesians 1: 7-10)

PREVIOUSLY we pointed out that we cannot be loved by God except through Jesus Christ, his only-begotten Son. For if the angels in heaven are not worthy to be reckoned by God as his children, except through the one who is their Head and Mediator, what shall we say of each of us who by our transgressions constantly provoke God's wrath, since we war against him? God must therefore look on us in the person of his only Son, otherwise he must hate and abhor us. Our sins, in a word, set such a distance between God and us that we cannot approach him without immediately feeling that his majesty is entirely against us, and is armed to crush us totally, as it were.

It remains for us now to see how God in his grace receives us through the work of our Lord Jesus Christ. Accordingly, Paul writes that *we have redemption in him through his blood, even the forgiveness of sins according to the riches of God's grace.* In the first place we learn that God's hostility to us comes not from his nature, but from the fact that we are corrupt. I speak of God's nature, for insofar as we are his creation it is clear that he cannot hate us. However, because we have become corrupt and because we give ourselves to every kind of evil, God must inevitably be, in a sense, our mortal enemy, our opponent, until the remembrance of our sins is blotted out before him. Until we are restored, we are guilty of everlasting death, for God, who is the source of all righteousness and integrity, detests the evil which he sees in us. Until our sins are wiped away, we cannot possibly hope that he will show us love or favour.

Notice the two words which Paul uses here in order to explain how we are reconciled to God. He speaks of 'ransom' or 'redemption'—words which have the same meaning. Then too he speaks of 'the forgiveness of sins'. How then does God's anger come to be appeased, so that we are reconciled to him and are even counted by him as his children? It comes about, says Paul, when our sins are forgiven us. However, because redemption is needed for this to happen, Paul includes it also.

It is true, so far as we are concerned, that in blotting out our sins God has recourse to his unmerited goodness. He looks for no payment, and is nothing if not generous. Where, indeed, is the man capable of making satisfaction for the very least offence he has committed? Supposing each of us as long as we lived strove to make amends for a single transgression, and thus to gain favour in God's sight, that would most certainly be a task entirely beyond our abilities. That is why God must receive us in mercy, without seeking any recompense or satisfaction from us.

Nevertheless the reconciliation which was completely free to us was most costly to God's Son. No other price was to be found except the blood which he shed. He went surety for us both in body and soul, answering for us before the judgment seat of God in order to obtain our absolution (1 Pet. 1:18, 19). Our Lord, I say, was exercised both in body and soul, for it was not enough that, in the sight of men, he should suffer so cruel and disgraceful a death. He also had to bear in himself the most terrible distress, as if God were his judge. He went so far as to make himself one with our sinful selves in order to render full satisfaction (2 Cor. 5:21). That is why Paul brings these two words together in this verse.

To begin with, then, we notice that we cannot find favour with God nor be received by him until our sins are swept away and until the memory of them is completely effaced. As long as God sees us as sinners, we can only be abhorrent to him: in us and in our nature there is only evil and shame. We are his enemies and he is our adversary, until we come to the remedy set forth here by Paul—the forgiveness of sins. What this shows is that no one can be loved by God by reason of his worthiness, for what explains God's love for us? As we have said, God must look toward our Lord Jesus Christ and take no account of us. This is made especially clear, however, when we see that, in forgiving us our sins and in adopting us, God makes us acceptable to him even though in his sight we are guilty of death. This, then, is the knowledge of salvation which is described for us in Zechariah's song (Luke 1:77). God has had mercy on us and forgives our offences, on account of which we were his enemies.

Reflect also on the fact that although we have forgiveness for our sins through God's unmerited kindness, this is only because of the ransom paid by our Lord Jesus Christ—paid not in silver or gold, as Peter writes in his first letter (1 Pet. 1:18), but by the spotless lamb who had to take this role upon himself. So whenever we seek to enjoy God's favour and acceptance, let us fix our minds on the death and passion of Jesus Christ, so that we might find in them all that is needed to appease the wrath of God. Since, moreover, our sins are wiped away by the satisfaction and payment he has made, be sure that we can bring nothing of our own, thinking that we can reach an understanding with God.

Here we plainly see how the devil has, by his cunning, extinguished all hope of salvation in the world, by making us believe that each must redeem himself in order to be on good terms with God. This is what the papists call good works, merits or virtues. For what is the point of the many practices which they have devised? Why do they torment themselves in so many ways, so that no one ceases night or day but runs to and fro and in endless circles? All that they do has this as its goal—to appease God. Thus all the good works which are so prized in popery are merely ways of making satisfaction for sin.[1] Now that is to do away with the ransom of which Paul is speaking here, for there is an unbreakable bond between these two things: God's wiping our sins from his memory, his casting them as it were into the depths of the sea, and his receiving payment offered to him in the person of his only Son. We cannot obtain one without the other. So if God is to be favourable to us, we must acknowledge that we are his enemies until, by his sheer grace, he forgives us our debts.

It is important to observe that Jesus Christ made himself our intermediary. His sacrificial death has the effect of obtaining a perpetual reconciliation for us; we must always look to it for refuge. True, our Lord Jesus Christ throughout his life made himself a ransom for us, for the obedience which he rendered while on earth to God his Father was meant to make amends for Adam's offence, and for all the sins for which we are accountable. However, in this verse Paul expressly mentions the blood of Jesus Christ, for we must turn to his death and passion as to the sacrifice which has the power to blot out all iniquity. That is why God, under the law, showed by means of symbols that this is the

---

[1] See further, on the Roman Catholic doctrine of satisfaction, *Inst.* III.4.25-27, IV.18.1.

only way for men to be reconciled to him. It is true that in his death Jesus Christ not only shed his blood but felt the terrors and the dread which ought to have fallen on us; but here Paul includes everything in the one category, as is the usual way with Scripture. In short, we should learn to find all our righteousness in the compassion which God, in his pure goodness, has shown us. Nor should we presume to lay some virtue or other of our own before him, in order to put him in our debt. It should be enough for us that he receives us, who deserve nothing, solely out of love, and only because in his sight the remembrance of our sins has been effaced.

Remember that none of this comes about apart from the death and passion of our Lord Jesus Christ. It is there that we must stop. That said, the apostle now adds that *all this is according to the riches of God's grace.* Paul has every reason to extol the grace which God displays when he receives us in his mercy, for we have seen how wilfully mistaken men are in their foolish arrogance. For the most part, they continually fancy that they can reach some understanding with God through their works of satisfaction or by some other device. It is because we are so deceived by our idle fancies that Paul dismisses the lot, declaring that we should delight rather in the riches of God's grace. He might have said that God does all things according to his grace; instead, he speaks here of enormous wealth, warning us not to bring mere pennies with us when there are a million crowns to be had!

Now it happens that the papists, when they refer to their works of satisfaction, do not claim that what they do can wholly suffice. Nevertheless they believe that, along with the death and passion of Jesus Christ, they can contribute something of their own, and that the bits and pieces that they provide will make God content and will placate him. Such is the devilish belief that exists among the papists, who establish Masses, gabble their many prayers, traipse about on pilgrimages, observe one feast-day or another, practise this or that devotion, and if need be wear the hair-shirt. All this they do in order to assist the death and passion of our Lord Jesus Christ, as if these were inadequate in themselves.

Paul, on the contrary, affirms that God's goodness as revealed in Jesus Christ is a treasure so great that everything else must cease and be thrown down. And when God displays such ample generosity as should fill us with delight, is it not hugely presumptuous of us to bring to him our paltry trifles—our pilgrimages, our acts of devotion—as if they were somehow commendable and worthwhile? Is it not as if the blood of Jesus Christ were insufficient to pay the price of our salvation—the ransom price, I say? This is why the apostle endeavours on the one hand to make short shrift of all the empty ideas which we conceive, in the belief that we can appease God's wrath by offering recompense and satisfaction. On the other hand Paul seeks to assist us in our weakness. For although we tend to convince ourselves that we can achieve marvellous feats of virtue, and although we give the impression that God is in our debt, when it is a question of calling upon him in earnest and of putting our hope in him, it is then that Satan tempts us to despair. We are shaken by trials and tribulations; we are so distraught that we cannot trust any of the promises of Scripture, or anything we are told about the death and passion of Jesus Christ. Thus, to remedy our sinful unbelief which is much too firmly rooted in us, the apostle spreads before us the rich treasures of God's goodness, so that whatever confidence we might have is overwhelmed by the vision of God's great generosity toward us.

We read next that *God has caused his grace toward us to abound in all wisdom and understanding*. Here we discover how we come to take possession of the things that Paul has spoken of already. Our entire blessedness, our sovereign good, lies in the fact that we are reconciled to God, who acknowledges us as his children and whom we may lawfully and with complete freedom invoke as our Father. Yet how can we obtain something so alien to us? Although we are told that we are worthless and helpless, we are also assured that in our Lord Jesus Christ we will find everything that we lack, and that his death and passion are a sacrifice sufficient to blot out the memory of all our offences.

If, however, we ask whether all share in this blessing procured for us by Jesus Christ, we must answer 'No'. Unbelievers have no part or portion in it: it is a particular privilege for those whom God gathers to himself. Hence Paul teaches that faith is necessary, otherwise Christ is of no use to us (Gal. 5:2, 6). So while Christ is, overall, the Redeemer of the world, his death and passion are fruitful only for those who accept the things that Paul presents to us here. Accordingly we see that, having understood the blessings which Jesus Christ has brought us and which he daily offers us in his gospel, we must be united to him by faith, for the Turks, Jews, papists and all others like them are cut off from Christ and estranged from him. They perish in their defilement, since they presume to do marvels. They, and all the heathen who have ever been, make the common claim that we must appease the wrath of God. How do they do that? In the many ways that they devise, according to what each man dreams up in his own head. Such people as these have no fellowship with Jesus Christ. Therefore if faith is the key which opens up for our enjoyment the treasures which Paul has just described, that is how we will have all the riches we need in order to be saved. We will lack nothing, if indeed we are united to Christ by faith.

It is, however, not without reason that Paul uses these two words, 'wisdom' and 'understanding'. His aim is to demonstrate that, to reach maturity, it is enough if we are instructed in the gospel. Anything added to this is merely dung, filth and rottenness. By these two highly reputable words the apostle designates the gospel, so that each of us should quietly listen to what God has to teach us through his only Son. We should be so teachable that we set ourselves to know nothing except what proceeds from his mouth. In all simplicity let us receive what he tells us, and let us persevere, however much the world may deride us and however much men may rise up against us. Let us scorn the world's cleverness, for there are many as we know who have itching ears and who want something new to be offered them each day.

Lest, then, we be so fickle, and lest we foolishly desire to know more than is permissible, note what Paul says here. As long as we make progress in the gospel, we will find in it all fullness of wisdom, so that we are able to dismiss everything else not only as superfluous but as harmful, since it might turn us from the pure truth which, in keeping with Christ's will, unites us with him.

Paul's purpose, briefly stated, is to show how priceless is the gift God grants us when he is pleased to call us to the knowledge of his only Son, our Lord Jesus Christ. When we have him, all else is to be despised. We must no longer be driven by the foolish desire to know this or that, for, as I have said, to know Jesus Christ is the most perfect knowledge we can have. Hence Paul tells the Colossians that he has been a faithful teacher who has sought to lead men to fullness of wisdom (Col. 1:28). He admits that he was rough and common in his speech (2 Cor. 11:6), and that he possesses neither wisdom nor eloquence, both of which were highly prized in the world (1 Cor. 2:1). Nevertheless he asserts that when people accept his teaching, they will find in it solid food which will fully nourish their souls, and which requires nothing else by way of addition. So when this is told to us today, we are warned to keep ourselves in check, to suppress all our stupid curiosity which is much too rooted in us, and to hold to the pure message of the gospel. It is there that we must stop. That, in essence, is what we need to remember about this verse.

We might notice here a point I made before, that whenever the gospel is preached, God's grace is poured out upon us. If we recognize his goodness and rich provision when he waters the earth, how much more, when the word of salvation is brought to us, ought we to see that God not only waters us for the salvation of our souls, but fills us so as to satisfy us completely? Paul, then, is not content merely to say that, when parched, we find a measure of refreshment in the gospel. It is as if God were pouring out on us water in abundance, so that we might drink and be restored, having the sustenance and energy to press on to the end. That is how we should value God's goodness when he is pleased to draw us to him through the gospel, and when, at the same time, he puts us in possession of the blessings won for us by our Lord Jesus Christ—blessings offered to us in the gospel and which God wants us to accept by faith.

To explain his meaning more fully, the apostle goes on to say: *It is because he has made known to us the mystery of his will, according to his good pleasure which he purposed before in himself.* Now this is something which should further enhance the worth of the gospel, namely that in it we have the secrets which were earlier hidden in God. Paul speaks this way not only here: we will see it explained at greater length in chapter 3 (Eph. 3:9-11). Nor is it only in this letter: everywhere Paul declares that the preaching of the gospel ought to thrill us, since in it God reveals what previously was beyond all human understanding—things which we could never have thought or believed (Rom. 16:25; 1 Cor. 2:7, 4:1; Col. 1:26, 27). At first God seemed to have chosen only Abraham's line, on terms suggesting that he had rejected everybody else. And it was marvellous to see how his gifts were poured out on all his people. Yet at the time when Jesus Christ came into the world, we know that this people had completely fallen away, and that God's truth had been so distorted that only superstition existed among the Jews.

Everything, then, seemed hopeless when, against all expectation, salvation suddenly appears and is offered to every nation! Suddenly Christ, the Sun of righteousness (Mal. 4:2), gives light to a world which until then lay in deep darkness— darkness so profound that escape from it was something no one dared to hope for. This is why Paul says that the gospel is where we learn the mystery of God's will.

It is true that, at first glance, God's will seems quite simple. Accordingly there are many rascals who believe that what the gospel contains is only for the ignorant. They think that, by dint of dreaming, they can come up with ideas which are far cleverer than anything taught by Jesus Christ. People like that do not deserve even to taste the things revealed to us here; they are made blind and wholly senseless by their pride.[2] However that be, the faithful feel deep down that there is divine majesty in the teaching of the gospel. Consequently Paul warns us in this verse that we should not come to the gospel expecting to learn anything ordinary: we come in order to be lifted above the world. We will never be amenable to God's teaching, and we will never be ready to make progress in his school, unless, being lifted high above the world, we worship the things which God tells us with his sacred lips. In short, humility is both an entry into faith, and its beginning.

Yet how can we be humble, if we do not know that what God reveals to us is far beyond our grasp and understanding? Paul's

---

[2] A probable reference to those whom Calvin, in a lengthy treatise of 1545, calls 'Spiritual Libertines', a somewhat amorphous but well-connected movement with pronounced antinomian and mystic tendencies, whose members laid claim to special revelation. Their leaders enjoyed the protection and esteem of Marguerite of Navarre (1492–1549), sister of the French king, Francis I. Cf. Calvin's letter to Marguerite of April 1545, in John Calvin, *Tracts and Letters*, ed. Henry Beveridge and Jules Bonnet, 7 vols. (Edinburgh: Banner of Truth Trust, 2009), 4:453-58.

intention, then, is that we should revere the gospel, conscious that it is not our place to judge whether God's words are right or wrong. We must regard it as settled that all that comes from him is infinite wisdom—wisdom beyond reproach. All our boasting must be cast aside, so that, modestly and soberly, we may worship the truth proclaimed to us in God's name. Such was Paul's purpose in speaking of God's 'mystery'.

In order to demonstrate how indebted we are to God, the apostle repeats the phrase which he used before, 'according to his good pleasure'. Paul means to exclude and rule out every idea of personal worth which our minds might conceive. There is no room for God's good pleasure unless men are denied all merit and unless they come empty to him. As soon as we presume to bring something or other of our own to God, we most certainly exalt ourselves in order to veil his grace, which loses the lustre and pre-eminence it deserves. To encourage us, therefore, to abandon all vain confidence, Paul again brings us back to God's good pleasure, declaring in effect that when the gospel is proclaimed to the world, it is all about God's generous and unmerited kindness.

Nevertheless, wishing to suppress all boldness on our part, he adds that *God had earlier, by his own decree and will*—by his own high and incomprehensible counsel—*purposed this in himself.* For why do so many people go so far as to question God, to debate with him and to argue their case against him, if not because they think these things should be clear and obvious to all? That is why Paul, understanding how impetuous and over-bold we are in inquiring into God's counsels, tells is that these are sealed letters, and that God has kept his counsel to himself. It is not lawful for mere creatures to rise to such heights; if they do, they will come to grief and break their necks!

We might indeed strive hard to know God's will, and rightly so, insofar as he reveals it to us. His word gives us light. When, however, God ceases to speak, he intends to keep us on a tight rein; we are to be held captive as it were, in case we stray too far. For we will enter into a maze—the depths of hell, even!—whenever we try to know more than is allowed, more than we should, more than God conveys to us in his word.

Observe, then, what Paul means to say here. When God keeps his counsel to himself, we must hang our heads and be willingly ignorant. Wisdom is accursed, and is liable to cast us into hell, when we presume to know more than what God has taught us. Conversely, in our ignorance, we are wiser than all the sages in the world when we seek to know nothing except as God's word leads and directs us. There is in God one single will, but he reveals it to us according to our capacity, and to the extent that is necessary and useful to us. As we saw when we spoke about the forgiveness of sins, this is an article of faith which we cannot do without. That is why Zechariah calls it the knowledge of salvation (Luke 1:77). So to know where we are to look for the forgiveness of sins is a matter of necessity. Apart from Jesus Christ we are always God's enemies; we have no means of finding peace or reconciliation apart from Jesus Christ.

Now while we know the things to which God's word testifies, we are bound, at the same time, to worship those that are hidden from us, as has already been said, and as we will see when we deal again with God's election. Here Paul speaks of 'God's earlier purpose', which shows that God predestined us before the creation of the world. Yet it remained hidden. 'Yes,' says Paul, 'but now it is made known to us.' This, then, is what we have to remember: it is not due to our own efforts that we have been called to the knowledge of the gospel; none of us can push ourselves forward or make God our debtor. God, in his infinite goodness, chose to illumine us, not because he suddenly thought of it, and not as men do, in fits and starts. This was decided in God's counsel, and it was decided from eternity. Furthermore, if our minds are so restless that we are driven to ask: 'What then? Did God choose us beforehand? Why did he not reveal it sooner? Why was there no obvious sign of it?'—Paul, to stop us being so reckless, tells us that this decision was shut up, so to speak, in God, until such time as witness was borne to it.

In sum, it is not permissible to know more than what the gospel proclaims to us; and what it proclaims is to be worshipped. Accordingly, the apostle adds this comment: *God chose to effect his purpose in the fullness of time.* From this we learn that it is useless to torment ourselves, for we are bound to fail. When we attempt to know more than God allows us, our minds dissolve in a haze of thoughts. Anyone who asks why God did not hasten sooner, shows by that very fact that he claims to be wiser than God. Is that not a mark of hellish pride? Does any creature deserve to enjoy the earth's sustenance when he exalts himself thus? That is why Paul affirms that the right to decide belongs to God. For if a man in his own house can say how his folk should be cared for, having this or that to drink, this or that bread to eat, this or that bed to lie on, how much more should we not concede such rights to God? Why should he have fewer privileges than earthworms? Let us learn, then, to allow God the authority to manage his church and to effect the salvation of his elect as he wills. As to the question of time, we should regard it as fully come when he is pleased to reveal it to us. We cannot act as judges or arbiters when it comes to measuring times, years, months or days. It should suffice that this was how God wished it to be.

People will nevertheless argue: 'How is it that four thousand years have passed since the time of Adam's fall? Could not God have remedied affairs by sending the world's Redeemer sooner? Think of all the poor wretches who were lost in darkness! As a result, the human race was ruined as in a flood which swallowed everything. Yet Jesus Christ remained hidden. And even later there were only a few who tasted him in a shadowy, symbolic way, for it was the Jews alone who expected a Redeemer who would bring them salvation. And they only had calves, sheep and brute beasts to assure them that their sins were pardoned, and that God would be favourable to them.' If, therefore, we ask, 'Why should all this be?', let us turn to what this verse tells us in a word: the time was not yet fulfilled. And why was that? Because God had not ordained it.

This is something which we noticed already in Galatians (Gal. 4:4, 5), where Paul similarly presses hard against the foolish speculations into which we stray when we seek to rise higher than we should.[3] We should judge that it is God's responsibility alone to decide the times and seasons; we should think of everything he does as timely. For although winter and summer come round regularly for us each year, if summer is late, we have got to keep our feelings in check and not grumble at God. We might find ourselves saying: 'Ah, if God were pleased to send us heat, that would be something to be wished!' Even so, we must come to this conclusion: 'God is rightly in control. He must rule and have authority.'

Thus if we have to show restraint in the natural order which is common to all of us, and in which God makes himself known in so familiar a way, what shall we say of the secrets of the heavenly kingdom, of the eternal salvation of our souls, of that mystery so high—the coming of the Son of God to restore that which had perished? Should we not all hang our heads and humbly accept what God tells us? Should we not acknowledge all that he commends? Accordingly Paul refers expressly here to the fullness of time. What he means is that we can never truly benefit from the gospel until we honour God by delighting in his sole will, by accepting it without demur and without voicing

---

[3] Calvin's sermons on Galatians (Nov. 1557–May 1558) immediately preceded the sermon series on Ephesians. They were translated from the French by Kathy Childress and published by the Banner of Truth Trust in 1997.

our objections. Let us glorify God and admit that his counsel is the rule of all that is wise, right and equitable.

To give us a better understanding of these things, Paul now adds that *God's purpose was to gather together everything, both in heaven and on earth, in Jesus Christ—even in him.* Paul uses the words 'gather together' to indicate that we are in a state of dreadful disarray until our Lord Jesus Christ restores us again—and not only us, but all created things. It is as if Paul were describing the whole of nature as disfigured, ruined and wrecked by Adam's sin, until we are again united in the person of Jesus Christ. For although we behold in all of God's creatures the wisdom, power, goodness and righteousness of God, the fact is that, high and low, we see the marks of sin. All creatures are subject to corruption (Rom. 8:21); everything is spoiled, for God abhors and rejects us. Restoration must therefore be the work of Jesus Christ.

That is what Paul means by 'gather together'. We should cease to love ourselves; we should feel shame at our inner decay; our guilt fills the whole world. The Holy Spirit warns us in this verse that we are not only in a state of ruin, but that we have involved the whole world in it. And we do so each day by our sins. The only remedy is for Jesus Christ to make total restoration, by gathering us together and by making us one so that we are united with our God. That is the first thing to remember about this verse.

Now Paul makes this point in few words. That is true, but it is worth pondering at greater length. We should endeavour to do this morning and night. When we look at ourselves, we should think, 'Who are you, poor creature? You have been separated from God since birth; you are his enemy, heir to his wrath. There is nothing in you which is not inclined to evil and wilfulness. Not only do you feel such disorder within yourself, but there is disorder also in the world because of your wilfulness.' We should therefore feel distraught and ashamed. But at the same time we should confess how great is our debt to God when he is pleased to bring us together in his only Son—we who, in a sense, had torn apart what he had arranged in so beautiful an order.

Moreover Paul is not content to speak only of men who were estranged from God by sin. He refers also to 'all things in heaven and on earth'. He thus includes the angels themselves, and although in them God's glory is resplendent, and although they have never been separated from him, they too needed to be gathered together by our Lord Jesus Christ. This happened in two ways. Although they never fell away and did not depart from their origins, and although God's righteousness—of which they are mirrors and models—is always evident in them, the fact remains that if God chose strictly to examine them, they are far removed from his perfect righteousness, as we read in the book of Job (Job 4:18). There is besides a second reason related to the first: the angels could not be as sure and steadfast as they need to be, if Jesus Christ had not ordained that they would never fall away. That, then, is how, on the one hand, they have been gathered together; but the gathering together of which Paul speaks is because they have been united with us.

We know that when we were banished from God's kingdom, we were cut off from all hope of salvation. The angels were bound therefore to be our enemies, and they still would be, if it were not for the unity which we now have with them through the work of our common Head. This also is why, in Jacob's vision of the ladder (Gen. 28:12, 13), God was said to be seated above it; it touched both heaven and earth, and the angels ascended and descended on it. Now our Lord Jesus Christ is the true and everlasting God; he touched heaven and earth, for in his person God joined his divine being with a human nature. In this way heaven has been opened, so that the angels begin to have dealings with us and even to act as our servants, as is said in the letter to the Hebrews, for they are commanded to care for our souls (Heb. 1:14). Similarly it is said in Psalm 34 that they encamp round about us, watching over us and protecting us (Psa. 34:7). We are thus united with the angels in heaven by our Lord Jesus Christ. This also explains why he said that, henceforth, we would see heaven opened and the Son of Man descending in majesty with his angels (Matt. 24:30, 31; Mark 13:26, 27). With these words he teaches that heaven was closed to us, and that we did not deserve to experience any of God's favours. Whereas now, since he has revealed himself as our Head, has reconciled his Father and us and fulfils the role of Mediator, he is not only Head of the faithful but also of the angels. He gathers us all together.

Accordingly, while the devils make war upon us and constantly seek to contrive our ruin, the angels are armed with infinite power in order to sustain us. And even though we do not see them visibly, we should be absolutely certain that they watch and keep us safe. Otherwise, what would become of us? The devil, we know, is like a roaring lion who seeks only to devour us (1 Pet. 5:8). We see just how many ruses he employs to deceive us. The angels must indeed, then, have endless power if they are to keep us safe. We need also to be kept under Jesus Christ's protection: he is their Head and ours.

Such is Paul's meaning in this passage. As he says, we who were once scattered have been gathered together, and not only have we been reconciled to God by the death and passion of our Lord Jesus Christ, but we are now also united with the angels, who are our brethren and companions. God has charged them with the task of guiding us, supporting us in all our ways (Psa. 91:11), watching over us, and battling continually against all the enemies who make war on us, until we are gathered together into our heavenly rest.

Now let us cast ourselves down before the majesty of our good God,
acknowledging our faults and praying that he may so make us feel

them that we are drawn to true repentance, and continue in the same all the days of our lives. Let us not cease to hope in him and to come before his face with all boldness, since our sins have been wiped away by the blood which was shed for our cleansing. May this message so strengthen us that we may always be conscious of our need to give ourselves fully to his service. And since he has been so kind a Redeemer to us, let us not doubt that he will daily continue to show us his goodness, in order to complete the work he has begun. May he sustain us in all our conflicts, until, being delivered from the cruelty of Satan and of all his ministers, we are taken out of this world and made to share in that blessed happiness to which he calls us.

4

THE HOLY SPIRIT'S SEAL

You also hope in Christ, having heard the word of truth, that is, the gospel of your salvation, in which you believed and were sealed by the Holy Spirit of promise, [14] *who is the pledge of our inheritance, until the redemption of the purchased possession, to the praise of his glory.* (Ephesians 1:13, 14)[1]

WE saw previously that Paul shows that God's unmerited goodness is the sole basis of our salvation, and that we must seek no other reason for his choice of some and his rejection of others. We must be content with his pure will, his counsel and his unchangeable decree. Anyone who goes further is bound to stumble in his recklessness into such an abyss that he will find that those who cannot humbly and reverently worship God's majesty and his secret counsel will be put to shame. So let us learn to ascribe all our salvation to God when it comes to delving into causes.

It is true that, in order to become children and heirs of God, we must belong to the body of our Lord Jesus Christ, which comes about through faith. We cannot, however, believe in the gospel unless God draws us by his Holy Spirit. Now as we see,

---

[1] Curiously, no record exists of a sermon on Eph. 1:11, 12, which directly addresses the question of God's predestination, counsel and will.

he does not deal equally with all, for although he is well able to enlighten everyone and to ensure that none are unbelievers, the opposite is what we find. Understand, therefore, that he chooses those he pleases, and that if we want to know the reason why, we will be climbing too high. That is why so many arrogant people risk breaking their necks, since they cannot agree that God rules us as he wills, as is his proper right.

Moreover, earlier on, Paul made Jews and Gentiles completely equal—a point we shall have to discuss at greater length.[2] Since God had chosen Abraham's descendants, we might have thought that they possessed some natural worth. Admittedly, if we consider the grace which God extended to the Jews, they were much more preferred to the rest of the world; but if we judge them in themselves, we see that they were empty of all righteousness. Accordingly we should always come back to this point, that God has no debt or obligation to anyone at all. If he freely adopted the Jews, it was not because they were better than others or had anything to boast about. Thus Paul insists that those who have believed in Jesus Christ are also included in God's election, but cannot boast of having greater merit than others. It is to this that we must keep coming back: from among the Jews and Gentiles alike God chose those he willed, so that his grace alone might be made known, every mouth stopped, and no one entitled to claim a contribution of his own.

When, therefore, the apostle compares Jews and Gentiles, he says that if we consider that God chose them as his inheritance, they were a holy race. He gave them his law and promises, making them superior to those he rejected and forsook. From God's point of view, however, all human boasting must be cast down. By declaring that our sins are forgiven and that we lay

---

[2] The reference is possibly to Calvin's earlier sermons on Gal. 3, where the Gentiles are said to be heirs of the grace promised to Abraham, and to be, with the Jews, 'the children of God by faith in Christ Jesus' (Gal. 3:26).

hold of God's grace by faith, Paul shows that this can only be attributed to God's compassion for us. As we noted before in Galatians, Paul told Peter that they were native-born Jews, and according to common belief those descended from Abraham's line were a holy race. 'Yes,' says Paul, 'but our only refuge and assurance of salvation is to believe in Jesus Christ. We are lost and ruined in ourselves, for we bring with us only God's wrath and curse' (cf. Gal. 2:14-16).

Now just as Paul, here and elsewhere, affirms that men are wrong to think that there is something of worth or merit in them, so now, to better confirm this truth, to suppress all argument and to end every objection, he takes us back to the source—not only to God's gift of faith to whomever he wills, but to his choice of us before the world was made. We must therefore bear in mind that we are all, from the greatest to the least, answerable to God, and that there is no one, however eminent or holy, who can except himself from the common lot of man. Having made that point, Paul then extols God's goodness, because the Ephesians have now joined with those who were earlier deemed to be God's people and servants in his church. Before they came to believe the gospel, the Ephesians were very different, as will be said more fully in the second chapter (Eph. 2:11-13). At any rate, the believing Jews who had been converted to Jesus Christ were, in a sense, brothers of the angels in heaven, since they were members of a common Head. The Ephesians, by contrast, were poor and wretched, strangers to the hope of salvation, enemies of God and totally accursed. Yet here we see God removing the distinction and putting them on an equal footing. God's goodness is therefore all the more conspicuous, which is why Paul tells how, having gathered his church together, he has so established it that the eldest are seen to rely wholly on him for mercy, while those who were rejected and even abhorrent to him, now have reason to glorify him, for he has freed them from destruction.

The outworking of God's grace thus illustrates Paul's previous remarks. Our election, as I have said, is hidden and beyond our comprehension. Scripture shows us the way: it is not lawful for us to inquire beyond the point to which it leads. However, although God's election is hidden, he testifies to it by the gifts he showers upon us—gifts like faith, which is granted by the Holy Spirit. That is one point. Now if faith were the kind of gift by which God causes his sun to shine upon both good and bad, allowing the earth to produce food for all without exception, that would count among his gifts and benefits. But faith is a particular gift which is not bestowed on everyone: God reserves it as a treasure for those he wills. The reason is that we are all children of Adam, and are thus part of the same mass. Why does he enlighten some and leave others in their blindness? His election is the only cause. So although we cannot understand by reason or proof why God should have elected us before the world was made, we know that this is so because he reveals it to us when we have the light of faith. Experience also makes this abundantly plain.

What makes me accept the gospel and adhere to it, while others remain mindless and stupid, or else grow bitter against the message of salvation? It would be sacrilege for me to think that it was all my own doing, for we must always come back to what we said before: 'What makes you superior?' (1 Cor. 4:7). Here Paul demolishes all loftiness in men, so that no one can come forward and claim anything for himself. We must not, Paul says, imagine that we are worthy in ourselves: it all comes from God.

In this present passage, then, Paul argues from experience that the Ephesians had been chosen by God, and that their faith must thus be grounded in God's unmerited goodness. They had heard the message of the gospel and had believed it. But how did that come about? Paul asserts that it can only have been because they had been confirmed in faith by the Holy Spirit. Now if they had been confirmed, the Holy Spirit must have been at work in them beforehand. To enter into so profound a maze as God's eternal election is out of the question. God points as it were with his finger to the fact that he has elected us, provided we are not ungrateful to him, provided we recognize the blessing he has given us and provided we are quite sure that he marked us out from all eternity—that is, set us apart for himself, to be his very own children.

Paul's meaning is therefore clear to us, which is why we should learn not to run round in endless circles, when all we need to do is confess that we owe everything to God's pure mercy. Evidence of this is furnished by the faith we have, for, as I said, it does not come from our natural disposition; it is a gift from on high which is not given indiscriminately, but to those whom God wills.

There are many words here which we need to weigh. On the one hand, Paul seeks to exalt the grace of the Holy Spirit, by insisting that we can have no part or portion in our Lord Jesus Christ or in all the benefits he has obtained for us, unless God allows us, by his Holy Spirit, to take possession of our salvation. That is one point to notice. On the other hand, the apostle is careful to reveal the priceless blessing that is ours through the gospel, when he calls it *the word of truth, the gospel of salvation.*

In the first place Paul aims to give us unshakeable assurance, so that we can call upon God free of doubts and misgivings, for as long as we are doubtful as to whether God loves or hates us, we cannot truly invoke him in prayer. That would be the end of our salvation according to the words of the prophet Joel (Joel 2:32). The general message of holy Scripture is that we cannot obtain salvation unless we turn for refuge to God in prayer and supplication. Without this assurance we would be excluded from salvation, as we will see more fully in the third chapter.

We must be truly certain, therefore, that God is our Father, and that he counts us as his children. But how could we have so firm a faith unless the message of the gospel were absolutely sure, so sure that we would be quite wrong to question it? That is why Paul calls it 'the word of truth'.

Naturally there are other truths, as when God threatens us, for he threatens not in pretence or in vain. His threats and his promises are sure to be carried out. However, since here it is a matter of correcting the distrust to which we are all too prone, Paul calls the gospel 'the message of truth'. He is saying this in effect: 'Friends, God has borne faithful witness to his will. It is as if in the gospel he was opening up his heart to you. You should therefore stop there.' Paul also makes the point that our salvation is wholly enclosed in the gospel, so that we might come to love and value it. Would we be so devoid of sense and so completely mad as to despise our salvation? Thus we are told that it all derives from God's pure mercy, from his eternal election, knowledge of which does not lie close at hand but which the gospel reveals to us. It is the means and agency by which we know. For though, through his sacrifice, our Lord Jesus Christ reconciled the world to his Father, what good would it have done us if we could not share in it by faith? Faith is not an idea that men imagine in their heads: it is a determination which we make that God can neither lie nor deceive. As we look expectantly to him, we must not fear that our hope will not come safely to port.

In sum, the apostle wants us to know that if we are able to benefit from the gospel, we will not remain shaken or worried. We will be able to call upon God with full voice, confessing that we are very much in debt to him, that we owe him everything, that we have no fear that he will disown us, will not welcome us or will fail to answer the prayers we make to him.

Let us do, then, as Paul urges us, and stick with the message of the gospel. Let it be as if God were visibly appearing to us—as if the very skies were opened! And let us remember the words which came from the lips of our Lord Jesus Christ, that when sins are pardoned through the preaching of the gospel, this is ratified at the same time in heaven (Matt. 16:19, 18:18; John 20:23). This, therefore, is the certainty we ought to have, so that we no longer doubt whether or not God will answer our prayers.

Now once we are taught to believe the gospel, Paul tells us that we should cherish it as a priceless treasure, since it is God's power for salvation to all who believe, as he writes in the first chapter of Romans (Rom. 1:16). Let us continue, then, to boldly defy the devil and all the trials he puts in our way, because it is God who calls us. He has abundantly testified to his love for us, and to his fatherly goodness.

We come now to the second part of the verse on which we briefly touched: *sealed by the Holy Spirit of promise*. Paul clearly shows that God, besides desiring the gospel to be preached to us, must work by his Holy Spirit and with particular grace. There are many, as we know, who happily admit that only God's generosity moves and prompts him to send the gospel to us. They imagine, nevertheless, that some accept it and others do not, because free will prevails. The result is that God's grace is diminished, for it is not enough that he should offer us his grace, as we might offer an apple to little children, so that whoever runs fastest gets it. If that was how God cast his grace about, our own strength and efforts would certainly account for the greater part of our salvation, and credit would remain with us. As it is, Paul first of all asserts that God daily invites us to become heirs of his heavenly kingdom—and this out of his free, pure generosity. He then adds that we must be touched by his Holy Spirit. True, he writes as if the Spirit supplied only part of grace; this, however, was because he had earlier assigned first place to the Spirit.[3] Paul is

---

[3] 'Part of grace', because at this point of his argument Paul is concerned not with the Spirit's work of illumination and regeneration, but with his work as sustainer and preserver. As Calvin will shortly say, the Spirit is 'doubly active' in the believer.

mindful that he had already argued that faith comes from God's free election. Yet for God to enlighten us by his Holy Spirit, to impress his grace on our hearts and to incline them to obedience was not sufficient; in addition he must strengthen us, maintain our faith and give us invincible perseverance to the end.

This is the point to which Paul seeks to lead us. Faith, we have already learned, comes from God's Spirit; we are illumined by his grace. We now learn that he keeps us safe so that we do not fail.

We will understand this better if, to begin with, we remember what was explained before, that as long as God leaves us in our natural state we are wretched and blind, wandering in darkness. We are shut out, alienated from the heavenly light until God has mercy on us and illumines our minds with his brightness. That is the first thing to bear in mind. In the second place, once we embrace God's grace by faith and find in Jesus Christ all that we need to be completely happy, we must be strengthened in that faith. Why? Just think of how changeable we are. Even those most disposed to follow God will immediately fall: we are so frail that at any moment the devil will throw us down if God does not take us firmly by the hand. Thus we read that God employs his power to sustain his elect whom he has given to our Lord Jesus Christ (John 10:28). Where, alas, would we be, if he did not fight for us? We would soon come to grief, and not only once, but we would fall, as I have said, countless times. Although we are on the path of salvation, our frailty, our fecklessness and inconstancy would lead us astray, unless, that is, God so worked in us that through his Holy Spirit we were victorious in our struggles with Satan and the world.

God's Spirit, accordingly, is doubly active in us so far as faith is concerned. He enlightens us, so that we grasp what would otherwise be hidden from us and accept God's promises with full obedience. That is the first thing. The second thing is that the

Holy Spirit must continue to work in us, giving us perseverance so that we do not fail half-way through. That is Paul's theme here. It is as if he said, 'Friends, you have known and experienced God's grace, by which he brought you to obey his gospel. You could never have come on your own if he had not taken pity on you. See, however, how God redoubles his grace by granting you perseverance. You might have gone on for three days, three years or more, but God would have helped you do it. You would have been continually shaken, numb with fear and without assurance, had not God promised to take care of you until you reached your goal and finished your race.'

Paul therefore says that we have been sealed—or stamped—by the Holy Spirit. Observe the image which the apostle uses here. We know that documents are authenticated by means of seals. It has been that way since time began. Seals, it is true, were not applied then as they are today, for instead of adding a hand-written signature, a seal or ring was employed. That was the form in which testaments, letters and every kind of contract were drawn up. Here, then, Paul declares that we must be sealed in our hearts. Strictly speaking, he should have said that it was the gospel which was sealed, but in order to remind us that it is we who are at fault, and that the gospel in itself is a fully genuine document, he sought to show that when God seals his truth, it is because we are so hard to manage, stumbling about and shaken like reeds in every wind, until we become strong in faith.

Notice, in any case, that the Holy Spirit is like a seal by which God endorses his truth. I have already said how needful this is for us, for although we confess that God's word deserves to be received without objection or dissent, we always doubt it, and there is much to convince us of that fact. Thus, whenever we are troubled and upset, we grow distraught. We would certainly feel less fear if we were sure of the goodness to which God testifies. All the trials that disturb us attest the fact that we do not benefit from God's gospel as we should. So he himself must authenticate it by his Holy Spirit; he must impress it on our hearts with such certainty that we can remain resolute. Our steadfastness cannot be undone by anything the devil might stir up and contrive in order to destroy our faith.

This will be all the easier for us to understand if we examine the weaknesses which I mentioned before. Supposing we accepted all the evidence in the world, we would not be wholly sure, or as sure as we should be, that God wishes to be favourable to us, and that amid the many perils of this world he has us under his protection. For here we are, as it were, all at sea: at every moment winds and tempests arise; it would take nothing to sink us. How then could we defy Satan? We are like wretched sheep, bereft of weapons, means and every other thing. How could we rejoice either in life or death, confident that Satan is powerless against us, unless we were truly and genuinely sealed?

In this verse, then, we are exhorted to rid ourselves of all presumptuousness and arrogance, so that God alone is praised and exalted. Let us also remember Paul's words that we have weapons with which we can effectively do battle (Eph. 6:13-17). Although our enemy is strong and sturdy, we will never be vanquished as long as we make good use of what we are told here—that God's Spirit seals the truth for us, and gives us certainty concerning God's promises in the gospel.

Now to this first image the apostle adds a second: *the Spirit is the pledge of our inheritance.* We should not be surprised that Paul so strongly reaffirms his message, for from the beginning of the world the devil has not ceased to inflate men's foolish belief in their wisdom and abilities. That was what brought Adam down when, seeking to become wiser than God, he tried to rise higher than was lawful. This was denied him. It is the same for us, but the devil still persists in his fight. By means of this ruse he was able to ruin the human race, and he still attempts to make us

believe that we are capable of one thing or another. It was therefore necessary for Paul to strip men of the false and accursed
idea they had of their free will and their powers, and to teach
them to refer everything to the Holy Spirit. That is one point.

A second point is that we are so ignorant and earthly that
we need someone to chew over God's message for us. We can
conceive nothing unless we see God's gifts with our own eyes
and touch them with our hands—gifts that are nevertheless
invisible! Consequently Paul had to resort to figures of speech
to explain how God's Spirit enables us to lay hold of the gospel
and of the good things it contains, and how he must support us
to the end.[4]

Contracts, as we know, are endorsed by the payment of
a deposit, which we call 'God's pence'. Thus, if we buy fields,
houses, inheritances or goods, although our word should be
enough on its own, men are so devious that if they feel they are
losing out they are not ashamed to break their word. As a result
the practice of the deposit was introduced. It is as if full payment
has been made and as if the transaction is irreversible. Paul's
message, then, is that God's Spirit is given in order to ratify our
salvation completely.

Now why is this? *'It is,'* says Paul, *'for your inheritance, for the
day of your redemption.'* True, as God's children we are already
his heirs. Recall, however, what we are told in the eighth chapter
of Romans: our salvation is enclosed in hope (Rom. 8:24). We
do not yet see it, and we do not yet enjoy it, as we read in the
third chapter of Colossians: 'We have died, and our life is hidden
with Christ in God' (Col. 3:3). Although we are God's children,
our enjoyment is not yet complete. John says the same thing in
his letter: our faith is not in doubt, but it is not yet manifest;

[4] Paul's resort to metaphor is the means by which we, who are slow to comprehend,
may more easily 'digest' the message of Scripture. Calvin is fond of representing God's
truth as food which the preacher must carefully chew over (*mâcher*), before it is offered
to the hearer.

we must await the day when we will be like God, having light enough perfectly to see what now we only believe (1 John 3:2). Further, we find Paul saying in Second Corinthians that as long as we are pilgrims on this earth, we are absent from God, because we walk in hope; we do not yet experience the thing as present, but see it only by faith (2 Cor. 5:6, 7). In short, even though, in John's words, we have passed from death to life (John 5:34), we are always struggling with an endless number of deaths, which beset us on every side.

In this verse, then, Paul joins these two things. On the one hand he affirms that we have not yet attained our redemption and inheritance; but on the other he gives us assurance that only our thanklessness can stop us glorifying God. We have no fear that we will not reach the heavenly life, a down payment on which we have through the Holy Spirit. We are united to our Lord Jesus Christ, so that all his benefits belong to us and are imparted to us by faith. Attend, then, to the words of Paul, when he tells us that the Holy Spirit is our pledge, and that because he is our pledge we can be sure of our redemption, which will be ours, fully and completely, on the last day.

It is abundantly clear, however, that we are poor earthworms, surrounded by decay and corruption. It is lamentable to see the misery to which we are exposed. The world curses and derides us for our singleness of heart; we are made to suffer hunger and thirst; we often feel that God has forsaken us, cut us off, and that he does not even deign to show us pity, as if we were the most contemptible creatures on earth. That is the appearance we present. There must thus be a remedy to give us assurance amid so much worry and distress.

So it is that Paul calls the Holy Spirit our pledge. Although the world feels free to plant its foot upon our belly, so to speak, although our Lord disciplines us with so many trials, although he humbles us so that we seem like lambs meant for slaughter, and although we have death, as it were, between our teeth, a sound remedy is not denied us. How? When the Holy Spirit rules in our hearts, we have reason to boast amid all our trials, as we read in the eighth chapter of Romans (Rom. 8:15-17). Not only are we able to call upon God, knowing that he counts us among his children; we are also irrevocably certain that, afflicted and troubled though we are, God is our Father; he will lead us to the heavenly glory. In this way our hope is tested and found true.

Besides this, we are taught to walk patiently. Since God has given us his Holy Spirit as our pledge, let us not be as feverish or hasty as we usually are. If God treats us roughly, we immediately start to grumble, and we soon get fed up with our suffering. God will not have us enter his kingdom in one bound, as we say. He wants us to pass through this world in the midst of many thorns and briars, and to experience much hardship and distress. Yet although he chooses to take us along this path, he supplies us at the same time with a sound remedy which should be sufficient for us. He strengthens us by his Holy Spirit, giving us invincible steadfastness so that we are equipped to fight until the time for victory is fulfilled.

Even today, it is true, our faith is victorious, but we do not yet fully enjoy its fruit. We must therefore always resolve to sigh and moan, but also to rejoice. There is nothing inconsistent in the cry we utter with Paul: 'Alas, wretched man that I am, who will deliver me from this bodily prison?' (Rom. 7:24). Let us all lament, then, and despair of self, since we are so much given to our evil desires and many failings. But let us also not cease to confess our thanks to God, content with the portion he has given us and which should certainly suffice, as we wait for him to complete the work he has begun. For we have his Holy Spirit dwelling in us, and we have his promise that we will never be without him to the end.

Here, then, we are urged to take the bit between our teeth and to proceed so steadfastly that none of this world's ills will prevent us from continuing our race, until we reach our goal. This is the reason why Paul speaks particularly of redemption. We have indeed been redeemed by our Lord Jesus Christ, who has been given to us for redemption, as is said in another place (1 Cor. 1:30). Its end result and fulfilment, however, are still to come. So redemption is twofold: that accomplished by Jesus Christ, and the other for which we wait and which will be revealed to us at his coming. Paul speaks about this in the eighth chapter of Romans, when he says that we should not be surprised if we groan and are in distress, for all of God's creatures keep us company, and are like a woman in travail just before birth (Rom. 8:22, 23). We know that the whole world is subject to corruption because of Adam's sin. Nevertheless, in the midst of our groaning we ought not to faint. We should restrain our feelings, for it is sufficient if we understand that our redemption has been purchased by our Lord Jesus Christ, and that he will confirm in us what he has already bestowed on us.

Such is Paul's meaning here. The Spirit of God is today a pledge for us, until such time as we are removed from this transitory life and freed from all our ills—from bondage to sin itself which is the heaviest burden we have to bear. Until we are delivered from these things, let us rest easy in the knowledge that God's Spirit dwells in us. As for the phrase 'purchased possession', we may take it to mean redemption already acquired, as when the Spirit is called 'the Spirit of promise', that is, the Spirit who confirms all of God's promises, or when he is called 'the Spirit of godly fear', for it is he who makes us obedient to God's righteousness. 'Purchased possession' thus points to redemption which has been already won, showing that even if we do not feel its actual effect, provided we are sure of what Jesus Christ has done for us, we need not fear that his sufferings were in vain. His sufferings would of course be pointless if they failed to reach us, if we gained nothing from them or if we reaped no benefit.

All this has therefore been won for us by our Lord Jesus Christ. As for us, he reins us in lest in our thanklessness we refuse the blessing which God offers us—the blessing, that is, of rejoicing in our afflictions, knowing that our salvation is assured, and that we are no longer in a position to defy God or to blaspheme against him. Let us go on our way, then, in peace, until, freed from this present prison, we are gathered together as one in our Lord Jesus Christ.

> *Now let us cast ourselves down before the majesty of our good God, acknowledging our faults and praying that he may make us feel them more and more, so that we, being brought to hate our sins and to confess how deep is the iniquity within us, may turn to him for righteousness and seek its source in him. And knowing that he is a merciful Father to us, may we not doubt his assurance that he adopted us before the world was made, to the end that, calling upon him in prayer with true perseverance, we may not faint.*

IV.

ELECTION IN CONTEXT

A SERMON ON EPHESIANS 3

FROM FIRST CREATION
TO SECOND

[To me this grace was given …] ⁹ *to proclaim to all the fellowship of this secret hidden from the beginning of time in God, who created all things through Jesus Christ,* ¹⁰ *that by the church God's manifold wisdom should be made known to the principalities and powers in the heavenly places,* ¹¹ *according to the eternal purpose which he realized in Jesus Christ our Lord,* ¹² *by whom we have assurance and access with confidence through our faith in him.* (Ephesians 3:9-12)

AS we said this morning, all of God's works deserve our reverence, for they bear the stamp of his boundless goodness, righteousness, power and wisdom. Nevertheless there are certain works which are more marvellous still, and which lift them out of the realm of the ordinary. God sometimes works in such a way that men, despite themselves, are forced to feel astonishment and dread. It is the same with doctrine: everything contained in the law and the gospel is wisdom, which should call forth our worship. Without these we would never understand anything, since God is said to teach the lowly and the humble (Psa. 19:7). In any case, part of what Scripture teaches can certainly be grasped by the ignorant and the unschooled. There are other things, however, which are loftier or more profound. This is what Paul means when he calls the preaching of the gospel, when compared with everything else, 'a secret'.

Although God determined, from time immemorial, to call the whole world to salvation, he delayed the execution of his plan until the coming of our Lord Jesus Christ; and when he came, it was as if something new and strange had happened. That, then, is what we should remember when Paul states that he was appointed an apostle *to impart the secret which previously had been hidden in God.*

Here Paul insists that although in men's eyes the proclamation of the gospel was new and unusual, this was no sudden or hasty action on God's part; he was simply giving practical effect to what, from the creation of the world, had already been decided and planned. So as we gaze upon God's works, let us not think that he has done, merely on a whim, something which he had previously kept hidden from us. Let us leave him free to plan, and when we see things happening, we should recognize that they had to be, since such was God's decree.

This is meant to humble us in many ways. First, we should understand how limited is our measure, so that we are led to worship what lies beyond our grasp. As to the implementation of God's counsel, we should keep an open mind, for it would be foolish and reckless of us to venture an opinion where future events are concerned. God, in fact, would laugh us to scorn! Thus those who go in for prophecy, on the basis of their own belief and with no calling from God to exercise that role, demonstrate their insolence. They deserve to be mocked by little children. Accordingly we must suspend judgment about things whose outcome God has not revealed to us. Let us acknowledge that he does nothing haphazardly and that everything is as he has ordained.

It is in this light, then, that we must judge the change that occurred when the Lord Jesus was sent into the world. If we ask why God delayed for such a length of time, we go too far in our desire to know. If we ask why, at that time, the Gentiles were ranked together with the Jews and were on an equal footing with them, since God had previously excluded them from his church, we must again worship his strict counsel of which Paul speaks here. All we must know is that God established things that way. If, therefore, we would learn to be sober, we would gain much more from God's works than do those worldly folk who bark in protest, even if they cannot bite. For nowadays we see many who are driven by a devilish frenzy to complain about everything God does, because they do not see a reason behind his purpose. They even spew forth their horrible blasphemies, as if God was not free to keep anything to himself, but had to admit men into his counsel and submit to them. Since, therefore, many in their base arrogance go so far as to tread God down, we ought all the more to put this teaching into practice, worshipping God's counsel and accepting, without dissent, what he has revealed to us as good and just, and so wisely done as to be beyond reproach.

The apostle, however, is not content merely to say that God kept his hidden counsel to himself. He further declares that *he desired his manifold wisdom to be made known*. The expression 'manifold wisdom' is deserving of notice. It is not that God alters or is changeable in himself, or that there are things in his counsel which are confused or complicated. Nothing like that is to be found in God. Paul is speaking in terms of our own understanding. When we try to comprehend God's wisdom we will be perplexed and dazzled, because it is infinite. Inherent in it are things that will make our minds reel and will totally overwhelm them. We will never be so clear and certain as to be able to say, 'That is how it is.'[1]

A lengthier explanation is perhaps needed if we would gain greater understanding. Sometimes when we look into mirrors

---

[1] Compare Calvin's comment in *Inst.* III.23.8: 'It should not be difficult for us to submit our understanding to God's boundless wisdom, so that it yields before his many secrets. In those things which it is neither lawful nor possible to know, to be ignorant is to be learned. The craving to know is a kind of madness.'

we see a hundred images reflected—a countless number, even. Seeing this, we are confused. This is how Paul describes God's wisdom, reminding us that our intellects are coarse and weak, and that we should not inquire too closely into what is beyond our reach and what God has determined in himself. If, then, we try to climb higher than is allowed and presumptuously intrude, hoping to know what lies in God's counsel and what he has explicitly determined, we will not get half way before we faint. We will catch sight of so many things that we will quite give up, confessing that it is not our place to reach into so vast and deep an abyss. But although, as Scripture says, wisdom lies in searching God's works with utmost care (cf. Psa. 92:5, 6), how, we might ask, can we confess that God is just, wise and all-powerful, if we are dazzled by his works? God indeed ordained the world to be a theatre in which we might behold his goodness, justice, might and wisdom. We must thus attend carefully to his works, but our minds faint when we think of them. Is there not a contradiction here?

Solving the problem is not difficult if we want soberly to know what God chooses to reveal to us and what will be of use to us, and if we have wit enough to see that he does not begrudge our learning from his works, our coming to him by this means and our calling with confidence upon him, so that we distinguish good from bad and walk according to his will. If that is so, we will understand from all of God's works what is needful for our salvation, provided we do not let our foolish, unruly passions have their way. Instead, we will be like scholars who wait for whatever their teacher is pleased to show them, which is why it is said in Job that we do well if we behold the outskirts of God's ways (Job 26:14).

We will therefore appreciate God's wisdom, justice, might and goodness when we see no more than the edges of his works; but if we seek to probe the innermost depths, we will discover the abyss of which we spoke before, which will overwhelm our minds. In sum, we must acknowledge that both God's word and works are mysteries to be wondered at, surpassing our comprehension and our competence. So when we look upon God's works we see marvels which amaze us even more than those we commonly see each day. Likewise in holy Scripture there are points that are not so obvious or so readily understood. Has that been our experience? Then we must first of all humble ourselves, and pray that God may enlighten us by his Holy Spirit, so that we may benefit from all his words and works. For the rest, let us learn what he has to teach us, and to be content with whatever measure he ordains for us. Let us not want to know more than what we learn in his school. That is the lesson for us here. Moreover when we act with moderation, our Lord most certainly will give us guidance. Although his counsel is beyond our grasp, and although the doctrine of the law and gospel are mysteries far above the world, they will be taught to us, for our profit and salvation. There is nothing, then, which we will find muddled, confused or complicated, for God will guide us by his Holy Spirit, giving us prudence and discernment, and enabling us to learn all that he knows is helpful to us. That is one point.

If, on the other hand, we are not teachable, and like a bolting horse run on further than is lawful, God's wisdom will be ever-changing. We will find it diverse in form, and possessed of so many facets that we will remain utterly perplexed and entirely bemused. The faithful, however, will take to heart what Paul is saying here. They are warned always to walk with fear and trembling, to keep a tight rein on themselves and not to want to know more than our Lord desires. So the question as to whether God intends his works to baffle us is now resolved. That is not what he intends, provided we allow ourselves to be taught by him. We are thus made to recognize the infernal arrogance of those rogues who go so far as to reject everything their reason cannot grasp. When they are told that God determines all things by his secret counsel, and that what we call chance or fortune has been decided from before the world was made, or that even the hairs of our head are numbered and that not one tiny bird falls from the sky unless God has foreseen and decided it (Matt. 10:29, 30; Luke 12:6, 7), up they come and protest, 'How is that? So if God tells us something different in his law, are we to think that he has not one but many wills? In that case he would be erratic and changeable. He would be prone to fickleness, just like a mortal being!'[2]

Now as I said before, these people do not know their limitations. Because they imagine that, unless God abides by what he has shown us in his word, he is inconsistent, since he possesses two wills, that's what makes them twitter on like this. The fact is that it is possible for God's will to be one, simple and self-consistent. For us, however, it will appear diverse, taking many forms. It is as if we were watching a hundred different images which dazzled our sight or which totally confused it. When Paul describes God's wisdom as diverse in many ways, it is like a painting which has a thousand hues, so that we cannot tell one exactly from the other. However, in speaking this way Paul did not mean that God's wisdom was so complicated that it was incongruous or at odds with itself. No, he is telling us that although God's counsel is consistent, although it follows

---

[2] The notion of a 'double will' in God was a theme familiar to medieval theologians. The concept arises from the fact that while Scripture sets forth God's will for men, there is in his secret counsel a 'hidden will' (*volonté cachée*), inaccessible to us, by which evils forbidden by God's law nevertheless occur according to his purpose. The Reformer, as we noted earlier, refuses to attribute disasters such as war to a merely 'permissive' will of God, contrary as the taking of life is to the sixth commandment. God's will, he holds, is one and simple; it is only our arrogance (*outrecuidance*), ignorance (*rudesse*) and sluggishness (*tardivité*) which lead us to think that God is inconsistent. Cf. *Inst.* I.17.1-2, 5; I.18.3; III.24.17. On the contradiction between God's decretive and prescriptive will, see John Murray, 'Calvin on the Sovereignty of God' (*Collected Writings*, 4 vols., Edinburgh: Banner of Truth Trust, 1976–1982, 4:202-04). Murray argues that the contradiction, though real, is consistent with God's perfection, since it is capable of being embraced by him in his determinate counsel and foreknowledge.

its natural path, although God does not alter or change and although the light which is in him is never dark, we who are human, when we try to draw near, become dazed and bewildered in our thinking. And if we proceed further and in our excessive boldness venture to intrude, we will ultimately come to grief: God will completely crush us!

It is in this light, then, that we must view what Scripture teaches us concerning the providence of God. It is true that we have clear instructions from God. He will not have us harm our neighbour, nor rob, nor extort, nor be greedy, deceitful or malevolent. These things he tells us. At the same time he bids us live chastely and refrain from all violence. However, when wars break out in the world, when there is bloodshed and countless acts of rape, will we say when these occur that God failed in his counsel to consider what was right? Do we think that he would let fortune prevail, as if he were asleep in heaven, or was enjoying a delightful rest? What a blasphemous idea! It would be like making God into an idol. And what would become of us if that were so? For Satan is a roaring lion who seeks to devour us as his prey (1 Pet. 5:8). We would continually find ourselves in his paws and between his teeth. If God did not determine everything in this world and keep Satan and all his evildoers in check, we would most certainly be doomed to perish a hundred times every minute of the day. Moreover, unless we realize that wars and similar things are judgments which God uses to punish our sins, we would surely not be brought to repentance. Let us therefore learn the lesson we are taught here, that God has a definite will, which is entirely uniform and which is neither capricious nor inconstant.

Whatever the case, we ought to worship God's counsels which are so high and deep as to be beyond our reach. As for the disputed questions which the devil sets before us—'How can God involve himself with sinners? How can he be the author of evil since he uses Satan and the wicked to set men against each other? How can he not incur guilt?'—though we may not manage to settle these questions, though they continue to confuse us and though these curs may keep assailing us with their blasphemies against God, let us arm ourselves with moderation, knowing what Scripture says about God's manifold wisdom, and knowing that though his will is many-sided, it is nevertheless always one. That, in brief, is what this passage teaches.

At this point Paul links the theme he has been expounding to a much broader statement which he now makes, declaring that *God created all things through our Lord Jesus Christ, that by the church his wisdom might be made known to the principalities and powers in the heavenly places.* Now when Paul says that God created all things through Jesus Christ, he is either taking us back to the beginning of the world, or he is speaking of God's restoration of what was lost and ruined by Adam's sin. For as we saw earlier, the task of Jesus Christ was to gather up all that had previously been scattered. Adam by his fall perverted and corrupted all order, creating utter confusion in heaven and on earth until all should be restored by Jesus Christ. Thus the renewal effected by our Lord Jesus Christ may well refer to this second creation, as if by his coming God had restored the world to the state it had before it was effaced.

In any event Jesus Christ accomplished both these things, the first creation and the second. This is a reasonable interpretation, since Paul by evoking the image of creation leads us from one to the other. Now all was created through Jesus Christ when he was ordained Head of both angels and men (Col. 2:10; Heb. 1:2). Yes, even supposing we had no need of a Redeemer, our Lord Jesus Christ had already been appointed as our Head. It was not necessary for him to be clothed with our flesh or to offer himself as a sacrifice to redeem sinners, since he was already entrusted with the task of reconciling God and men, and of uniting them with the angels in heaven. This is how all things were created through Jesus Christ.[3]

Here, however, the apostle wants particularly to point us to the restoration achieved by Jesus Christ when he was given to us as our Redeemer. Although the world had assuredly been formed, although the sun and moon gave forth their light and the earth produced its fruit, we know that, as Paul says in the eighth chapter of Romans, all creatures groaned as a woman does in travail (Rom. 8:22), for they saw themselves subject to corruption because of Adam's offence, since he was cursed. In sum, whereas God had shown himself to be our enemy, he became our Father; and whereas Adam's sin perverted what had been destined for our use, all was repaired at the coming of our Lord Jesus Christ. In this way he gathered up everything that had been scattered, and the world was changed, just as the prophets had said (Isa. 11:6-9, 65:17, 66:22; Jer. 3:17; Mic. 4:1-7; Hab. 2:14). Although they did not try to assign the work of renewal to a definite period of time, nevertheless, by announcing the coming of our Lord Jesus Christ and of the grace which would be given to the church, the prophets speak in these terms: 'Behold, I create new heavens and a new earth.' This is what God says through the prophet Isaiah (Isa. 65:17), and more than once, for these words are commonly found in all the prophets. So Paul, according to the usual style of Scripture, declares that all things were created through Jesus Christ.

Now this verse refers specifically to the church, for while the world has not yet been renewed, we already share in the promised restoration. Through the work of Jesus Christ we enjoy

---

[3] Note the (unreal) conditional: 'Even supposing …'. It is rare for Calvin to entertain a hypothesis which has no scriptural support. His meaning here is not that Christ's incarnation and cross were superfluous to God's purposes of grace, but that the Son's headship over creation and the restoration of all things through him were determined by God's counsel in eternity. Reconciliation was purposed from eternity; its fulfilment took place in time, and in a given space, between Bethlehem and Golgotha.

the things which God created but of which we were previously deprived. When the sun and moon illumine us, and when we are fed with the produce of the earth, we know that these things belong to us because we are children of God. How is that so? Because he has adopted us in Jesus Christ. What we have sung in the Psalm concerning man, should be applied to the Son of God himself.[4] As Paul faithfully explains, we see no righteousness today in humankind, since all is corrupt and defiled. We must therefore come to our Head by whom we are restored. We could not be blessed by God in our eating and drinking, nor could we enjoy all that he has made, if our Lord Jesus Christ had not restored us, and ensured that the world is given to us as our inheritance, so that, with a good, clear conscience, we might enjoy the gifts he showers upon us. All was thus created through our Lord Jesus Christ, inasmuch as God restored the church, and for his sake and through his agency he allowed us to share in the inheritance which he obtained for us.

Having shown us, then, that we have been created through God's Son, and that he is our Head, since all are joined to him by faith, the apostle adds that *this wisdom was not known to the angels themselves*. Consequently they benefit from our salvation, and have cause to worship God for introducing them to something which had been buried, as it were, until then. Some who think that this is a strange idea believe that Paul was referring to the devils. Here, however, he is speaking explicitly of the heavenly places, and clearly means to distinguish the angels from the reprobate. And supposing the devils learned God's wisdom from our salvation, what then? There would be no point in that at all! There are others who, unable to get to the bottom of this verse of Paul's, think that the angels are present among us, in the

---

[4] A marginal note refers to Psa. 8:5: 'You have made him a little lower than the angels; you crown him with glory and honour.' Metrical versions of the Psalms were sung in the Genevan church in a fixed order over a 28-week cycle. Psalm 8 was assigned to the Sunday afternoon service of the third week.

manner of students who come to hear the message preached. This is a most absurd and childish speculation. We know that because of our ignorance God adapts both his teaching and the use of the sacraments to our capacity. The angels in heaven, however, have no need for either baptism or the Lord's Supper, since they are completely spiritual beings. But because we crawl upon the earth, we need means which are appropriate to our infirmity, in order to help us come, little by little, to God. So the doctrine that is preached to us is not intended as instruction for the angels. What sense would it make to say that the angels might learn from what is taught in the church today?

Remember, in the first place, that although the angels behold God's face, this does not mean that they have yet attained the perfection which is promised to us. That is kept for the last day, when everything will be fulfilled. Today the angels know only in part. Admittedly we must not assign to them the status and condition which are ours: they receive a more intimate form of instruction, because they come closer to God than we do. Be that as it may, they still need to close their eyes, as we read in the sixth chapter of Isaiah, in the vision given to the prophet (Isa. 6:2). Although, then, the angels are heavenly spirits and live intimately with God as servants of his kingdom, their eyes are covered, showing that they do not yet understand everything, and that they know only in part. God must make it clear to them that they are created beings, ensuring that they are always held in check. They must humble themselves and keep to their rank. Furthermore it is said that the angels do not know when the last day will be, for it is hidden from them (Matt. 24:36). Why is that? It is to make us abase ourselves even more, so that we will not be ashamed to be ignorant of things which God has not revealed to us.

So that we should not feel hurt that God keeps many things hidden from us, the example of the angels is set before us, demonstrating that they do not yet know everything. Rightly, then, it is said that they did not know what would be achieved and done at the coming of God's Son—that is, that all nations without distinction should be called to the truth of the gospel, and that all should be adopted in order to be made spiritual children of Abraham (Gal. 3:7). True, the angels well knew that Jesus Christ was the Head of the whole human race, but how that would come to pass, at what time and by what means, was hidden from them. Hence Paul says that they benefit by seeing how our Lord dispensed his gifts. It was not enough to say that men should be astounded by such a miracle, namely that God should gather into his house those who before had gone astray, should join himself to those who until then had been his deadly enemies, and should summon those who once were abhorrent to him. It would not have been enough to say that we would have been amazed by this. When Paul, therefore, says that this was news indeed to the angels and that they would wonder at this display of God's great riches, we are taught that whenever mention is made of our calling—how God in his mercy forgot our sins, remade us in his image, restored us who in Adam were lost and doomed to deepest hell, and drew us into the kingdom of heaven; when we are taught that God was not content to show us his lavish provision in this world, but gave us a share in his immortal glory and the crown of life in his kingdom—when all of this is made clear to us, we must learn to marvel and to accept with all due reverence such high, worthy and outstanding gifts.

It is not only here but elsewhere that Paul calls the angels 'principalities', in order to show that we cannot conceive of anything, however noble and lofty, which is not inferior to Jesus Christ. This we see more fully in the first chapter of Colossians (Col. 1:16). For because in those times some were exalting the angels and veiling the majesty of our Lord Jesus Christ, Paul teaches that although the angels are in a sense God's powers and the arms he uses to perform his works, although they exercise dominion and might, Jesus Christ has total pre-eminence and authority over them. Just as the sun obscures the light of the stars, so must whatever dignity the angels possess be thrown down. It must not stop Jesus Christ being the one to whom all should turn and look; all should know that in him lies fullness of blessing. Paul makes this same point in our present passage.

There is something further we must note. Today, as we know, the papists are happy to appeal to the virtues of the apostles, the Virgin Mary and other saints, making idols of them. On the other hand, they think that if we do not worship or invoke them, and do not ascribe to them the worship which belongs to God alone, we are more or less doing away with them. That is why they cry: 'What? Why should the Virgin Mary not be our advocate, since she led so holy a life, was a mirror of all perfection and was so pleasing to God?' Really? As if the excellence that God placed in his creatures was meant to rob Jesus Christ and force him to retreat! Be sure, then, that anything we might say and preach about the virtues and eminence of the Virgin Mary, the apostles and the rest, including the angels in heaven, must not detract from the majesty of our Lord Jesus Christ, must not turn us away from him or permit his work to be assigned to this person or that.

What then? Let us be clear that virtues are so apportioned to all of God's children that Jesus Christ alone is the source of all goodness (John 7:37, 38). Let us therefore come to him, and let God's creatures always keep their place; let Jesus Christ be pre-eminent as their Head. That is what these words of Paul are telling us. How miserable it would be if we now abandoned Jesus Christ and went in search of angels, given that they marvel at the riches God displayed when he united us to the body of his Son, and called us to himself to be his children! So the fact that the angels wonder at our salvation ought to make us more obedient to our Lord Jesus Christ, so that, without deviating in the slightest, we steadfastly cling to him.

Accordingly Paul adds a final word: *by him we have boldness and access with confidence through our faith in him.* Here Paul effectively accuses of ingratitude those who are not content to have Jesus Christ, but who believe they must have additional help. He therefore asks what more can we ask than to be made one with God. Is that not bliss in all its fullness? The fact is that, through our faith in Jesus Christ, we are confident that we can draw near to God and that we have been given access to him. But more than confidence is involved: we also have boldness to come to him with heads held high, not presuming anything of ourselves or coming to him in a careless frame of mind. We must always practise the words of the Psalm which says that, while relying on God's goodness, we must always worship him with fear (Psa. 34:8, 9). At any rate, we can always come before God's throne with absolute boldness, knowing that his majesty is no cause for dread, since in the person of his only Son he shows himself to be a Father to us.

The apostle's intention, then, is to keep us abiding in Jesus Christ. And this shows just how wilful we are, for Paul's earnest concern that we should steadfastly cling to God's Son reflects the wisdom of the Holy Spirit, who knows our feebleness and instability. If we had an ounce of common sense, this would be enough to teach us that through the gospel we can possess God's Son who gives himself to us, and that in possessing him we have everything we could want. To say this in a single word should have been enough, as Paul has already demonstrated. We see, however, that he repeats himself, and reinforces his remarks as if this were a thing difficult to believe. In truth it is very difficult, for we are only too prone to distrust and unbelief. Besides, to believe for just one day is by no means everything. Perseverance is required, which is something very rare in this world, because we are always flitting aimlessly about. That is how people more or less consciously deprive themselves of what has been given to them. And since this is how things are, and since we can only with great difficulty be induced to stop and go no further, let us make use of the remedy which Paul offers here.

To begin with, we should notice that Jesus Christ is the door; by him the heavens are opened to us for, as we read, the veil of the temple was torn, allowing us to enter directly into God's sanctuary (Matt. 27:51; Heb. 10:19). Not some physical temple as it then was: we can now come before the face of God and seek refuge in him, just like a child who throws itself into the lap of its father or mother. God undoubtedly surpasses in kindness and goodness all the mothers and fathers in the world! If, then, we know that, what more can we desire? Do we want something, whatever it may be, that is better and more exalted than God? Then we would need to look for it in the depths of hell, for although we may run round in as many circles as we like, we will never find anything in creation, high or low, which is worth a straw compared with God, as the prophet Isaiah says (cf. Isa. 44:8).

Thus because God has given himself to us in Jesus Christ, and because all fullness of deity dwells in this great sanctuary, symbolized under the law by the visible sanctuary (Heb. 8:2)—because all this is ours, should we not be completely satisfied and find our rest there? And although our feelings and desires are unstable, let them be kept captive and in check, so that we cry: 'Let us cling, let us cling to our God!' David says the same: 'My every joy and blessing is to be united with my God' (cf. Psa. 73:25, 26). And in another place he says: 'God is the fount of life and light' (Psa. 36:9). As we also sang this morning: 'He is my portion; I can have nothing better. I will make him my delight' (Psa. 16:5).[5]

---

[5] A paraphrase, not an exact quotation. Metrical versions of Psalms 16 and 36 were appointed for use in the Sunday morning service of week 3.

Notice also the various steps which Paul identifies here. First of all we must have faith, for although Jesus Christ consecrates by his blood the pathway to God his Father, an opening is not given to all. Unbelievers cannot enjoy this blessing, to which Jesus Christ is the key. True, the door is close at hand and can be easily opened provided we have the key—provided, that is, we accept the gospel with true obedience of faith. This is why the apostle tells us that it is not enough for Jesus Christ to display the riches of God's boundless grace and mercy: we for our part must accept them by faith. Not that we can do so in our own strength, but in any event we cannot draw near to Jesus Christ, nor share in the good things he offers us in the gospel, unless we put our faith in him.

Then from faith we must come to trust. We must, that is, be fully persuaded that God will always receive us and will be propitious to us, despite the fact that we are wretched sinners who do not deserve to be upon the earth. We know that when we reach heaven we will still be acceptable to him. Hence faith is joined to trust, and from this comes courage or boldness, which is as it were the topmost step, so that, although we should feel desperate considering who we are, we nevertheless come with head held high to offer ourselves to God. Now why is that? It is because he sees us in the person of his only-begotten Son, whom he calls his beloved (Matt. 17:5; Mark 9:7)—not for his sake, but for the sake of us who are members of his body.

Here, then, is what we should gather from this passage. When we receive the message of the gospel with true obedience of faith, we possess Jesus Christ, and through him we are led to God his Father, so that we attain fullness of life, light, and all goodness. In the meantime we are exhorted to grow in faith, until we reach the assurance that, in battling with the trials which may assail us, we will be victorious through faith. In the end, as Paul says in the eighth chapter of Romans, we will be able to boast, in the face of life and death and of powers high and low, that we scorn every difficulty, for we know that nothing can separate us from the love which our Lord Jesus Christ has for us, and which is displayed by God his Father in the person of his Son (Rom. 8:38, 39).

For this reason also our prayers must be grounded in full assurance, for, as James says, the man who doubts is mistaken if he thinks that he can obtain anything (James 1:6, 7) We must therefore find assurance in the gospel promise that God is ready to receive us in mercy when we come to him. We are convinced, then, that Paul did not speak in vain when he said that, if we have faith, we should not look for anything else than Jesus Christ. May he be all our treasure, for in him we possess everything we need to make us joyful and content.

> *Now let us cast ourselves down before the majesty of our good God, acknowledging our faults and begging him so to make us feel them that we despise them more and more. Yet may we also rejoice, since he has been so merciful to us in and through his only Son, for he has rescued us from hell's abyss, and has opened his kingdom to us. May he further bless us by enabling us to come to him with true faith, and by delivering us from those worldly enticements which turn us away from him. May we learn to renounce all vainglory, for we are empty of all goodness, to the end that we may seek whatever we lack in him who is the fount of every blessing—a fount which never runs dry.*

APPENDICES

APPENDIX I.

ELECTION: DOCTRINAL FORMULATIONS

THE first of the following texts is one of the earliest statements concerning election written from a Reformed perspective. It was composed by Calvin's compatriot, Guillaume Farel, missionary-evangelist to the French-speaking Swiss, and appeared in a doctrinal handbook titled *A Summary, or Brief Explanation of Certain Points Most Necessary for Every Christian to Place his Trust in God and to Help his Neighbour.* The work was first published in Lyons in 1529, then revised and reissued in 1534. Whereas Calvin initially attached election to ecclesiology, the doctrine of the church, Farel attaches it to eschatology, the final judgment. For both of them, however, election serves to establish the freeness of saving grace, the incorporation of believers into Christ and their eternal security in him.

The remaining texts outline various formulations of the doctrine as found in three major Confessions of Faith, of which the first two appeared in Calvin's latter years, and the last, some fifty years after his death.

1. *Summary, or Brief Explanation* (1529/1534)

Chapter XLII: The Day of Judgment

The glory of the elect, their welfare, salvation and life, and the consummation of all things for which every creature yearns, will be revealed at the triumphant and victorious coming of our Saviour and Redeemer.

When all his enemies are placed beneath his feet, and when everything is made subject to him, the elect will come before our Lord in the air. There the great power and glory of our Lord Jesus will be seen. What anguish and distress there will be for those who have persecuted him and who have hated him in deadly earnest, slaying him in malice and in actual deed, beginning with Abel, the first of the righteous ..., and ending with the last of the righteous elect. For whatever is done to the elect is done to the body of Jesus: they are his body, flesh of his flesh and bone of his bone. But let us leave this thought to those murderers who have shed the blood of the faithful, save that in this very thing we will have cause to give thanks to our good Father, who has set us apart and has separated us from among them, making us his own, not because of our works or merits but through his grace and boundless goodness.

Then the elect who have been written and numbered in the book of life before the world began, true children of God by adoption and grace, separated from the wicked and exalted on high at God's right hand, will hear the voice which is full of gentleness, grace and mercy: 'Come, you blessed of God my Father, receive as your inheritance the kingdom prepared for you from the beginning of the world.' Here you can see that those who have the Father's blessing come to Jesus and are made heirs of God with him. These were those who were promised to Abraham, when it was said that by his seed (that is, by Jesus) they would be blessed. For them the kingdom of heaven was prepared from the very beginning of the world ... For all receive by faith fullness of grace in Jesus; they are his members, united to him and appointed to life from the beginning of the world.

Before the world was created God foresaw and chose his own. Therefore he does not say: 'Come, you who are circumcised and baptized, or numbered among my apostles and disciples, or who are called Jews or Christians or by some such name.' But to every tongue and nation Jesus says: 'Come, you to whom my Father has given his blessing and for whom he has prepared the kingdom from the beginning of the world.' Nothing can hinder God's election and immutable purpose, whether a person is born and brought up in Turkey or dies in his mother's womb. Since he has been appointed to life, he is loved by God, as Jacob was in his mother's womb. God's purpose is firm, for his election and grace, and the Spirit of God by whom he sanctifies his own in Jesus, are tied to no particular time, place, person or operation. They are given freely, with no consideration of the kinship, nationality, place or manner of life of those to whom God gives them.

On the other hand, to be sons of Abraham or Isaac according to the flesh, is of no advantage to the unbelieving and the reprobate. Grant them all the sanctification afforded the body by all the baptisms and cleansings possible. Have them taught by all the most holy prophets and apostles, and even by the lips of Jesus himself. Get them to remember and to teach what they have learned, and to perform all good works and miracles. Let them have every appearance of holiness—it avails them nothing. If they are not God's chosen, they will be rejected.[1]

[1] *Le Sommaire de Guillaume Farel, réimprimé d'après l'édition de l'an 1534*, ed. J-G. Baum (Geneva: J-G. Frick, 1867), pp. 118-21.

2. *French Confession of Faith* (1559)

Article XII: The Eternal Election of God

We believe that from this general corruption and condemnation in which all men are plunged, God withdraws those whom, in his eternal and unchangeable counsel, and by his goodness and mercy alone, he has elected in our Lord Jesus Christ, without consideration of their works, leaving the rest in this same corruption and condemnation, in order to display his justice in them, just as in the former he causes the riches of his mercy to shine forth. For some are no better than others, until such time as God distinguishes them according to his unchangeable counsel which he determined in Jesus Christ before the creation of the world. Nor can anyone, by his own strength, enter into such a blessing, since by nature we cannot have one good impulse, feeling or thought, until God first acts and disposes us accordingly.

3. *Belgic Confession* (1561)

Article XVI: Eternal Election

We believe that all Adam's descendants, having thus fallen into perdition and ruin by the sin of Adam, God showed himself to be as he is, merciful and just. He is merciful in withdrawing and saving from this perdition those who, in his eternal and unchangeable counsel, have been, by his pure goodness, elected and chosen in Jesus Christ our Lord, without any consideration of their works. He is just in leaving the others in their ruin and fall, into which they plunged themselves.

4. *Canons of the Synod of Dort* (1618–1619)

I. Election and Reprobation

Article VI.

That God in his good time gives faith to some and not to others, proceeds from his eternal decree. For *known to God are all his works from eternity* (Acts 15:18); and *He does all things according to the counsel of his will* (Eph. 1:11). According to this decree, he softens the hearts of the elect, however hard they are, and he inclines them to believe; but, in his just judgment, he leaves those who are not elect in their wickedness and obstinacy. Here is chiefly displayed the profound, merciful and at the same time just distinction between men who are equally lost, as also the decree of election and reprobation revealed by the word of God, a decree which the perverse, the impure and the ill-assured twist to their own destruction, but which brings inexpressible comfort to holy and devout souls.

Article IX.

Election was not made on account of foreseen faith, the obedience of faith, holiness, or of any other quality or disposition in men which would be the cause or precondition of their election; rather, it was made in order to bestow on them faith, the obedience of faith, holiness etc. Election is therefore the fount of every saving good, and of eternal life itself, which are its fruits and effects, as the apostle declares: *He chose us* (not for what we were, but) *so that we might be holy and blameless before him in love* (Eph. 1:4).

Article XVI.

Those who, in truth, do not yet feel a living faith in Jesus Christ, an assured confidence of heart, peace of conscience, an earnest concern for filial obedience and a glorying in God through Jesus Christ, but who nevertheless make use of the means of grace by which God has promised to produce these things in us, ought not to lose heart at the mention of reprobation, nor should they rank themselves among the reprobate. Rather, they should carefully persevere in the use of these means, and with fervent desire devoutly and humbly wait for a time of more abundant grace. Much less should those take fright at the doctrine of reprobation who, while seriously desiring to turn to God, to please only him and to be delivered from this body of death, cannot yet advance as far as they would like to godliness and faith; for God, who is merciful, has promised that he will not quench the smoking wick nor break the bruised reed. This doctrine, however, is rightly a cause for dread to those who, as long as they are not converted to God, disregard him and the Saviour Jesus Christ, and are wholly enslaved by the cares of this world and the cravings of the flesh.

APPENDIX II.

CRITICS OF CALVIN'S DOCTRINE

THAT Calvin's twofold doctrine of predestination or, in its single form, of election, should find no support among Roman Catholic theologians, was scarcely surprising. The Church's official teaching, which made man a co-worker with God in the work of grace, could not countenance a view which attributed salvation solely to God's determination. Man's free will, it was held, though wounded by sin, was not so weak that it could not, when predisposed by grace, claim for itself pardon and life. The concept of election was not explicitly denied. What was denied was its severance from all consideration of human worth or effort. Aquinas, for example, with characteristic subtlety, conceded that God does not reward merits which are prior to the grace of election. He does, however, grant a reward for the sake of future merits: 'We might say that God preordained to give glory on account of merit, and that he preordained to give grace to merit glory.'[1] Three centuries later, the Council of Trent, in its decree on justification (January 1547), spoke in similarly ambiguous terms. It agreed that initial grace is predestined, but taught that man, by virtue of his free will, is able to cooperate with God in order to receive the gift of justification (Chapters 5 and 6). No one, however, can know with absolute certainty that

[1] Aquinas, *Summa theologiae*, Ia 23.5.

he is among the predestined, nor can he be sure, when justified, of being able to persevere to the end. To believe otherwise is to be guilty of presumption (Chapters 12 and 13).

Rome's opposition was entirely expected and reluctantly accepted. Harder for Calvin to bear was the unwillingness of Protestant colleagues fully to endorse the doctrine and to defend it with vigour. The Lutherans were a case in point. Luther himself was a convinced Augustinian in his belief in, and advocacy of, predestination. Melanchthon, however, as we noted in our Introduction, was far more cautious, and not until his *Commonplaces* of 1535 did he confront the issue directly, warning that it had the potential to perplex godly minds and to provoke unhelpful curiosity. In his 1543 revision of that work, he contended that free will consists in the ability to apply oneself to grace. Writing to Calvin in May of that year, he expressed doubt as to whether it was ever possible to resolve the tension between divine providence and human or natural agency ('contingency'). He was suspicious of any view of God's sovereignty which risked making God the author of sin, and preferred to explain the existence of evil wholly in terms of man's depravity. 'Let us blame our own will,' he wrote, 'since it is we who fall; let us not seek the cause in God's counsel, and let us not rise to accuse him. Let us know that God is willing to help and assist those who truly struggle.'[2] When, in 1546, a French translation of the *Commonplaces* was published in Geneva, Calvin supplied a preface in which, in a spirit of compromise, he commended Melanchthon's eminence and his desire to set forth God's truth in as plain a manner as possible. Positively, Melanchthon is said to defend the doctrine of free grace and of man's total inability to save himself. The Holy Spirit alone is able to illumine and regenerate the sinner. If, Calvin goes on, the author's remarks on predestination are brief, it is because he wishes to discourage

[2] *CO* 11:541-42.

speculation and to avoid unhelpful disputes. 'I confess,' he adds (so that no one might mistake his meaning), 'that of all that God has been pleased to reveal to us, nothing should be suppressed, come what may. But anyone who seeks to benefit readers by his teaching deserves to be excused if he stops at what he knows to be profitable.'[3]

Relations with Melanchthon nevertheless remained strained, nor were they helped when opponents mischievously sought to pit Melanchthon against the author of the *Institutes*. The differences between them, Calvin argued, were more apparent than real. However, in a lengthy defence of his position to the Genevan authorities, the Reformer described Melanchthon as 'a timorous man' (*un homme craintif*), who spoke more as a philosopher than as a theologian, and whose attempts to steer a middle course were like those of a man 'swimming between two currents'.[4] In a personal letter to Melanchthon of November 1552, Calvin bluntly asserted that 'in teaching the doctrine of election, you seem to have no other purpose than to suit yourself to the common feeling of mankind.'[5] In a further letter of August 1554, he accused his correspondent of needlessly dissembling his opinion and of doing a disservice to the church of God. 'What else,' he wrote, 'can I suppose of a man of the most penetrating judgment, and profoundly learned in heavenly doctrine, when what you conceal as a thing unknown to you cannot but force itself on the observation of every one who is, however superficially, versed in the Sacred Scriptures?'[6] Together with the controversy over the Lord's Supper, the issue was to

---

[3] *CO* 9:848-49. Compare Paul Helm (*Reforming Free Will*, Fearn, Ross-shire: Mentor, 2020, p. 66), who regards Calvin's preface as evidence of his initial enthusiasm for Melanchthon. It is rather to be seen as an olive branch offered to an important but wary interlocutor.

[4] Calvin, *Tracts and Letters*, 5:368 (letter dated 6 October 1552). As early as 1539, Calvin had noted Melanchthon's reputation for 'softness of disposition' (*Tracts and Letters*, 4:125).

[5] Calvin, *Tracts and Letters*, 5:379.

[6] Calvin, *Tracts and Letters*, 6:61-62.

plague relations between Reformed and Lutheran for years to come.[7]

Among the Reformed churches, it was, as we have seen, the arrest and trial of Bolsec in the autumn of 1551 which occasioned most concern. A question of biblical interpretation had flared into an open dispute about the very basis of Calvin's doctrine of election. Bolsec's criticisms were by no means new. He affirmed (1) that fallen man retained free will; (2) that Christ had come to enlighten every man, since God desired the salvation of all; (3) that salvation is lost only through men's carelessness; (4) that election discourages moral effort and effectively makes God the author of sin.

When, in the course of Bolsec's trial, the Genevan authorities sought the advice of the Bern, Basel and Zurich churches, the outcome for Calvin and his fellow pastors was less than satisfactory. Bern recommended tolerance, and suggested that further discussion cease for the sake of the church's peace and tranquillity. Both Basel and Zurich supported the doctrine of election, but counselled moderation and stopped short of condemning Bolsec. Bullinger, head of the Zurich church, in a personal letter to Calvin, expressed surprise that he had had to pronounce on a subject which, although 'sublime', was touched on only sparingly by the apostles, and only when circumstances obliged them to do so. Bullinger much preferred God's free grace to be proclaimed to men through the gospel, without reference to a doctrine which many good men found uncongenial.[8] How deeply Calvin was wounded by Bullinger's letter is clear from

---

[7] Melanchthon's caution was mirrored in later years in the Lutheran *Formula of Concord* (1577), which affirmed God's will to save all, and which recognized predestination in a positive sense as extending 'only to the godly, to the beloved children of God, being a cause of their salvation' (Article XI/4).

[8] *CO* 14:214-15. Bullinger's surprise arose in part from the fact that, in negotiating with Calvin an accord on the sacraments in August 1549, he had twice affirmed the doctrine of election (*Consensus Tigurinus*, Articles 16 and 17). He saw no need for the Zurich church to offer the Genevans further assurance.

the lines which he penned a week later to his colleague Farel in Neuchâtel: 'Should you be displeased with the general letter of the Zurich men, let me tell you that Bullinger's private letter to me was not a whit better … It is not fair that I should be troubled with his trifles while he, at the same time, is looking down on our wants with supreme contempt.'[9] In his reply to Bullinger of January 1552, the Reformer was equally frank: 'When he [Bolsec] accused us of holding impious doctrine, we deferred to your judgment out of respect to you. I fail to see why this should annoy you … For you to plead in defence of a man who seditiously disturbed a peaceful church, who strove to divide us by deadly discord …, was the extreme of absurdity. Altogether, I feel grieved beyond measure that there is not a better understanding between us.'[10]

Fresh trouble soon arose when Jean Trolliet, a former monk turned notary and a member of Geneva's council, declared to anyone who would listen that Calvin's doctrine of predestination, as outlined in the *Institutes*, attributed Adam's fall exclusively to God's will, thus making sin a necessity for which God was directly responsible. Trolliet further complained that in a sermon of 12 June 1552, Calvin had implicitly defamed him by denouncing those who would not be guided by God's word as riff-raff (*canaille*) who should be cast out of the church. The resulting litigation, initiated by Trolliet, ended in November 1552 in what Calvin could only regard as an ambiguous verdict. The Reformer was declared to be a 'true teacher in this town' and his *Institutes* to be 'well and holily done'; his doctrine of predestination was not to be further impugned. No charge, however, was

---

[9] Calvin, *Tracts and Letters*, 5:329.

[10] Calvin, *Tracts and Letters*, 5:332-33. Further details may be found in Cornelis P. Venema, *Heinrich Bullinger and the Doctrine of Predestination* (Grand Rapids, MI: Baker Academic, 2002), pp. 58-63. On Bullinger's general doctrine, see Richard A. Muller, *Christ and the Decree. Christology and Predestination in Reformed Theology from Calvin to Perkins* (Grand Rapids, MI: Baker Academic, 2008), pp. 44-50.

entered against the plaintiff, who was judged to be *un homme de bien*—'a good man'.[11]

The last decade of Calvin's life brought no end to the controversy. The opposition of Bern, Geneva's most powerful political ally, was such that, in February 1555, the Reformer offered to present his case, in person, to a synod or similar body. His proposal was rejected, but by way of sanction Bernese subjects were forbidden to participate in the Lord's Supper in Genevan churches.[12] Two years later Calvin was embroiled in a heated exchange with a former associate, Sebastian Castellio, who, he believed, was circulating from Basel books or papers which assailed his teaching on predestination. He first replied with a short piece in French, titled *Reply to the Calumnies and Blasphemies by which Certain Evildoers Try to Make the Doctrine of God's Predestination Odious* (1557). Calvin's God, Castellio had allegedly asserted, was indistinguishable from Stoic Necessity, and was no less cruel if it were true that he had created human beings in order to damn them. If, on the other hand, God was rightly said to take no pleasure in the death of the wicked (Ezek. 33:11), how could his will to save not be universal, and how could men who still bore his image not be free, of their own volition, to claim his grace? There is more than a note of weariness in Calvin's response to the arguments of what he calls this 'muddler' (*brouillon*).[13] Two further polemical works, composed in Latin and published in 1557 and 1558, sought to

---

[11] Cf. Jean Rilliet, *Calvin, 1509–1564* (Paris: Fayard, 1963), pp. 180-81; Bruce Gordon, *Calvin* (New Haven: Yale University Press, 2009), pp. 204-09. Documents relating to the dispute will be found in *CO* 14:371-85.

[12] Calvin, *Tracts and Letters*, 6:136-37, 151-52.

[13] Text in *CO* 58:199-206. Castellio had formerly been appointed, on Farel's recommendation, principal of Geneva's Collège de Rive. Following friction with Calvin and the city council, his employment was terminated in 1544 and he left Geneva for Basel. In the wake of Servetus' execution he published, pseudonymously, a treatise denouncing the punishment of heretics (1554), Calvin being his obvious target. Authorship of the document which provoked Calvin's *Reply* of 1557 has never been established. The Reformer identifies the culprit as 'Sebastian Castellio or someone similar'.

bring Castellio to heel, but failed to advance the debate either way.[14]

In the absence of any consensus regarding the doctrines of election and reprobation, positions were taken up which were never abandoned. Some six years after the Bolsec affair, we find Calvin complaining to a correspondent that anyone aspiring to a pastorate in Bernese territory, but holding the same views as himself, is sure to be rejected.[15] In the event, Geneva's ministers held firm to the agreement reached in the course of the *congrégation* of December 1551.[16] For his part, Calvin continued to proclaim election as crucial to a true and proper understanding of salvation. Thus, in the Confession of Faith which, in the name of the Reformed churches of France, he composed for presentation to the Holy Roman Emperor at the Diet of Frankfurt in 1562, he affirmed that since the human race is totally corrupt, 'God looks upon us with pity, in order to be merciful to us. He has no other grounds for showing us mercy than our own misery. His goodness toward us proceeds from his choosing us before the creation of the world. He sought no reason for doing so outside of himself and apart from his good pleasure. This is our first foundation, namely that we are acceptable to God because he was pleased to adopt us as his children before we were born. In this way, as a particular privilege, he has rescued us from the general curse in which all men are immersed.'[17]

Enough, perhaps, has been said to show that, in the Reformed camp, there were more than a few who were unwilling to abandon free will in favour of God's foreordination, and who preferred

---

[14] Texts in *CO* 9:257-66, 273-318. A translation of the 1558 tract will be found in Calvin, *The Secret Providence of God*, ed., with introd., Paul Helm, tr. Keith Goad (Wheaton, IL: Crossway, 2010). See also Hans R. Guggisberg, *Sebastian Castellio, 1515–1563*, ed. and tr. Bruce Gordon (Aldershot: Ashgate, 2002), pp. 144-48, 183-85.

[15] Calvin, *Tracts and Letters*, 6:433.

[16] See further, E. A. de Boer, 'The Consensus Genevensis Revisited', *Acta Theologica*, Supplement 5, 24/2 (2004), pp. 51-77.

[17] *CO* 9:756. Cf. Calvin, *Tracts and Letters*, 2:142.

to put the universal call of the gospel before the doctrine of particular grace. There were others, closer to Calvin, for whom it was more a question of tone or balance than of substance. The author of the *Institutes*, it was felt, might have argued just as effectively had he been less ready to respond to provocation, more measured in his polemics and more cautious in positing a decree of reprobation parallel to, and in appearance symmetrical with, the decree of election.

As we noted earlier, the Reformer readily understood that, for many people, election was a 'dangerous sea'.[18] He maintained, however, that it need not threaten shipwreck, provided we allow Scripture to be our guide. His position was, as Wendel has rightly said, essentially simple: if election is taught in Scripture, it should be acknowledged; if it is acknowledged, it should be openly preached.[19] And—we would add—if it is openly preached, it should be allowed to work as and when God wills.

---

[18] *Institutes*, p.487.
[19] F. Wendel, *Calvin, sources et évolution de sa pensée religieuse*, p. 205.

APPENDIX III.

CALVIN AND THE PREACHING
OF ELECTION[1]

READERS of Calvin's treatise of 1552, *Concerning the Eternal Predestination of God*, might be forgiven for thinking that no doctrine, no article of faith, was of deeper concern to him, or of more lasting importance, than this. It is the strongest and most sustained statement which the Reformer ever made on the subject. Written to refute the arguments of two Roman Catholic apologists, Albert Pighius and Giorgio Siculo, but with the Bolsec controversy also in mind, the work mounts a spirited defence of sovereign grace, divine justice, definite atonement, effectual calling and final perseverance. The author's position could not be clearer. 'God,' he writes, 'by his eternal goodwill, which has no cause outside itself, destined those whom he pleased to salvation, rejecting the rest. Those whom he dignified by gratuitous adoption he illumined by his Spirit, so that they receive the life offered in Christ, while others voluntarily disbelieve, so that they remain in darkness, destitute of the light of faith.'[2] It is this treatise, together with what is also said in the

---

[1] The substance of this paper was first presented at a forum organized in Dec. 2018 by the Presbyterian Reformed Church, Epping, N.S.W., to commemorate the 400th anniversary of the Synod of Dort.

[2] *Concerning the Eternal Predestination of God*, ed. and tr. J. K. S. Reid (London: James Clarke, 1961), p. 58.

Institutes, which accounts for the popular view of Calvin as the dour, unyielding predestinarian.

Election is not, however, an indispensable requirement of what is sometimes—improperly—called Calvin's 'system'. The doctrine of creation and providence is sufficient to establish the fact of God's power, majesty, benevolence, fidelity and wisdom; and the doctrine of redemption to establish his grace, justice, mercy and love. What the doctrine of election does is to anchor God's saving work not in the uncertain will or tenuous merits of those who are its beneficiaries, but in God's will alone—not, however, in his bare volition, but in his complete and full personality. We do well to remember, as Francis Davidson observes, that 'it is not the will of God that elects and predestines, but God in his act of will.' And he who wills and acts is the God and Father of our Lord Jesus Christ.[3]

Election, as Calvin often asserts, undoubtedly has its uses, but if it were not found in Scripture it would not occupy him to the extent that it does. There is no reason to doubt the Reformer when he says he would never have spoken of the subject 'if the word of God had not led the way'.[4] And since God's word contains nothing superfluous, nothing except what is necessary for us to know, it must be proclaimed. From Calvin's published works we know how he proclaimed election visibly, so to speak, in the written word. How did he proclaim it audibly, in his sermons?

To survey all of Calvin's sermons presently in print—almost 1,400—is out of the question. A more realistic alternative is to sample as widely as possible the Reformer's 345 sermons on New Testament texts, where the doctrine of election comes to its fullest expression. It is on these that the comments which follow

---

[3] Francis Davidson, *Pauline Predestination* (London: Tyndale Press, 1959), pp. 16-17.
[4] *Concerning the Eternal Predestination of God*, p. 61.

are based.[5] It should be noted that no record exists of sermons on the Gospel of John and the Letter to the Romans, which would otherwise offer a rich field for investigation. Among the New Testament sermons which were recorded and which have been preserved, there are full sets on Galatians, Ephesians and all three of the Pastoral Epistles. Partially preserved are sermons on the Synoptic Gospels—the so-called *Gospel Harmony*—the Book of Acts and First Corinthians. A small number of special sermons commemorating Christmas, Easter and Pentecost also exist, together with a single sermon on Second Thessalonians and another on Hebrews. Calvin's extant New Testament corpus, it will be seen, is far from complete, but is, we think, adequate for our purposes.[6]

The place of election in Calvin's sermons

A first question to be asked concerns the place which Calvin accords the theme of election in his preaching. How often, and how deeply, does the doctrine occupy him?

The answer has everything to do with the way in which the Reformer organized his pulpit ministry. Except for the special occasions listed above, topical preaching on isolated texts was abandoned in favour of *lectio continua*, that is, the systematic exposition of a whole book from beginning to end, as was also the practice in the Strasbourg and Zurich churches. The preacher's task was to allow doctrine to emerge from the text in which it was embedded, verse by verse, chapter by chapter. The biblical text determined the doctrine, not the other way round. If, therefore, the doctrine of election is front and centre of the passage which lies before him, Calvin will comment on it as

---

[5] *CO* contains a total of 292 sermons on New Testament texts. A further 53 appear in the *Supplementa calviniana* series (= SC), Neukirchen: Neukirchener Verlag, 1961ff., Vols. 7 and 8. A further volume of sermons on 1 Corinthians 1–9 is in preparation.

[6] On Calvin's New Testament sermons and their dating, see T. H. L. Parker, *Calvin's Preaching*, pp. 62–64, 153–54.

fully as his text—and time—allow. If, on the other hand, election is only incidental to his text, if, so to speak, it merely hovers around the margins, he will be suitably brief, and may even omit it altogether.

It cannot, however, be assumed that if the text entirely ignores the issue of election, the preacher will do likewise. Other factors, other themes, may draw his attention to the doctrine and may persuade him to include it in his exposition. Two themes in particular act as catalysts: God's lavish providence, and the nature of his church.

Thus, in expounding Paul's letter to the Galatians which says nothing about election, Calvin remarks that God's bounty, great as his fatherly care is for his creation, 'is as nothing compared to the special love which he reserves for his elect, his flock. This is not due to any merit to be found in them, but rather because it has pleased him to make them his own.'[7] Or again, he tells his hearers that in order to experience God's free bounty, 'we must lay down all ideas of worth or merit, and first look to God's free election … God chose us before we were born, indeed, even before the creation of the world.'[8] As to God's church on earth, it is, by any estimate, a mixed body, whose members too often behave badly, to the scandal of many. Why, the preacher asks in a sermon on Titus, should this be? It is because not all are elect. 'To have faith and to obey Christ's gospel we must be members of Christ's flock, which we are by special gift of God … God has chosen us because of his immutable election and because of the unmerited goodness which he showed in adopting us as his children.'[9]

Asides of this kind are never forced improperly on the scriptural text, nor are they allowed to distract from the preacher's

---

[7] *Sermons on Galatians*, tr. Kathy Childress (Edinburgh: Banner of Truth Trust, 1997), p. 18.

[8] *Sermons on Galatians*, p. 77.

[9] *Sermons on Titus*, tr. Robert White (Edinburgh: Banner of Truth Trust, 2015), pp. 13-14.

main theme. They occur often enough, however, to suggest how closely election is bound up for Calvin with the recurring themes of God's goodness and of the community of the redeemed.

The content of Calvin's preaching

What exactly does Calvin say about election in sermons addressed, it must be remembered, not to a specialist audience, but to a largely uninitiated congregation of townspeople and visitors? What essential truth or truths does he want them to know?

A useful starting point will be found in one of the early sermons on the *Gospel Harmony*. A simple statement like that of Zechariah: 'He has raised up for us a horn of salvation in the house of his servant David' (Luke 1:69), allows the preacher to establish three vital facts:

> David is called God's servant so that we should know that salvation was from his house. It was not founded on any human worth but on God's free election. Inasmuch as God was pleased to act this way, we need look for no other reason than his infinite goodness.[10]

In brief compass the fact of salvation is established; the source—election, independent of human merit—is stated; and the motive—God's goodness—affirmed. This, we might say, is the core position from which Calvin never retreats. Whatever variations he weaves on the theme of election, the essentials do not alter. The pattern followed here is the pattern set twenty years earlier when, in his Catechism of 1537, the Reformer first posited election as the precondition of saving faith.

More substance to this bare outline is provided by an important group of sermons on the letter to the Ephesians. Of the forty-eight sermons which compose the set, four, on Ephesians

---

[10] *Sixty-five Sermons on the Gospel Harmony*, Sermon 15 (*CO* 46:172).

1:3-14, concentrate largely on the doctrines of election and reprobation. From the outset the preacher's theme is God's initiative
in choosing the unworthy for salvation out of the sinful mass.
Those who argue the case for God's foreknowledge are sharply
called to order. What, asks Calvin, could God possibly foresee,
except our depravity? On what basis, then, does God choose?
Why does he discriminate?

It is often said that Calvin does not answer the question. He
answers it as far as he is able, but not with a view to satisfying our
curiosity. His answer is not from faith to unbelief, but from faith
to faith. In his Ephesians sermons he affirms that God's choice
is determined by his 'secret', 'hidden' or 'narrow' counsel. Our
creaturely status makes it impossible for us to plumb the mystery
of his will. His purposes lie beyond our reach: they are 'incomprehensible'. We have no other option but to be 'willingly ignorant'.[11]

To be ignorant, however, is not to be deaf. Election made in
eternity issues in God's call which is specific to time and place.
God calls his elect outwardly by his word and inwardly by his
Holy Spirit. In this work of 'double grace', sinners are led to
repentance and faith. They are attentive to God's voice which
does not thunder as at Sinai, but speaks gently, graciously, famil-
iarly: 'Here am I. Here am I. Although you have scorned me, I
condescend to come to you, for I care for your salvation.'[12]

To embrace salvation, says the preacher, is to embrace, by faith,
Christ as Saviour. And just as God's call is mediated by his Spirit,
so too is faith. Faith is the bond which unites us to Christ our
Head and which makes us one with him; with him we are sons
and daughters of the same heavenly Father. We cannot come to
God as we are: we can come only through Christ; it is in him that

[11] Sermon on Eph. 1:7-10 (*CO* 51:291). B. B. Warfield expresses the implications of
Calvin's thought this way: 'God in his love saves as many of the guilty race as he can get
the consent of his whole nature to save' (*The Plan of Salvation*, 1955, p. 74).
[12] Sermon on Eph. 1:3, 4 (*CO* 51:260). On the notion of 'double grace', see *Sermons on
Galatians*, p. 77.

we are chosen, called, and received into God's family. 'God,' says Calvin, 'deigns to look upon us in Christ, for Christ is the book in which our names are written ... He looks on us as in a mirror, and sees that which makes us pleasing to him.'[13] We are blessed only in Christ, loved only in the Beloved: our election is in him.[14]

In expounding Ephesians the preacher has one more, decisive, point to make. Election is not an end in itself; it is the means to an end—holiness. Justified by faith, the elect are called to sanctification by the Spirit, to lead lives that are more like Christ's, more conformable to God's will, more agreeable to him. Progress, Calvin warns his hearers, may be painfully slow. We are not reformed from the very first, nor are we ever completely remade in this life. Perfection is not to be had while we are in the body. God does not 'bring' his own to perfection, the Reformer declares, he 'draws them toward it'. To argue for perfection here below is to display 'diabolical pride'. There is, however, a perfection which lies within our grasp:

> Our real perfection is to know our weakness, and to turn to God that he may correct our faults and uphold us in his infinite goodness. And whatever good works we are enabled to do must redound to his glory, not to ours.[15]

[13] Sermon on Eph. 1:4-6 (*CO* 51:275-76, 281). We might note that of all the ways in which Scripture speaks about redemption, the image of adoption is the one preferred by Calvin. It might be said that for the Reformer, the choicest blessing conferred by election is the privilege to call God 'Abba, Father', to call upon him in prayer, to look to him for aid, and to know that nothing can part us from his love.

[14] Calvin's thought should not be misunderstood at this point. In his preface to *Concerning the Eternal Election of God*, J. K. S. Reid, for example, echoes an earlier criticism by Karl Barth when he reproaches the Reformer for conceiving of Christ's role in election as purely instrumental (p. 41): 'He [Christ] must be regarded as not merely the agent but as the *fundamentum* of the decrees, so that they are framed not in his absence but really in him.' Calvin understands the phrase 'chosen in him' as referring not to the incarnate Christ, but to the eternal Son who, co-equal with the Father and the Spirit in the unity of the Godhead, and co-author of the divine decrees, is present and active from the very beginning. The elect are chosen not only in, through and for him, but by him. Cf. Richard Muller's discussion in *Christ and the Decree*, pp. 40-43.

[15] Sermon on Eph. 1:4-6 (*CO* 51:273).

One thing is clear: the grace of election can never be an excuse for inertia. God treats us not as blocks of wood but as responsible moral agents. As his children, we must actively seek to do what pleases him, and when we fail we must actively repent.

In expounding Ephesians, Calvin does not shrink from confronting the issue of reprobation, a theme, be it noted, that does not appear in Paul's letter. The key to the problem, says Calvin, is found in God's particular providence, by which the non-elect are condemned to remain in their sin. The preacher's language is unambiguous: God is said to reject (*rejeter, réprouver*) or dismiss (*débouter*) the unsaved, to leave them alone (*laisser, délaisser*) so that they are shut out (*forclos*) of the kingdom of heaven. The result is that among the many who hear the gospel, some 'return home without having profited, and even with hearts hardened against God, displaying a rebelliousness which before was hidden.'[16] Nowhere, however, in the Ephesians series are people said to have been appointed (*ordonnés*) to destruction, and no mention is made of a specific decree of reprobation.[17] The corresponding absence of the concept of 'double predestination'—a term, be it noted, that Calvin did not use—suggests that, despite the firm position taken up in his more formal works, the preacher adopts a noticeably milder, pastoral tone as he places each of his hearers, without exception, within reach of God's inexplicable grace. None among those who heard him could possibly conclude that they were condemned to perdition despite themselves, that an iron law of necessity was laid upon them, and that, when invited to repent and believe the gospel, they were constrained to refuse.

---

[16] Sermon on Eph. 1:3-4 (*CO* 51:259-60).

[17] Only once among the sermons which comprise this present volume does Calvin cite Scripture (Prov. 16:4) to the effect that God 'has ordained the loss' of the unsaved (Sermon 3 on Gen. 25:21-23; *CO* 58:45).

Election and the preaching of the gospel

Calvin's doctrine of election is inseparable from his doctrine of salvation. Salvation, and the effects bound up with it—justification, sanctification, glorification—flow from election as a stream from its source. Election, says the Reformer, 'is the very foundation of our salvation', 'the first foundation of our faith'.[18] It follows then that 'if we dispense with election, there is no salvation to proclaim'.[19] Election validates the gospel in the sense that it makes redemption uniquely a work of sovereign grace, and ensures that Christ's offering of himself actually redeems those for whom he died.

Nevertheless election cannot be said to constitute the gospel—not, at least, the gospel which Calvin regularly preached to his Genevan congregation. That gospel, articulated at different times and in different ways, centred on the person and work of Jesus Christ, who, at the cross, as perfect Man made reparation for man's sins, and who, as the eternal Son of God, vanquished evil and rose to give life to the lifeless.

Consider, by way of a single example, how the preacher frames his message in a sermon on Matthew 1:18-21. We have a Redeemer, he says,

> who took all our burdens on himself, becoming accursed for us and paying what he did not owe in order to clear our debt. He made himself a sacrifice in order to appease God's wrath. He shed his blood in order to wash and cleanse us of our defilement and stains … The faults which we committed are not imputed to us, since Jesus Christ made full and complete satisfaction for them.[20]

[18] *Sermons on 1 Timothy*, tr. Robert White (Edinburgh: Banner of Truth Trust, 2018), pp. 190, 194; *Sermons on Titus*, p. 14.

[19] *Sermons on 2 Timothy*, tr. Robert White (Edinburgh: Banner of Truth Trust, 2018), p. 57.

[20] Sermon 21 on the *Gospel Harmony* (CO 46:257). Cf. *Sermons on 2 Timothy*, p. 393, where Calvin defines the 'essence' of his gospel in similar terms.

Dense as this statement is, it is not election which lies at its centre, but the atonement. Election does not bypass the cross; it does not render the cross superfluous, but leads us inevitably, inescapably to it. It touches us in time and space, and only takes effect when, quickened by the Spirit, we are reconciled to the Father by the passion and death of his Son.

To preach the gospel is, therefore, to preach Christ as the elect Son, who on the cross and in our stead bore the burden of reprobation merited by our sins, and who for our sake and in our name confessed himself momentarily forsaken. To preach the gospel is also to proclaim Christ as the risen Lord who has overcome death, who reigns in glory at the Father's right hand and who opens the kingdom of heaven to all believers. To preach the gospel is, finally, to issue an open invitation to all who hear—to all, says Calvin, 'white or black, old or young, upright or wicked, rich or poor, loved or unloved, handsome or plain'[21]—all without exception are invited, in the preacher's down-to-earth phrase, to stop beating about the bush and to come straight to Christ, to receive Christ, to accept Christ. How, asks Calvin, could anyone refuse so clear and gracious an invitation? 'What excuse,' he says, 'can we offer when we refuse to come to Christ and to accept him as the one whom the Father has given to us? What excuse, when by his righteousness he has made us acceptable to God and heirs of the kingdom of heaven?'[22]

Assurance of election

Calvin does not often in his preaching pose the question of assurance. If, it might be asked, election is hidden in God's secret counsel, what knowledge can the faithful have of it? What assurance is open to those who have committed themselves to Christ? Calvin's reply is that just as God's effectual call comes by way of word and Spirit, so does assurance of election.

---

[21] *Sermons on Galatians*, pp. 134-35.
[22] Sermon 31 on the *Gospel Harmony* (*CO* 46:378).

In the first place, he insists on the evidentiary value of the gospel, which he likens to a transcript or copy (*double*) of an original record held in heaven, and on whose absolute authenticity we may rely.[23] Elsewhere he compares the gospel to a last will and testament, by which God makes over to the elect the inheritance of the kingdom prepared for them.[24] Consequently assurance depends from first to last not on the quality of faith, which is only a proximate or instrumental cause, but on the witness of God's word to his grace in Christ.

If the gospel is the evidence of our election, the Holy Spirit is its pledge and guarantor. 'Does God in due course touch us by his Holy Spirit?' asks the preacher. 'Then we are grafted as it were into the body of our Lord Jesus Christ, and we receive the pledge of our adoption. This is the guarantee which we are given by way of complete assurance that God keeps us safe and counts us as his own.'[25] Calvin is thus in complete accord with Zwingli, who held that certainty of election comes from the seal of the Spirit, 'by which the believer knows that he is truly free, that he is of God's family and not a slave'.[26]

It goes without saying that, while God is able to make all things work for his people's good, and while he gives them many proofs of his love,[27] material success and personal prosperity are on no account to be construed as evidence of election. To think otherwise is not only to misread Calvin's thought but to parody it. According to Christ's promise, those who follow him will have tribulation in this world (John 16:33). Popular representations, which interpret success as a sure token of God's favour, completely miss the mark, since God reserves the right to try

[23] Sermon on Eph. 1:4-6 (*CO* 51:281); *Sermons on 2 Timothy*, pp. 61, 69.

[24] *Sermons on 1 Timothy*, p. 193.

[25] *Sermons on 1 Timothy*, p.193. Cf. *Inst.* III.24.5, where the Spirit's gift of communion with Christ is said to be sure proof of believers' inclusion in the book of life.

[26] Zwingli, *An Exposition of the Faith* (1530), art. 6.

[27] See above, p. xiv, note 12.

us and to deny us the advantages which by nature we crave. Self-examination is thus constantly enjoined on believers in order to identify weaknesses, to humble pride and to encourage confession and amendment of life.[28] Even so, they are bidden to look for assurance upward and outward, not to their feeble achievements—for what else can they be but unprofitable servants?—but to the one whose promise is to be trusted, whose will is sure, and whose mercy is everlasting.

Conclusion

A study of Calvin's preaching establishes the fact that, surprising as it may seem, the Reformer addresses his congregation without prejudging any who gather before him. From the pulpit he may—and does—deplore instances of spiritual laxity and misbehaviour both in and out of church, but that is a very different issue. When preaching, he does not mentally separate the sheep from the goats, but makes his appeal to all freely and without conditions.[29] Election is never conceived as a hurdle which the unconverted must clear before God's offer can be entertained. For the hearer to ask: 'Am I elect?', is to ask quite the wrong question. The only question which he or she needs to pose is: 'Am I willing?', and everything that the preacher says indicates that where there is will, there is ability.[30]

---

[28] Compare the Synod of Dort, whose canons list several spiritual marks by which believers may, positively, judge the reality of their election (Canon 1, art. XII; Canon 5, art. X).

[29] It is important to recall what was said in our Introduction (p. xviii), that none are to be denied the church's ministry of proclamation and pastoral care on the grounds that their standing is uncertain. 'Since we do not know those who belong to the company of the predestined, we should be so minded as to desire the salvation of everyone' (*Inst.* III.23.14).

[30] The Reformer's practice suggests, as Auguste Lecerf has said, that 'the gospel message contains the offer of power to the sinner to accept it, in the sense that the infirm man is able, at Christ's command, to stretch out his hand (Matt. 12:13).' (*Etudes calvinistes*, Neuchâtel/Paris: Delachaux et Niestlé, 1949, p. 38.) Cf. Calvin's comment in his sermon on Gen. 25:21-23 (pp. 81-82, above): 'The promises in the gospel *certainly contain our salvation in themselves*, and we are not deceived if we rely upon them.' (Our emphasis.)

In Calvin's hands the doctrine of election is no bar to confident preaching and to honest evangelism. Any preacher who proclaims God's offer of pardon and life knows that it will be taken up by all whom God calls. True, he has no warrant for believing that those whom God calls will have led a hitherto virtuous life: God may permit his elect to go badly wrong (*se débaucher*) and to stray (*s'égarer*) before he finally draws them to him. The preacher has no warrant, either, for thinking that God will effectually call each time the gospel is preached. The Spirit's saving operations are not ours to command. God's choice of time and place is a matter entirely for him. Such is the sense of the question which Calvin poses in his *Institutes*:

> Who will deny that it is right that God should dispense his gifts freely, according to his good pleasure? That he should enlighten such nations as he wills? That he should cause his word to be preached wherever he likes? That he should bring forth from it as much or as little fruit as he chooses?[31]

The minister of the gospel is thus required to be both faithful and patient as he looks to God's Spirit to work as he wills. 'Men's conversion,' declares Calvin, 'does not depend on them. It is God who refashions them and who makes them new creatures. Shall we stop God from working a miracle which far exceeds our understanding? Let us expect more from God's grace than we can ever conceive.'[32]

Least of all does the 'dread decree' of reprobation prove to be an impediment. The implications of Calvin's practice are well summed up in the Second Helvetic Confession of 1566, written by Bullinger two years after the Reformer's death:

> Although God knows those who are his, and here and there mention is made of the small number of the elect, yet we

---

[31] *Inst.* II.11.14 (French text).
[32] *Sermons on 2 Timothy*, p. 251.

must hope well of all, and not rashly judge anyone to be a reprobate.[33]

The mystery of God's hidden counsel notwithstanding, Calvin despairs of none who come under the sound of the gospel. Nor should any who claim to follow in his steps.

[33] Second Helvetic Confession (1566), Ch. 10, art. 4.

INDEX OF
SCRIPTURE REFERENCES

INDEX OF
PROPER NAMES

INDEX OF
SUBJECTS